Employment Forecasting

The World Employment Programme (WEP) was launched by the International Labour Organisation in 1969, as the ILO's main contribution to the International Development Strategy for the Second United Nations Development Decade.

The means of action adopted by the WEP have included the following:
– short-term high-level advisory missions;
– longer-term national or regional employment teams; and
– a wide-ranging research programme.

Through these activities the ILO has been able to help national decision-makers to reshape their policies and plans with the aim of eradicating mass poverty and unemployment.

A landmark in the development of the WEP was the World Employment Conference of 1976, which proclaimed inter alia that 'strategies and national development plans should include as a priority objective the promotion of employment and the satisfaction of the basic needs of each country's population'. The Declaration of Principles and Programme of Action adopted by the Conference will remain the cornerstone of WEP technical assistance and research activities during the 1980s.

This publication is the outcome of a WEP project.

Employment Forecasting

The Employment Problem in Industrialised Countries

Edited by
M.J.D. Hopkins

A study prepared for the International Labour Office within the framework of the World Employment Programme

 Pinter Publishers, London and New York

© International Labour Organisation, 1988

First published in Great Britain in 1988 by
Pinter Publishers Limited
25 Floral Street, London WC2E 9DS

British Library Cataloguing in Publication Data

Employment forecasting : the employment
  problem in industrialised countries.
  1. Employment forecasting
  I. Hopkins, M.J.D.
  331.12′5′091722   HD5701.55

  ISBN 0–86187–938–4

Library of Congress Cataloging-in-Publication Data

CIP data is available from the Library of Congress
  ISBN 0–86187–938–4

Photoset by Mayhew Typesetting, Bristol, England
Printed by Biddles of Guildford Ltd.

The designations employed in ILO publications, which are in conformity with
United Nations practice, and the presentation of material therein do not imply
the expression of any opinion whatsoever on the part of the International
Labour Office concerning the legal status of any country, area or territory or of
its authorities, or concerning the delimitation of its frontiers.

The responsibility for opinions expressed in studies and other contributions
rests solely with their authors, and publication does not constitute an endorsement by the International Labour Office, of the opinions expressed in them.

Reference to names of firms and commercial products and processes does not
imply their endorsement by the International Labour Office, and any failure to
mention a particular firm, commercial product or process is not a sign of
disapproval.

Dedication

I should like to dedicate this book to my father and my father-in-law, both of whom fought valiantly for their country in the Second World War but, after a lifetime of activity, spent their twilight working years suffering the indignity and stress of unemployment.

Contents

List of Tables and Figures

Tables

Figures

Preface

The purpose of this volume is twofold, first to analyse feasible alternatives to unemployment which can be implemented within the next ten years, and second, to assess the experience and methodologies for medium- to long-term employment forecasting of experienced practitioners in this field. Most of the experience in this area has been gained in industrialised market economies and hence the focus of the volume is there. However, some experience has been gained in the larger newly industrialising countries and a chapter has therefore been included on one of them, namely Mexico.

This book is based on contributions received at a workshop on this topic especially designed to produce the present volume, held in Geneva in September 1983. The delay in presenting these edited contributions has been due partly to the editor's leaves of absence from the ILO. First, in the Netherlands Antilles during 1984 and 1985. Even in that tropical paradise, the two-tone call of the brightly coloured Trupial bird was sometimes shadowed by the angrier tones of the unemployed. Second, in Tunisia during the period 1986–7. There, too, high levels of unemployment have contributed to tensions and fears of insurgency.

The contributors are all eminent in their respective fields, and many have acted as the economic conscience of governments both in proposing forecasts of the evolution of employment and related topics, such as hours of work, labour supply, sexual composition of labour and working time, as well as unemployment, and in examining policy alternatives to the crisis of unemployment.

The case studies in this book were selected mainly because each of the groups involved have been influential in drawing the attention of their respective governments to the impact of policy on employment and unemployment. As is the case with all models, one can never claim that policy makers actually 'use' the models to create and take policy decisions. Policy formulation is much more complicated. Models are used as a testbed for ideas and to allow alternative policy experiments to be examined without subjecting actual economies to the stresses and turbulence involved. Nevertheless, even though the studies are now somewhat dated, the sceptical reader will be surprised to see how each of the major forecasts have stood the test of time.

The case study of the United Kingdom, written by the leader of the University of Cambridge growth project, has consistently alerted policy makers to the impact of their policies on unemployment. The group's model has also had one of the best records of the relatively numerous forecasting groups in the UK. Unfortunately the Keynesian flavour of their work and the consequent criticism of government policy has not helped them to continue to receive the funding support from the UK government that they had previously enjoyed.

The case study of France discusses the DMS model. The chapter has been contributed by the Director of France's influential National Institute of Statistics and Economics. The DMS model and its updates have been used on a regular basis as a testbed for policies for each of France's national plans.

The study of Belgium is refreshing in that it provides an unusual critical look, by an insider, at some of the methods and data used in the Belgian Planning Office to assess the impact of policy on employment.

In the case of Holland the team responsible for the medium-term model used by Holland's key Central Planning Bureau present their work and some policy simulations.

Project LINK, lead by Nobel prize winning economist Larry Klein, is reported here by Peter Pauly of the University of Pennsylvania to illustrate how national models are linked together to produce a consistent world forecast. This model has been important in recent years in helping the United Nations to produce short-term forecasts of the world economy.

A glimpse into the way the OECD produce their economic and employment forecasts for the *OECD Economic Outlook* is given by OECD economist Peter Sturm in his chapter.

Finally, an application of the Cambridge growth project's model to a developing country is discussed by Ajit Singh of Cambridge University. How the model and its results were used, and what influence it had while Ajit Singh was adviser to the Mexican President José Portillo are explored.

Each of the chapters follows, in general, the broad outline:

1. A description of the main forecasting techniques and major assumptions (detailed information is given in a list of annotated references);
2. A statement of the major trend in unemployment and the structure of employment in the medium-term future for the country or group of countries being studied;
3. A discussion of the alternative scenarios examined as a likely way out of the crisis;
4. The major policy conclusions arising out of the work relevant to the unemployment problem;
5. The limitations of the approach in terms of its ability to evaluate alternative policies;
6. A comment on future areas of work and outstanding unsolved problems.

The chapters cover three major areas: country case studies in industrialised market economy countries (United Kingdom, France, Belgium, the Netherlands); multi-country studies stressing international linkages in Organisation for Economic Co-operation and Development (OECD) economies; and one case study of a single semi-industrialised country (Mexico). There is also an introductory and a concluding chapter.

It is hoped that the volume will be read by those interested both in the techniques underlying the forecasting of employment and in the policy alternatives leading towards full employment. Hence academics, government planners, and policy advisers may be interested; and both developed and developing country readership is envisaged.

Acknowledgements

I should like to thank the participants in the workshop on employment forecasting held in Geneva in December 1983, where most of these papers were presented and discussed. Those who presented papers and/or participated in discussion were:

T. Barker, University of Cambridge, United Kingdom
R. Courbis, Université de Paris, France
M. Demotes-Mainard, INSEE, France
D. Freedman, ILO, Geneva
J. Galtung, Institute of Advanced Study, Berlin (West)
S. Gupta, Planning Commission, India
C. Koellreuter, BAK group, Basel
J. Kok, Central Planbureau, Netherlands
J. Martin, ILO, Geneva
J. Mesa, GATT, Geneva
J. Mouly, ILO, Geneva
P. Pauly, University of Pennsylvania, United States
P. Richards, ILO, Geneva
G. Rodgers, ILO, Geneva
J. Royer, UNCTAD, Geneva
O. Ruyssen, FAST, EEC, Brussels
S. Schulmeister, Institut Wirtshaftsforschung, Vienna
A. Singh, University of Cambridge, United Kingdom
G. Standing, ILO, Geneva
P. Sturm, OECD, Paris
M. Vanden Boer, Planbureau, Belgium
R. van der Hoeven, ILO, Geneva
W. van Ginneken, ILO, Geneva.

I should also like to thank Thelma Viale and Nancy Burford for typing the drafts.

Introduction

Michael Hopkins

This introductory chapter describes what is in each chapter and gives the main policy conclusions for each of the studies.

OVERVIEW OF CHAPTERS AND POLICY CONCLUSIONS

The United Kingdom

Chapter 2, by Terry Barker, reviews some of the experience of using a large-scale economic model – the Cambridge multisectoral model (MDM) – to examine the prospects for unemployment and employment in the United Kingdom over the 1980s. The chapter also presents a number of forecasts of unemployment performed before June 1983 by different groups in the United Kingdom. All were based on the current policies of the pre-June 1983 election, all forecast an increase in unemployment over the period 1982 to 1990 and all made the same assumption that the labour force would increase over the period. The forecast expected major further losses of jobs in manufacturing, a trend which has been evident since the 1950s.

Despite the fact that the source of new jobs in the past has been mainly in the service and government sectors, Barker doubts that this will continue. This is because, first, the recession of the early 1980s saw a loss of jobs in the service sector; second, banking, insurance and other services are becoming automated so that they may redeploy labour rather than increase their employment; and third, government policy is to reduce employment in the public sector.

In order to examine policy alternatives to reduce unemployment, Barker examined three main strategies: first, a continuation of the policies of the Conservative government of 1983 with a tight financial strategy but with some easing of the public sector borrowing requirement (PSBR) so as to allow faster growth in social capital formation; second, a protection strategy where tariffs and quotas on manufactured imports are combined with substantial domestic reflation; and third, a high investment strategy with a permanent incomes policy that is combined with extra investment in exporting industries.

The results of the two reflation strategies succeeded in reversing the rise in unemployment experienced in 1980–82, with the protection strategy succeeding better. The protection strategy was more successful because it had the highest growth in government expenditure over

1986–90. However, both strategies have limitations. The protection strategy is limited because of the danger of tariff retaliation; new investment may be in the wrong industries going against decades of international specialisation and the tariff must escalate in order to preserve the momentum of growth. The investment strategy is limited because a permanent incomes policy, difficult to preserve, is required; a much higher public borrowing is needed and there is the danger that the extra investment will be in the wrong projects.

The major policy conclusion of the Barker study was that a major shift is needed to reverse the increase in unemployment in the United Kingdom since 1979, let alone to reduce it to the 200,000 of the 1960s. Substantial reflation, including a 15 per cent depreciation of sterling and a reduction in VAT from 15 to 5 per cent, only reduces unemployment by one million from expected levels over three million. A crucial issue is whether inflation will become a problem once again if there is substantial reflation. Although United Kingdom money supply has grown well above target rates, the rate of inflation fell sharply from 16 per cent in 1980 to 6.7 per cent in 1983. In that this was due to the increase in unemploymnent and fear of redundancy then, as unemployment levels stabilise and then fall, wage rates are likely to rise again.

Finally, Barker concludes that as a result of the increased interdependence of national economies, co-ordinated reflation is more effective than ever before and the costs of unilateral reflation in the form of import expansion, balance of payments crises and unplanned depreciation are correspondingly greater. Therefore attempts by the United Kingdom to reflate, on its own, are likely to fail through balance of payment crises or inflation, or to lead to trade wars.

France

In Chapter 3 Jean-Pierre Puig, the Director of INSEE, gives an exposition of the functioning of the labour market in the DMS model of France, presents some of the forecasting results and points out the principal shortcomings of the model. The DMS model's medium-term projections were used in the preparation of the seventh, eighth and ninth economic plans for France. For the ninth plan (1984–88) three scenarios relating to the international environment were devised.

The first assumes that the world economy will recover slowly and that the trends apparent during 1975–80, between the two oil shocks, will resume. The annual rate of growth of production of France's main trading partners would thus be 2.7 per cent and inflation 7.1 per cent per annum. The second scenario assumes that there will be persistent economic stagnation leading to a deflationary spiral and increasing compartmentalisation of the world economy. Annual growth rates of production of France's trading partners would then be 1.5 per cent per annum over 1984 to 1988 coupled with 5.4 per cent inflation. The third scenario assumes that the United States policy of disinflation and stabilisation will be successful, thus giving a new boost to world economic growth led by the most advanced countries (the United States and Japan). The growth of France's partners would be 2.8 per cent, much as in the first scenario, but with lower inflation at 4.5 per cent.

In the ninth plan five other domestic scenarios were variants on a steady increase in public spending, a rapid growth of purchasing power and a reduction in working hours. The remaining scenarios assumed a more rapid modernisation of the industrial sector led by the public sector. The best results for employment occurred when there was intensive investment in the industrial sector in order to ease the pressure on the balance of payments.

The macro-economic strategy for the ninth French plan, therefore, combined a massive capital stock modernisation campaign so as to lessen France's external dependence coupled with an attempt to halt the increase in the per capita purchasing power of the average wage. Finance for the investment meant that a special effort was made to increase household savings, especially as earnings would be increasing much more slowly than in the past.

It was felt that, despite the test of this strategy on the DMS model, unpredictable results might still occur. This was because the conditions for implementing the strategy were not basically dependent upon government decision, since reallocation resources between investment and consumption demands a consensus of all the economic partners – a consensus that government action may facilitate but cannot possibly guarantee.

Belgium

In Chapter 4 Marc Vanden Boer of the Belgian National Planning Office discusses unemployment and forecasting in Belgium. He begins by noting that the problem of unemployment is extremely acute although the 'official figures' show a remarkable stability, with the same number being employed in 1981 compared to 1970 and only unemployment having shown an upward trend – 0.8 per cent and 4.4 per cent in 1970 and 1981 respectively. He warns, however, that the official figures use restricted definitions of employment and unemployment and that because of the economic crisis the content of the two notions has changed, and this has not been taken into account in official data. For example, the official figures of unemployment take no account of the part-time unemployment that has increased because of the recession, and they ignore a large number of people occupied by the public sector in special absorption programmes that did not exist before 1975. He reasons that these and other similar problems mean that the official figures for unemployment in Belgium are underestimated by as much as

13.4 per cent, ie the 'real' unemployment in Belgium could have been as high as 17.8 per cent in 1981.

The explosion in unemployment in Belgium in the early 1980s was not solely due to the worldwide economic crisis as the baby boom of the 1950s and 1960s meant that a larger number of young people than usual entered the labour force. Thus, despite a doubling of school attendance within 20 years, the number of young females entering the labour force in 1980 was 28.7 per cent higher than in 1970, and the number of young males was 8.1 per cent more in 1980 than 1970.

In the rest of the chapter, Vanden Boer examines a possible solution of the unemployment problem by reducing individual working time. This he examines in two simulation models, SERENA and Maribel, that were used by the Belgian Planning Office. Both models are rather mechanical in their treatment of reductions in working time. Unsurprisingly, reducing working time is seen as a possible solution but Vanden Boer wisely regards his results as premature. In the last section of his chapter, Vanden Boer provides some employment forecasts for Belgium using a simple 17-sector model of the economy.

The Netherlands

In Chapter 5, Hasselman, Kok and Okker present the Central Planning Bureau's model of the Netherlands (FREIA) and examine some simulations with possible employment policies. The world recession, which started in 1980 – the most serious since the 1930s recession according to the authors – faced the open Netherlands economy with a slow-down in world trade, in particular, in oil refinery products; and high real interest rates and a decline in the demand for natural gas with a corresponding drop in prices. All this, coupled with a high growth in labour supply, as in the Belgian case, contributed to a sharp rise in unemployment from 5.25 per cent in 1980 to 13.5 per cent in 1983. The Netherlands economy is characterised by underutilisation of capital and labour, large surpluses on the current account and a low rate of inflation – for all of which an expansionary policy would be an appropriate remedy. Unfortunately government budget deficits have risen to a dangerous level so that their reduction has become a primary goal. As a result, an expansionary policy is hardly possible. On the other hand, though a reduction of the government deficit would have the effect of lowering interest rates, the impact of lower interest rates on investment is lessened by the high underutilisation of capital. In that situation, the propensity to invest, and so create new jobs, is low.

Three scenarios of employment were simulated with the FREIA model: first, an expansionary set of policies financed through borrowing on the capital market; second, policies involving a reduction in wage rates; third, policies involving a reduction in working time.

In the first scenario the short-run positive effects of an expansionary policy on employment cause unemployment to fall initially, but it begins to rise again after a few years. This is because of the 'crowding out' phenomenon, that is, the displacement of private expenditure by public expenditure through high interest rates. Investment outlays initially rise but drop after a couple of years because the higher long-term interest rate makes itself felt and investment declines. Employment moves in line with labour requirements and capacity utilisation rates. Therefore unemployment falls initially and rises later.

In the second scenario, moderate wage reductions (a once-and-for-all 2 per cent reduction in the wages paid by enterprises in 1983 was tried and so was an annual reduction of 2.5 per cent combined with an annual reduction of taxes on wage income of 0.5 per cent of net national product for four years) spread out over several years has a positive impact on employment. This was because of a slowing-down of the scrapping process. (ie the substitution of capital for labour), an increase in exports and decrease in private consumption and imports. In order to prevent too sharp a fall in private consumption, the authors thought that wage reductions could be combined with tax reductions to an extent permitted by a controlled budget deficit in the long run. Unfortunately this may lead to a 'beggar my neighbour' policy since, if applied all over the world, it would further depress the world economy.

In the third scenario the impact of a 10 per cent reduction in the number of days worked per year spread out equally over a period of four years was simulated. The result of this initially led to lower-capacity production but not to higher-(capacity) labour requirements. The reason is the lagged influence of real labour costs on scrapping, in contrast to the immediate impact of effective labour time. In terms of employment the reduction in the number of working days had a 40 per cent effectiveness. If wages compensate less than fully for the decline in productivity, however, then the effects on employment will be less favourable. Furthermore, a decrease in the number of working days per year easily lead to an increase in the labour supply because of the greater opportunities for part-time work.

The authors conclude that the results of the testing of possible employment policies are rather pessimistic. The fact that any policies that will increase the budget deficit are out of order make expansionary policies difficult to stimulate by the public sector alone. Like Terry Barker, the authors believe that only an internationally co-ordinated expansionary policy could possibly solve the unemployment problem within a reasonable period. However, unlike Barker, they conclude that, coupled with such an expansion, only a very strong 'beggar my neighbour' policy without reaction from its trading partners could help the Netherlands economy because of its extreme openness.

OECD

In Chapter 6, in the first of the chapters looking at many countries at once, Peter Sturm of the OECD reports on ongoing work on the OECD Interlink model. The model includes six country models – for the United States, Japan, the Federal Republic of Germany, France, the United Kingdom and Canada. The Interlink system is used to generate the baseline forecasts, including employment and unemployment, for the OECD's semi-annual *Economic Outlook*. In the chapter a brief description is given of the production systems and their interaction.

The baseline projection for the years 1980 to 1985 is given for each country under the main assumption of unlinked and fixed exchange rates (this essentially corresponds to the forecasts presented in *Economic Outlook* 33, July 1983. In this projection, total employment is expected to increase for Canada, the United States and Japan, drop slightly for France, fall for the Federal Republic of Germany and drop sharply in the United Kingdom between the first half of 1980 and the first half of 1985.

Four diagnostic simulations are reported in which each of the major prices in the economy are varied (wages, prices and cost of capital) and the level of aggregate output is increased. Next, six policy simulations are reported. None of the results are particularly dramatic in terms of increasing employment levels, nor are clear pointers given to a strategy that may drastically reduce unemployment.

The 'consensus' simulation, discussed in the chapter, is the one that achieved consensus amongst OECD countries in mid-1983. Because of the dominant policy preoccupation with inflation and the resulting reluctance to use expansionary demand management in the face of high unemployment, the 'consensus' scenario combined income tax reduction with wage restraint and accommodation of monetary policy. The employment increases fostered both a positive substitution and demand effect. Sturm believes that this strategy has the most chance of success if the resulting increase in enterprises' income leads to increased expenditure, and if labour does not respond to this pick-up in demand (and employment) by wage demands in excess of productivity increases. Then a protracted period of real wage growth below the productivity advance appears necessary, no matter what policy levers are used to stimulate demand.

LINK

In Chapter 7, Peter Pauly reports on the use of the econometric world model of Project LINK to simulate alternative recovery scenarios for the period 1983–88. The purpose of the LINK system is to tie together major macro-econometric models being used in each of the main countries or regions of the world and to generate a consistent model system for studying the world economy. In the systems used here there are models for twenty-four OECD countries, eight centrally planned economies, and four regional models for developing countries. Essentially the linkage system receives a set of import and export prices from each country or area model and passes back a consistent set of prices so that world trade equilibrium can be achieved.

Three sets of scenarios are examined in the chapter. The first set looks at a number of different domestic policies for industrial countries. These focus on traditional domestic monetary and fiscal policy instruments in the major industrial countries. The second set of scenarios focuses on a number of alternative international conditions – a reduction in crude oil prices, a 10 per cent depreciation of the deutschmark and yen against the United States dollar and a worldwide reduction of tariff rates on manufactured goods by 5 per cent. Quite surprisingly the first two experiments do not significantly change unemployment levels, but recognisable though not overwhelming positive effects on unemployment result from the third experiment because world trade is powerfully stimulated by tariff reductions. Remarkably, this latter experiment pictures quite well the surge in world trade (around a 9 per cent increase in 1984 compared to 1983) that occurred in 1984 due to the revaluation of the United States dollar – although, of course, no one predicted that such a massive revaluation would occur (eg around 40 per cent depreciation of the deutschmark against the United States dollar).

The third set of scenarios look at directly improving prospects for the Third World. These are: stabilisation of LDC export prices, fulfilment of the targets for official development aid and a reduction in tariff rates for broad commodity groups excluding energy.

In general, Pauly concludes that from an international point of view it is quite striking, given the degree of interdependence of the world economy, that a substantial recovery in the OECD is almost synonymous with a corresponding recovery in developing countries. But the converse is not true. From the point of view of employment and unemployment, the prospects for the short and medium term (1984–88) given in the chapter are rather disappointing. None of the packages considered by LINK can be expected to bring about spectacular reductions in unemployment rates. This is particularly true for the European economies.

Mexico

In Chapter 8 Ajit Singh, of Cambridge University, illustrates a form of technology transfer when he describes in his chapter how two models, developed at Cambridge to study the United Kingdom economy, were adapted to Mexico and used to explore a number of policy options and strategies.

In the early 1980s Mexico was faced with a major economic and currency crisis, yet it was blessed with huge reserves of oil, amongst the world's largest. The central policy issue was how to translate this oil into economic development rather than substituting for existing sources of wealth as had been the experience of many oil-producing countries, both rich and poor. Mexican oil was essentially presented with two kinds of long-term strategies. One strategy consisted, basically, of seeking closer integration of the Mexican economy with the world economy coupled with fast development of Mexico's oil resources. The other, a 'nationalist' strategy, consisted of slow integration into a world economy not expected to grow very fast in the medium term coupled with retaining existing import controls, slow development of oil resources and a fast growth of internal demand.

Both strategies were simulated on the adapted Cambridge models. Briefly, the results were that under the old strategy the long-term rate of growth of employment fell far short of the projected growth of the labour force, while under the nationalist strategy, because agriculture and industry were able to expand rapidly, employment was able to expand at a rate adequate to absorb the new entrants to the labour force. In the event, neither strategy was fully implemented.

As well as these longer-term strategies, the short- to medium-term effects of a number of alternative economic policies were simulated. Three sets of policies were considered: deflation and a reduction in the rate of economic expansion; devaluation and slower economic growth; selective direct controls on manufactured imports and a high rate of growth maintained at 8 per cent per annum. The results showed that a policy of deflation alone, to achieve a balance of payments target, led to severe shortfalls in provision of jobs compared to the government's employment target. Devaluation yielded a much higher rate of economic growth and employment absorption, but this was at the cost of hyper-inflation. Finally the policy of import controls limited the rate of growth of manufactured imports and led to a high economic growth compatible with exchange rate and (relative) price stability.

Concluding chapter

In the concluding chapter the treatment of the labour market in each of the models is summarised, followed by a discussion on the major employment variables of forecasting interest. Then an attempt is made to evaluate the accuracy of perhaps the best-known employment forecasting efforts, those of the OECD. There it is concluded that the OECD unemployment forecasts are quite accurate and, in general, outperform a naive model – where next year's unemployment is simply made equal to this year's. The exercise also demonstrated that a model to forecast employment performed better than the naive model. Unfortunately, it was concluded that there is no guarantee that more informed forecasts based on better and often more elaborate models will lead to better forecasts.

Therein lies a dilemma. Informed forecasting performs better than naive forecasting, but how much investment should be made in the former? This is not easy to answer because the modelling process, namely the testing of hypotheses against data, leads to a better understanding of how economies function. Such understanding is intended to lead to improved economic policy and, in the subject-matter of this book – employment, to identify how best to create employment and eliminate unemployment. That the OECD forecasting has improved, albeit slightly, over time suggests that investment in improving employment forecasting models is worthwhile, in order to help improve our understanding of the economics of employment, even if it may not lead to great improvement in our ability to forecast.

Finally, some of the broad alternative scenarios that need to be considered with respect to their employment implications are discussed, and the policy conclusions of the studies are evaluated.

Chapter Two

The Cambridge multisectoral dynamic model and alternative strategies for full employment in the United Kingdom

Terry Barker, Department of Applied Economics, University of Cambridge, United Kingdom

2.1 INTRODUCTION

This chapter[1] uses a large-scale economic model of the United Kingdom to examine the prospects for employment and unemployment over the 1980s and alternative economic strategies to move towards full employment.

Section 2.2 summarises the model and its properties, discussing the wage equation in detail. Section 2.3 looks at the unemployment problem in the United Kingdom, giving the forecasts of different medium-term groups. Section 2.4 describes the Conservative government's medium-term financial strategy and two alternatives to it, protection with a mixture of import tariffs and quotas and an investment-led expansion. Both alternatives include substantial reflation and elements in them correspond very loosely to the economic programmes proposed by the Labour and SDP/Liberal Alliance in the June 1983 election. Section 2.5 decomposes the alternatives into effects given by the different policies within them. Finally, sections 2.6 and 2.7 conclude with some limitations of the study and the main lessons for policy which come out of it.

2.2 FORECASTING WITH THE CAMBRIDGE MULTISECTORAL DYNAMIC MODEL

2.2.1 A general description

Version 6 of the Cambridge Growth Projects model[2] of the United Kingdom economy distinguishes 40 industrial sectors, giving annual projections up to the year 2000. The model is a disequilibrium one in that it does not assume full employment, balance of payments equilibrium or a stable and satisfactory financial outlook. Projections of a 'balanced' economy can be obtained by suitable government policies and movements in wage rates, the exchange rate and interest rates, but there is no guarantee that these policies and changes will be acceptable or that they will materialise by the free operation of market forces. Although some of the behavioural equations in the model assume optimising behaviour by agents, there are no such assumptions for the operation of the whole economy. Economic development is seen as essentially a historical process with the outcome in any year depending on that of earlier years. Expectations are treated as adaptive with the fundamental assumption being made that agents, as well as model-builders, are largely ignorant and uncertain about the consequences of their actions and decisions on the economy. Lawson (1981) contrasts this Keynesian approach with that of the rational expectations school. The model is seen as a means of organising data and judgements derived from economic theory and practical experience. One of the most important parts of that organisation, especially in a large and comprehensive model, is the imposition of identities within an accounting framework.

The model is a comprehensive one, including the determination of output, prices, incomes and expenditures, treating the whole economy as comprising 40 industries plus the government and personal sectors. It has recently been extended to include the holdings of financial assets and liabilities by institutional sectors, with an option for interest and other financial returns and payments to be derived from these holdings. It contains over 8,000 variables with over 3,000 of them as endogenous and about 800 of the endogenous variables determined from stochastic equations.

The model is based on the accounting structure of the System of National Accounts (SNA) (United Nations, 1968). It is estimated by conventional econometrics analysis of time series (usually ordinary least squares or full information maximum likelihood for systems) from annual data 1954–78 and by deriving a set of input-output and other coefficient matrices from a detailed cross-section analysis of a base year, 1975 in version 6 of the model (Barker, van der Ploeg and Weale, 1983). The cross-section coefficients are updated through the projection period to allow for technical change and other expected movements. The time-series estimates are characterised by the same form of equation being estimated for every sector in a particular classification. This has a number of advantages: it allows for easy comparisons across sections of parameter estimates; it acts as a deterrent to *ad hoc* explanations for particular sectors; it saves both human and computer resources in estimating a very large model; and it means that the algebraic and numerical structure of the model remains reasonably clear despite its large size.

2.2.2 The economics of the model

The version of the model used to generate the employment forecasts in this paper has the following economic structure and properties.

The exogenous variabels of the model are divided into three groups.

First there are economic policy variables such as tax rates, national insurance contributions, government expenditures, the rate of interest and the strength of incomes policy. The exchange rate is also included in the group, although it is not independent of the rate of interest and the two variables must be set together. The second group comprises rest-of-the-world variables such as industrial production and wholesale prices in world areas and the prices charged by the United Kingdom's competitors in overseas markets. The third group is of domestic resources such as the working population and the output levels of North Sea oil and gas (though these may be treated as policy variables in some exercises).

Demand is endogenous. It is built up for each of the 40 commodities from separate demands by industries for current input and for invest-ment, by private consumers, the government and exporters. In these sets of relationships, demands are affected by current and past levels of output, real income, production abroad, relative prices and various tax levels and rules. Interest rates play a part in explaining fixed investment, especially that by households in new dwellings. The consumers' expen-ditures are constrained to add up to a total derived from a consumption function which includes real wealth and real income acting on the expenditure with a distributed lag.

Supply is met by domestic production and imports, the ratio deter-mined by the level of total domestic expenditures, the relative price of the imported to the home-produced commodity and an index of excess demand. Industrial output levels and changes affect fixed investment, stock building and labour demand through stochastic equations usually involving lags in the response.

Labour demand is found from sets of equations determining total hours worked and average hours worked, assuming that workers and hours are substitutes. The change in total hours worked is determined by the change in output, the ration of investment to output (to allow for productivity changes associated with investment) and the change in unemployment. The change in average hours worked is determined from normal hours, allowing a trend and with a lagged adjustment, and the level of unemployment. Employment is found by dividing total hours worked by average hours worked.

Prices are built up from costs allowing for variations in capacity utilisation and for competition from imports to affect prices set by some industries. Costs are divided into costs of materials, services and fuels calculated from the current requirements of each industry, plus the wage bill and any industrial taxes. The wage bill is the product of the average wage rate for the whole economy, the wage differential (exogenous in this version of the model) and the numbers employed. It is one of the main inflows of income to the personal sector, the others being transfers from the Government and interest, profits and dividends distributed from the company sectors.

Since the model is designed for making long-term projections of the economy and analysing alternative policies and economic environment, we have imposed certain properties derived from economic theory or from experience in forecasting. For example, long-term price homogeneity is imposed in the equations so that a 10 per cent increase in all prices and in the nominal stock of wealth has no effect on real variables. Estimates of price elasticities are usually constrained to be in the expected direction.

2.2.3 The explanation of wage inflation

The model contains a behaviour equation explaining wage rates which has been estimated by Lawson (1982). This is particularly important at a time when the main concern of economic policy is the reduction of inflation and the main criticism of alternative reflationary strategies is that they will cause a return to the high inflation rates of the 1970s. The equation explains annual changes in money wages over the period 1955–79 and takes the form:

$$
\begin{aligned}
\Delta \log \varrho = \ & \Delta \log(\Pi_\epsilon/\tau_\epsilon) + 0.0205 \\
& + 0.491\,[7.6209 + 0.0205\tau - \log\Lambda^{-1}(\varrho\ \tau_\epsilon/\Pi_\epsilon)] \\
& (0.053) \\
& - 0.0186\ \Delta\log\ \bar{u} \\
& (0.007) \\
& - 0.0184\ \delta_{ip} + 0.036\ \delta_{72} \\
& (0.002)
\end{aligned}
$$

$$R^2 = 0.981;\ DW = 1.98;\ SEE = 0.0007$$

where ϱ is average value of earnings per person-year in £
Π_ϵ is the consumer price index, 1975 = 1,000
τ_ϵ is the retentions ratio (disposable wages/wages)
τ is a time trend with 1975 = 0
$\bar{u}$ is the unemployment rate (unemployment/(employment + unemployment))
δ_{ip} is an estimated incomes policy variable
δ_{72} is a dummy variable for 1972
Δ denotes the change and Λ^{-1} the log

(The numbers in brackets are standard errors).

Here the change in money wages is determined so that any changes in prices or in retentions are fully compensated with wage bargainers aiming at a fixed increase in real wages of 2 per cent a year – 'the target' – hence the coefficient on $\Delta\log\ (\Pi_\epsilon/\tau_\epsilon)$ is restricted to unity in the estimation. Naturally, there is usually a shortfall between actual increases and the target and part of this, 'the catch-up', is made up (about half) each year. This difference between the target and actual real wage rates is shown in square brackets in the second line of the equation with the actual wage rate as the last term. Increases in unemployment and incomes policies act so as to depress actual wage rates temporarily. Any shortfall below the target is accumulated and made up in later years.

This equation performs very well in explaining wage movements up to 1979: it is structurally stable and the estimated coefficients appear to be reasonable. The only doubt is the persistent lagging of actual wages below the target towards the end of the period, so that in 1979 the actual wage rate is 8 per cent below target. This implies that in spite of the considerable increases in real incomes, 1978–81, there remain considerable pent-up wage demands.

When the equation is allowed to forecast wages over the period 1979–83 in the model, it overestimates the rate of inflation. This can be interpreted in four ways:

1. The present and previous governments have been in effect operating a strong incomes policy. In moving away from consensus politics the government has radically shifted the old wage negotiating framework. Lawson (1982: 11) cites Peston (1980) in support of this interpretation.
2. The increase in unemployment and its exceptionally high level are having an effect over and above what would be predicted by the equation. On closer examination it appears that even a doubling of the rate of unemployment from 5 per cent to 10 per cent (an extra one million unemployed) has only a small (1 per cent) depressing effect on money wages according to the equation. This is half the estimated effect of an incomes policy at its weakest, for example in 1979 after it had broken down.
3. There has been a radical downward revision in the target increase in real earnings.
4. Wage earners have finally abandoned the attempt to catch up on the accumulated shortfall of actual wages below target wages.

The first interpretation is the only one consistent with the stability of the equation but frankly it does not have much appeal. It is true that the government is imposing strong restrictions on the growth in public sector wages but it is only able to do so because of the low increases in the private sector and the general fear of unemployment. Accordingly, we have imposed an unemployment effect on the equation which operates when unemployment rises above 1.25 million.

This unemployment effect is shown in Figure 2.1: when unemployment rises to two million, this depresses money wage inflation by 2.6 percentage points; when it rises to three million, inflation falls by 4.8 points. The Figure shows the strength of incomes policy required to achieve such reductions in inflation; thus an incomes policy slightly less

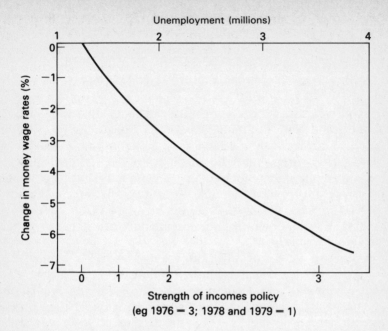

Figure 2.1: Unemployment effects and their equivalent incomes policy strengths, 1980–90 unemployment (in millions)

strong than the social contract of 1976 would have the same effect as three million unemployed on this reckoning.

Imposing this effect and assuming that the experience of mass unemployment has reduced target growth in real wage rates from 2 per cent to 1.5 per cent in 1980, we find that we can explain the actual and expected increase in money wages over the years 1980–83 with the wage equation. It should be noted that this treatment leaves the pent-up wage demands of 1979 more or less intact and that as the level of unemployment stops growing from 1983 onwards, wage inflation will gradually reassert itself. It also means that as unemployment is brought down, then substantial wage inflation will reappear unless there is a very substantial increase in real incomes. Both features seem to be plausible characterisations of the late 1980s.

2.2.4 The method of comparative dynamics using a forecasting model

The model is used to compare the expected outcome under a continued medium-term financial strategy as embraced by Conservative governments from 1979 with two alternative strategies, the first being protection of the economy and the second being a policy of massive investment in export-oriented industries. Both the alternatives are intended to reduce the level of unemployment substantially by 1990.

The value of this approach to the issues is apparent. The theoretical arguments about protection, for example, can be put in the context of the United Kingdom economy in 1984 with high unemployment, strong underlying inflationary pressures and a high propensity to import both on average and at the margin. The limitations of the theoretical analysis (eg Corden, 1971) assuming a static model, perfect competition and constant returns to scale, can be set aside and the tariff effects measured more comprehensively, though for a specific economy over a specific period.[3] Since the model is disaggregated, the partial and general effects on individual industries can be distinguished and non-traded inputs and output can be properly included in the analysis. Since the model has trade, quantity and price equations estimated on United Kingdom data, the terms of trade effects and substitutions between domestic and foreign goods can all be taken into account.

However, there are disadvantages to the approach. Since the model is very large, complex and non-linear, it is not possible to obtain an analytical solution so as to decompose the effects of tariffs, retaliation, extra investment, reflation and exchange rate depreciation. These separate effects can be measured by standardised comparisons as is done later, but there are strong interactions between the components, especially if the overall strategy is designed to raise employment by over two million. Furthermore, because the approach is specific, there is always the difficulty that the results may be significantly and unexpectedly different if the strategy is implemented in a different period, at a different scale or for a different country.

For plausibility the alternative strategies should each satisfy certain criteria in terms of financial balances (public sector borrowing requirement – PSBR – and the balance of payments) and available supplies of labour and other real resources. The results can also be compared with similar exercises done by others,[4] in particular the projections of the protection strategy published by the CEPG,[5] using different assumptions and a different model.

2.3   THE DIMENSIONS OF THE UNEMPLOYMENT PROBLEM IN THE UNITED KINGDOM[6]

2.3.1   Forecasts of unemployment

After remaining at about 1.5 million (1976–79), unemployment in the United Kingdom began rising in 1980. At the end of June 1980 registered unemployment was 1.7 million; it climbed rapidly through 1981 and by January 1982 it was 2.8 million; since then the rise has slowed and the June 1983 figure was 3 million although this new figure is based on a new definition with the removal of certain groups from

Table 2.1: Different forecasts of unemployment (in millions)

	1980	1981	1982	1983	1984	1985	1990
CEF 83/3 (June 1983)	1.8	2.6	3.0	3.3	3.5	3.7	4.3
CEF 82/3 (June 1982)	1.8	2.7	3.2	3.2	3.2	3.2	3.3
CEF 0 (June 1978)	1.9	2.0	2.3	2.5	2.8	2.7	—
CEPG (Dec 1982)	1.6	2.5	—	—	—	—	4.5
LBS (July 1983)	1.6	2.4	2.8	3.1	3.1	3.0	—
IER (Summer 1983)	1.7	2.7	2.8	3.1	3.2	3.1	2.9

Note: There are differences in definitions as explained below.
     — denotes not available.

Sources: CEF: Cambridge Econometrics Forecast. CEF 0 is from T. Lawson and A. Winters 'Macroeconomic Projections for the United Kingdom 1978–85', Conference on the Industrial Implications of Economic Policy, Pembroke College (1978), which launched the service. Projections of total United Kingdom unemployment, including school-leavers and excluding adult students.

CEPG: Cambridge Economic Policy Group, *Economic Policy Review*, **8**, **2** (1982: 7). Annual average monthly figures, United Kingdom, excluding school-leavers and adult students.

LBS: London Business School, *Economic Outlook* **7**, **10** (1983: 3). Projections of United Kingdom unemployment, excluding school-leavers and adult students, average monthly figures.

IER: Institute for Employment Research (formerly Manpower Research Group) University of Warwick, *Review of Economy and Employment* (1983: 16). Projections are of United Kingdom registered unemployment, including school-leavers measured as claimants to benefit.

the register. This represents an unemployment rate of 12.4 per cent of employees in employment.

Table 2.1 shows some early forecasts of unemployment in the United Kingdom. The general picture was that it would either continue to rise steadily through the rest of the 1980s, reaching over four million by 1990 (the Cambridge groups) or that it will remain at about three million up to 1985 and beyond (LBS and IER). These are all forecasts on the broad basis of 'present policies', interpreted so as to include fiscal relaxation if appropriate: for example, the CEF 83/3 forecast allows for a reduction in the standard rate of income tax from 30 per cent in 1983 to 25 per cent in 1988. The forecasts all assumed no change in the official definitions of unemployment.

The table also shows two earlier Cambridge Econometrics[7] forecasts, the one which launched the service: CEF 0 which anticipated as far back as 1978 a rise in unemployment to 2.7 million by 1985 and CEF 82/3, the forecast which is used as the basis for comparisons with the alternatives in this paper. The Cambridge Economic Policy Group (CEPG) and the Warwick group have also published early forecasts of a massive rise in unemployment. The early CEF forecasts were based on two factors. First, North Sea oil was expected to produce huge foreign exchange gains for the United Kingdom starting 1979–82, which would allow sterling to be revalued or prevent substantial devaluation or depreciation required to keep the economy competitive. These gains were increased by the increases in oil prices (1979–80). Second, there have been long-established official forecasts of an increase in the working population through the 1980s, adding one million or more to the labour force. To these factors must be added the pursuit of deflationary monetary and fiscal policies by the 1979–83 Conservative government and the effects of the international recession (1981–82).

These views are confirmed by *ex post* analyses of the contributing factors to the recession done by the National Institute of Economic and Social Research (NIER, 1981) and the London Business School (Budd *et al*, 1981). This work concludes that about 40 per cent of the shortfall in output (1978–80) was due to fiscal policy effects, about 30 per cent was due to the exchange rate not maintaining constant competitiveness and about 20–30 per cent was due to the increase in the price of oil.

2.3.2 Forecasts of employment structure

Table 2.2 shows recent forecasts of employment structure given by the medium-term groups. All are on the basis of current policies and all were completed before the re-election of the Conservative government in June 1983. They show a diversity in the expected structural changes, although all the forecasts expect an increase in unemployment (1982–90), and all make the same assumption that the labour force will increase by between 500,000 and 600,000 over the period.

Table 2.2: Forecasts of United Kingdom employment structure (in '000s)

	Level 1982	Changes 1982–90			
		CEF 82/3 June 1982	CEF 83/3 June 1983	CEPG Dec 1982	IER Summer 1983
Manufacturing	5,905	– 645	– 736	– 1,135	– 99
Private services and construction	11,110	1,022	520	26	519
Government	5,365	231	– 210	7	98
Other	1,321	– 230	– 195	– 41	– 121
Total employment	23,701	405	– 621	– 1,143	397
Registered unemployment	2,800	105	1,221	(1,700)	100
Total labour force	26,800	500	600	550	600

Notes: 1. All figures include the self-employed.
2. Total labour force figures are rounded to nearest 50,000.
3. Figures in brackets are estimated by the author using the sources available.
4. Levels are taken from the IER *Review of Economy and Employment*.

*Sources:*CEF: Cambridge Econometrics Forecasts 82/3 and 83/3. Manufacturing figures exclude food manufacturing and building materials. Construction figures include building materials.

CEPG: Cambridge Economic Policy Group, *Review of Economy and Employment* (1982).

IER: Institute for Employment Research, *Review of Economy and Employment* (1983).

The three Cambridge forecasts expect a further major loss of jobs in manufacturing which continues a trend evident since the 1950s. The source of net new jobs in the past has mainly been in the services and government sectors but there is doubt whether this will continue. There are several reasons for this: first, the recession has been a loss of jobs in the service sectors; second, banking, insurance and other services are becoming more automated so that they may redeploy labour rather than increase their employment; and third, government policy is to reduce employment in the public sector. The forecasts with the highest unemployment (CEF 83/3 and CEPG) also have the lowest number of new jobs in services and the Government. Indeed, the change from CEF 82/3 to CEF 83/3 reflects a forecast of much slower growth of government expenditure over the 1980s and hence some loss in employment, as well as a change towards higher productivity growth in the service sectors.

2.4 THE UNITED KINGDOM MEDIUM-TERM FINANCIAL STRATEGY AND THE ALTERNATIVES

2.4.1 The medium-term financial strategy

The United Kingdom medium-term financial strategy (MTFS) began when the Conservatives took office in June 1979 and has been the basis for official policy ever since. It is described in successive annual financial statements and budget reports beginning in 1980 (United Kingdom Treasury, 1980) and it is assumed below that it will continue to guide policy through the decade.

Inflation has to be brought down by controlling the money supply (originally measured as sterling M3 but later modified to become a range of monetary measures). The exchange rate must be allowed to vary or domestic money will not be controlled, though this principle has been relaxed on occasion when the authorities have wished to prevent too sudden and too rapid depreciations of the currency. A prime consideration, which has become a target for the strategy, is the progressive reduction of the PSBR. Since this was to be achieved at the same time as reducing direct taxes, this meant that indirect taxes have been raised and attempts have been made to cut public expenditure. The cuts have had effect, but mainly on the capital side.

The MTFS is a clear break with the post-war tradition in the United Kingdom of full employment as an important target for policy, if not the main one. The move towards monetary targets began in 1976 after the IMF visit in the autumn, but the full abandonment of demand management did not come until 1979 and later when the consequences for effective demand (and indeed inflation) of an increase in oil prices, an increase in the rate of value added tax (VAT) from 8 per cent to 15 per cent and later the international recession, were all ignored.

2.4.2   The assumptions for the projections

The assumptions for a continuation of present policies within the MTFS and for the alternatives of protection and high investment are given in Tables 2.3, 2.4 and 2.5. The strategies are:

1. Present policies: a continuation of the present financial strategy after 1984 but with some easing of the PSBR target so as to allow faster growth in social capital formation.
2. Protection: tariffs and quotas on manufactured imports combined with substantial domestic reflation so as to bring unemployment down to 1979 levels by 1990.
3. High investment: a reflation strategy with a permanent incomes policy combined with extra investment in exporting industries.

2.4.3   The protection strategy for full employment

A substantial reflationary package is assumed to be introduced from the start of 1984 with a reduction of VAT from 15 to 10 per cent and a further cut in employers' national insurance contributions (NIC). Government expenditure is also to be increased in the strategy but it takes longer to react (there are already some increases built into the projection of present policies). In 1985 VAT and the NIC came down to remain at the lower levels (5 per cent VAT) for the rest of the projection. Trade union co-operation with the strategy is assumed in the form of wage restraint in 1984 equivalent to the 'incomes policy effect' estimated for 1978 (Lawson, 1982). Wage restraint is also assumed for the period 1986–90 when worsening inflation threatens the strategy.

The reductions in taxes are financed by a 15 per cent tariff on imports of manufactures – but this must gradually increase thereafter in order to maintain domestic growth and the balance of payments. It is assumed to be impractical to impose tariffs on imports of services. The increasing tariff revenues allow a gradual increase in personal allowances from 1986 to maintain domestic expenditures. Extra protection is assumed in the form of selective quotas for three industries – electrical engineering, motor vehicles and textiles. This has been repeatedly advocated in a protectionist package, for example, by the Trades Union Congress (TUC) in its *Economic Review* (1982: 36). The quotas are set so as to maintain the ratios of imports to domestic output in the selected industries at the values of the ratios in 1983. The strength of the quotas is measured by comparing the imports which would have come in without the quotas with the restricted levels. It turns out that quotas do not reduce textile imports over the period or electrical imports in 1984 and 1985, because the tariff is sufficient to keep the quota ratio at 1983 levels. However, the motor vehicle quota reduces imports by 8 per cent in 1986, increasing to 18 per cent in 1990 and the electrical quota

Table 2.3: Key tax rates and national insurance contributions (in percentages)

		1983	1984	1985	1986–90
VAT	Present policies	15	15	15	15
	Protection	15	10	5	5
	High investment	15	10	5	5
Income tax standard rate	Present policies	28.5	28	25	25
	Protection	28.5	28	28	28
	High investment	28.5	28	28	28

In addition: 1. Income tax personal allowances are increased with protection by an extra 2.5 per cent in 1986 and 5 per cent in 1987, rising by 12 per cent in 1990.
2. Employers' national insurance contributions are reduced with protection and high investment by 1 percentage point in 1984 and a further percentage point in 1985.

Table 2.4: Public expenditure (in percentages per annum)

		1983	1984	1985	1986	1987–90
Public authorities current expenditure	Present policies	0.9	1.5	1.5	1.5	1.5
	Protection	0.9	2.2	3.0	3.0	3.9
	High investment	0.9	2.2	2.2	2.2	1.5
Social capital formation	Present policies	0.3	10	10	10	10
	Protection	0.3	10	15	15	15
	High investment	0.3	10	15	15	15

In addition, both protection and high investment have extra investment in nationalised industries of 5 per cent base levels in 1984 rising to 10 per cent in 1985, 20 per cent in 1986 and 30 per cent from 1987 onwards, except electricity, where it remains at 20 per cent.

Table 2.5: Exchange rate and interest rates

		1983	1984	1985	1986	1987–90
Effective exchange rate (percentage change)	Present policies	− 3.3	− 1.5	− 0.7	− 0.2	− 0.2
	Protection	− 3.3	− 16.3	− 8.1	− 0.2	− 0.2
	High investment	− 3.3	− 16.3	− 0.7	− 0.2	− 0.2
Banks' base rate (percentage)	Present policies	12.8	10.5	10.5	10	9
	Protection	12.8	12.0	13.0	13	13
	High investment	12.8	12.0	13.0	12	11

Table 2.6: Special assumptions

Protection	Tariffs of 15 per cent on manufactured imports in 1984 rising to 30 per cent by 1990.
	Import quotas on electrical goods, motor vehicles and textiles from 1984.
	Retaliation in the form of an extra 10 per cent foreign tariff on United Kingdom manufactures in 1985 and a reduction in United Kingdom exports to the EEC of 2 per cent in 1985, rising to 5 per cent in 1986 following United Kingdom withdrawal.
	Incomes policy of 1978 strength introduced at the end of 1985.
High Investment	Extra private investment funded by special investment loans from 1985 onwards. This is channelled towards exporting and is assumed to raise exports of selected industries by 3 per cent above base levels in 1987, 6 per cent above in 1988, 8 per cent above in 1989 and 10 per cent above in 1990.
	A permanent incomes policy is introduced with a small but increasing effect: by 1990 the policy is at strength 2.

reduces these imports by 4 per cent in 1986, rising to 26 per cent in 1990 (see Table 2.6).

Retaliation is an acknowledged danger of this strategy but its likely scale is very difficult to judge. There are usually strong protectionist pressures in most countries waiting to emerge when the time is right. The experience of the 1930s was of a wave of strong retaliation after the United States had passed the Hawley-Smoot Bill in 1930 (Jones, 1934). However, the United Kingdom is less important now in trade than the United States was in 1930; in addition, the existence of the European Economic Community (EEC) provides a safeguard against the piecemeal European retaliation of the 1930s. The CEPG have assumed (in their 1980 *Economic Policy Review*) retaliation reducing United Kingdom non-oil exports once and for all by 5 per cent, but more recently they have judged that it could be stronger at 10 per cent (CEPG, 1982). The assumption adopted here is that tariffs would be imposed on United Kingdom manufactured exports at an average rate of 10 per cent implying, with an average price elasticity of 1.5, a reduction of 15 per cent. This average is somewhat misleading, however, as the price elasticities differ considerably across export goods. Table 2.7 shows the estimated elasticities in the model and the lagged responses of exports to the foreign tariff.

The projection also assumes withdrawal from the EEC during 1984 with the consequent reduction in food prices as tariffs are removed from food imports and ending of any United Kingdom net contribution to the EEC budget. This withdrawal, combined with the protection measures, is assumed to provoke further EEC retaliation amounting to a 2 per cent cut in United Kingdom exports to the EEC in 1985, rising to a 5 per cent cut in 1986 onwards.

Table 2.7: Elasticities of United Kingdom exports of manufactures and the volume responses to a 10 per cent foreign tariff

Export group (1–5 non-manufactures)	Own-price elasticity	Response to a 10 per cent foreign tariff (percentage)	
		After one year	After two and more years
6. Chemicals	− 0.733	− 2.5	− 7.0
7. Textiles	− 2.163	− 6.0	− 12.0
8. Iron and steel	0	0	0
9. Non-ferrous metals	− 0.621	− 3.0	− 6.0
10. Metal manufactures	− 2.988	0	− 30.0
11. Mechanical engineering	− 1.502	0	− 15.0
12. Electrical engineering	− 1.849	− 9.0	− 18.0
13. Transport equipment	− 1.694	− 8.5	− 17.0
14. Instruments, etc	− 1.041	− 5.0	− 10.0
15. Clothing, etc	− 2.399	− 12.0	− 24.0
16. Rest of manufactures	− 2.092	− 10.5	− 7.0

Source: Winters (1981)

2.4.4 The high investment strategy

This strategy combines reflation with a permanent incomes policy and substantial increases in investment in export-oriented industries.[8] As in the protection strategy, VAT is reduced to 5 per cent and national insurance contributions are abolished but the depreciation of sterling is limited to 15 per cent in the first year and the government expenditure increases are more restrained.

The incomes policy is assumed to have the strength as shown in Table 2.8, when it is compared with the strengths of past policies as estimated in Lawson (1982). Thus the last Labour government's policy reached a strength of 4.5 in 1977 compared with an assumed strength of 0.25 in the first year of permanent policy. Thus only mild restraint is necessary in the first year or so of this strategy when the VAT reductions, together with the high levels of unemployment, are helping to moderate inflation. Later on in the 1980s, as the level of unemployment falls and real wage pressures build up, the incomes policy must become increasingly severe, building up to a strength of 2 in 1990. This is required so that price inflation will be held under this strategy to the same rates as those forecast under present policies (1987–90).

The industrial policy which also characterises this strategy is one of strong government support, mainly in the form of cheap finance for investment in a number of key industries.[9] The policy is based on an analysis of the relationship between investment, growth and trade. It appears that those countries which have high ratios of investment to GDP also have high income elasticities of exports (Barker, 1981b). Raising the income elasticity of exports by a programme of selective

Table 2.8: Estimated and assumed strengths of incomes policies in the United Kingdom

Period	1965	1966	1967	1968	1969		
Strength	1.0	1.5	1.0	1.5	1.75		
Period	1975	1976	1977	1978			
Strength	1.3	3.0	4.5	1.0			
Period	1984	1985	1986	1987	1988	1989	1990
Strength	0.25	0.25	0.75	1.25	1.5	1.75	2.0

Source: Lawson (1982).

investment may be one way of overcoming the problem of deindustrialisation which has been a feature of United Kingdom economic development (Singh, 1977; Blackaby, 1979).

Table 2.9 shows the assumed increases in investment and the assumed consequential increases in exports. Financial services' investment in plant and machinery is assumed to increase by the same proportion as that in the selected manufacturing industries since much of it is equipment leased to manufacturing. Extra investment is also assumed for the nationalised industries in electricity, transport and communications. The overall effect is to raise the investment GDP ratio from 17.3 per cent in 1984 to 20.0 per cent in 1990. This suggests an increase in the income elasticity of exports from 0.99 to 1.37 after a delay of one or two years, and this is reflected in the extra growth of exports shown in the table.

2.4.5   A comparison of economic effects

The two reflation strategies succeed in reversing the rise in unemployment experienced in 1980–82, with protection getting unemployment back to 1979 levels. This is despite a rise in the working population projected at over 700,000 for 1979–90. The protection strategy is most successful because it has the highest growth in government expenditure (1986–90): 700,000 of the extra jobs in this strategy are in the government sector. This is a return to the increases in government employment of the early 1970s.

The reduction in unemployment shown in Figure 2.2 is probably overestimated since it assumes that every extra person employed is one less off the unemployment register. In fact as unemployment falls, participation rates are likely to increase, making any unemployment target for policy that much more difficult to reach.

Present policies are likely to hold down the increase in money wages through the 1980s by keeping unemployment at high levels.[10] In fact the relationship we have imposed between unemployment and inflation indicates that the slow-down in the growth of money wages may not

Table 2.9: Assumed extra investment and exports by selected industries in the high investment strategy (in percentages above present policies)

Multisectoral dynamic model industry	1985		1986		1987		1990	
	Invest-ment	Exports	Invest-ment	Exports	Invest-ment	Exports	Invest-ment	Exports
Plant and machinery								
5 Cereal processing	5	—	10	—	20	3	30	10
6 Food processing	5	—	10	—	20	3	30	10
11 Chemicals	5	—	10	—	20	3	30	10
14 Mechanical engineering	5	—	10	—	20	3	30	10
15 Instrument engineering	5	—	10	—	20	3	30	10
16 Electrical engineering	5	—	10	—	20	3	30	10
18 Motor vehicles	5	—	10	—	20	2	30	5
19 Aerospace	5	—	10	—	20	2	30	5
28 Printing & publishing	5	—	10	—	20	3	30	10
30 Manufactures n.e.s.	5	—	5	—	20	3	30	10
38 Financial services	5	—	10	—	20	3	30	10
All assets								
33 Electricity	5	—	10	—	20	—	20	—
35 Transport	5	—	10	—	20	—	30	—
36 Communication	5	—	10	—	20	—	30	—

persist, simply because wage negotiators get used to the high levels of unemployment; this effect has been neutralised by the assumption of a mild incomes policy in the period 1987–90. The high investment strategy relies on a permanent incomes policy to hold down wage and price inflation. This does not have to be as strong as the 1976–77 social contract but does need to increase gradually in strength from the time that it is introduced. Protection adds rising tariffs and a further depreciation to the inflation pressures to the other strategies. Even with a moderate incomes policy, inflation is back to the rates of 1976 and 1977 (Figure 2.3).

The fluctuations in the United Kingdom growth rate for 1970–81 have been considerable, judged by earlier experiences (or by that of other countries: 1973 growth was one of the highest and 1981 one of the lowest in the OECD). Some recovery from the 1980–81 recession is expected (1982–83); the policies of substantial reflation extend the recovery to 1984 and 1985, with high investment being the most

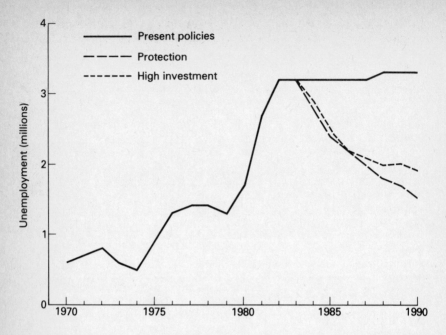

Note: Unemployment includes school-leavers and those on temporary schemes after 1982

Figure 2.2: Unemployment in three policy strategies, United Kingdom, 1970–90

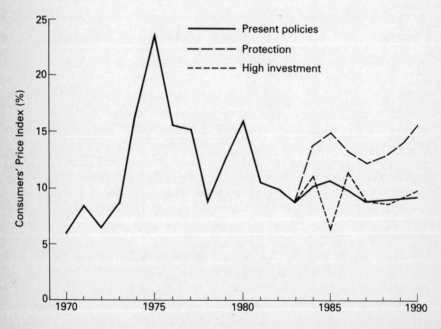

Figure 2.3: Inflation in three policy strategies, United Kingdom, 1970–90

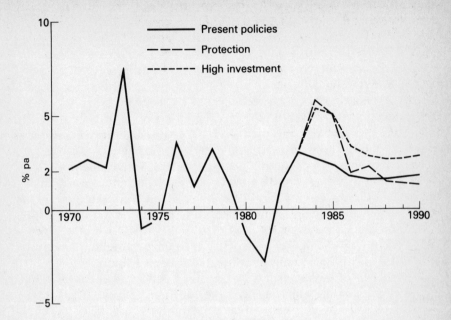

Figure 2.4: Growth in three policy strategies, United Kingdom, 1970–90

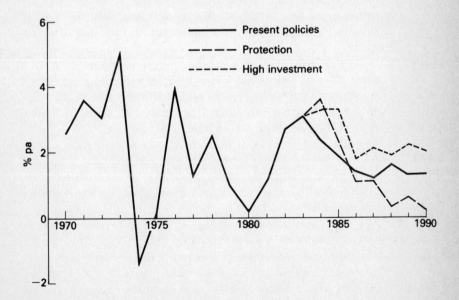

Figure 2.5: Growth in productivity in three policy strategies, United Kingdom, 1970–90

successful at sustaining growth rates above 2 per cent per annum (Figure 2.4). Note that these views do not anticipate a renewed world oil crisis in 1983–84 so that we are not expecting another sharp recession, comparable to those following earlier crises in 1974 and 1979–80.

Growth in productivity has fluctuated less than that in GDP. (Figure 2.5). The substantial fall in 1979 and 1980 is a cyclical phenomenon and repeats the fall of 1974. The recovery, in evidence in 1981 and 1982, is most cyclical. However, all the projections envisage that the rise will be sustained at higher levels than after 1975, although protection does not have rather low growth (1988–90). As expected, the highest sustained growth in productivity comes with high investment.

Protection reduces the PSBR most because tariff revenues are substantial and increasing (Figure 2.6). The lower income tax rates and high social capital spending, assumed with present policies, raise the PSBR ratio from the low rates of 1982–84. The highest PSBR is in the investment strategy. These figures include loans to finance the investment so that much of the borrowing does have real assets behind it.

The balance of payments has shown huge deficits in the mid-1970s and is at present showing equally huge surpluses (Figure 2.7). All the projections have a return to deficits in the mid-1980s followed by a cyclical recovery. The most protracted deficit comes with high investment mainly because 'best practice' technology tends to be imported. The protection strategy is likely to be less able to tolerate balance of payments deficits because of tariffs and the EEC withdrawal.

Figure 2.8 presents the average industrial growth (1983–90), the five fastest-growing industries and the five slowest-growing industries out of the 40 industries distinguished in the model. These are shown for the three categories.

On average, industrial growth is 2.2 per cent per annum (1983–90) under present policies, 3.0 per cent per annum under protection and 4.1 per cent per annum with high investment. The dispersion of individual industry growth under protection is smaller than with the alternatives, perhaps because the economy is less open.

The same industries tend to appear in the fastest-growing group, whatever policies are followed: instrument engineering, other manufacturing, electrical engineering and chemicals. And the same is true of the slowest-growing group: textile fibres, non-ferrous metals, shipbuilding, tobacco manufactures and iron and steel. However, it is interesting to note that two service industries – business services and communications – appear as fast growers with present policies, whereas with more reflation nearly all the fast growers are in manufacturing and none are in services. These service industries do have faster growth with reflation, but they do not respond as much as manufacturing industries to the extra demand.

Table 2.10 shows the distribution of the increase in employment on the alternatives over five sectors in the economy. General reflation

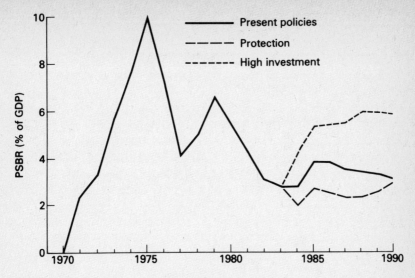

Figure 2.6: The PSBR in three policy strategies, United Kingdom, 1970–90

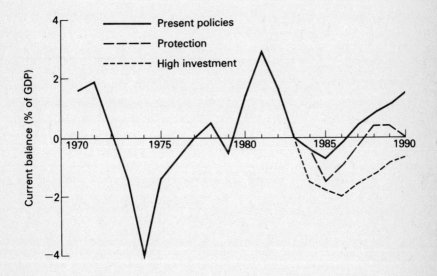

Figure 2.7: The balance of payments in three policy strategies, United Kingdom, 1970–90

includes those elements of reflation and sterling depreciation taken as common to both the protection and high investment alternatives. This shows that most of the extra employment is as a result of this reflation, whilst the rest is due either to more government expenditure, in the case of the protection strategy, or more service employment with high investment as a result of the higher growth in this strategy.

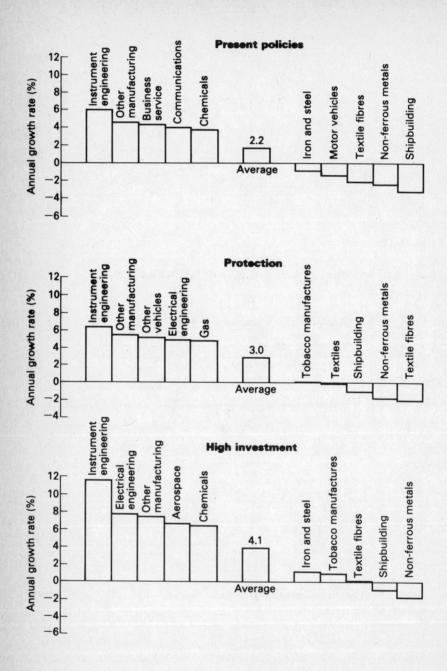

Figure 2.8: Fast and slow industrial growth in three policy strategies, United Kingdom, 1983–90

Table 2.10: Structural changes in employment in the alternatives, United Kingdom, 1990 (in '000s and in percentages)

	Primary sector	Manufacturing	Construction	Services	Government	Total
General reflation	18 (2)	238 (4)	152 (10)	465 (4)	134 (3)	1,007 (4)
Protection	28 (3)	334 (6)	249 (17)	360 (3)	805 (17)	1,777 (7)
High investment	23 (3)	329 (6)	171 (12)	723 (7)	134 (3)	1,380 (6)

Note: The figures in brackets are the percentage differences between the levels of employment in the alternatives and in the projection to 1990 under present policies.

2.5 AN ANALYSIS OF THE ALTERNATIVES

2.5.1 The protection strategy

The theoretical literature on protection emphasises the concept of effective protection, which includes the effect of a tariff on an industry's inputs as well as its outputs (Corden, 1971). The analysis of protection in a general equilibrium framework also goes further and includes the indirect effects on the economy through the government adjusting fiscal and monetary policy and the foreign exchanges adjusting the exchange rate both so as to maintain internal and external balance (ie full employment and balance of payments equilibrium). In the present exercise, tariffs and quotas are part of a general strategy and the effects of tariffs in reallocating resources between industries are overwhelmed by the general effects on an economy in conditions of unemployment with potential balance of payments problems.

In an empirical study of protection the following responses seem worth distinguishing:

1. the effects of the nominal tariff on trade, industrial prices and output, taking into account input structure and all the price responses and substitutions estimated as part of the overall model but holding wage rates as exogenous;
2. the response of wage bargainers to the higher cost of living and employment effects of the tariffs and quotas;
3. the response of other countries to the protection in the form of retaliation;
4. the response of the government to the tariff revenues which can be used to reduce tax rates or increase its own spending on health, education and other services;

5.   the response of the foreign exchanges to deficits or surpluses on the
balance of payments or indeed the imposition of tariffs on the
economy.

All these responses are part of the protection strategy presented above.
However, in addition, there is a 'Labour government effect' included in
the assumptions. This comprises the lower wage demands in the year
after Labour takes office, with the further depreciation of sterling of 75
per cent the following year and a mild version of social contract from
the year after that.

Table 2.11: An analysis of the effects of protection, United Kingdom, 1986

Decomposition	Unemployment '000s	Consumer prices %	GDP %	Exports %	Imports %	Balance of payments £ thousand million	PSBR £ thousand million
General reflation effect on present policy view	− 841	3.6	5.8	9.7	9.7	− 8.4	+ 9.5
Labour government effect on reflation	− 233	4.4	1.7	4.9	1.0	+ 0.5	0
Protection effect with no wage response	− 79	1.7	0.5	− 2.2	− 5.8	+ 8.7	− 17.4
Wage response to protection	113	4.2	− 0.8	− 2.4	− 0.4	− 1.7	+ 3.2
Retaliation effect	225	− 1.2	− 2.3	− 7.2	− 5.0	− 2.5	+ 2.3
Fiscal effect (spending the tariff revenues)	− 121	0.6	0.3	− 0.3	0.5	− 1.1	+ 1.3
Total	− 905	13.9	5.1	1.6	− 0.8	− 4.5	− 1.1

Note: The effects are measured by successively adding components to the present policy
view with real wage resistance assumed. They are percentage or absolute differences
between variables projected for 1986 in the successive model runs.

Table 2.11 decomposes the strategy into six parts. They will be
described as though they were sequential, but in fact they interact and
overlap. The assumptions and the results in the table allow for such
interactions. The table shows the effects of successively adding sets of
assumptions to the present policy view with real wage resistance
assumed. At each stage the effects of the new set of assumptions is
measured; in 1986 they cumulate to give the total effect of the

protection strategy although the model solutions cover the whole period 1984–90.

First, there is a general reflation effect, the elements of the reflation assumed to be in common with the high investment strategy discussed. The main elements are a cut in VAT to 5 per cent, reductions in employers' NIC, a depreciation of sterling by 15 per cent and increases in government spending. This package reduces unemployment by over 800,000 with a moderate worsening of inflation of about 1 per cent per annum (1983–86), but it does seriously worsen the balance of payments and doubles the nominal PSBR from its present levels.

The particular effects of a Labour reflation, following the assumptions above, are shown in the second line of the table. Although inflation is worsened through the further depreciation forced on the government, the economy is more competitive through the wage restraint of the trade unions and expands further with a slight improvement in the balance of payments.

The next two lines of the table show the effects of the tariffs and quotas imposed because of the serious deficit on the balance of payments. The first results are without allowing any wage response to the higher prices involved and the second ones allow a full response. Protection turns out to have a very modest effect on unemployment and growth, but a huge financial effect, reducing the PSBR and more than wiping out the balance of payments cost of general reflation. However, even without wage response, prices rise by another 1.7 per cent and even this assumes some monitoring of the industries with tariffs to prevent a full price response to the tariff. When wage rates are allowed to vary, the inflation worsens by a further 4.2 per cent, thus the overall effect of the tariff protection is an increase in the rate of inflation by 2 per cent a year (1983–86). Sterling devaluation has just as damaging effects but these are mixed up with the favourable effects of reducing VAT in the general reflation.

Retaliation reduces total exports by 7.2 per cent. This would be much worse if it were not confined to reductions in manufactured exports and exports to the EEC. In fact the retaliation is close to the gain to exports from the 15 per cent initial deflation. However, much of the potential effect on the domestic economy is lost through a further cut in imports. Unemployment goes up and there is a small improvement in inflation.

The fiscal response shown in the table is the result of the extra reflationary package assumed possible given the large revenue from tariffs. It takes the form of an increase in personal allowances of 2.5 per cent in 1986 and faster growth in public expenditure (1984–86). The result is similar to general reflation but without extra exports from a devaluation.

The overall effects have been discussed earlier. What the decomposition shows is the tendency for nearly all the components of the strategy to worsen the rate of inflation. Furthermore, it is clear that, taking protection and retaliation together, there is no improvement in unemployment – this must come through the spending of tariff revenues. But even if these are spent to the extent of bringing the balance of payments back to its original position, the reduction in unemployment is only about 200,000 whilst there is an extra 7.2 per cent rise in prices.[11] Equally unpalatable results could be obtained by looking at devaluation on its own without the reduction in VAT to compensate for its effect on inflation.

2.5.2   The high investment strategy

This strategy has been broken up into four parts:

1. The effects of the sterling depreciation of 15 per cent in the first year.
2. The combined effects of the reflationary package associated with the depreciation. This, together with the depreciation, gives the total general reflation which is common to both the protection and the investment strategies.
3. The effects of a permanent incomes policy gradually increasing in strength through the period 1984–90.
4. The effects of the substantial injections of investment into exporting industries and the transport, communications and electricity infrastructure.

Table 2.12 shows the decomposition on a comparable basis to that in Table 2.11. The 'general reflation' of the earlier table is here broken down into the effects of depreciation and those of the reflation. The depreciation, by 1986, has raised domestic prices by almost the full 15 per cent, but GDP and exports are at an appreciably higher level. The balance of payments is almost unchanged because the terms of trade effects (mostly higher import prices) outweigh the gain from extra exports. The PSBR is higher mostly because all nominal values tend to be higher in the economy. The net effect of the depreciation on unemployment is to reduce it by 271,000.

The reflationary measures have the most impact on unemployment, bringing it down a further 570,000 by 1986. The reduction in VAT and national insurance bring down consumer prices by 9.4 per cent almost offsetting the depreciation effect. GDP exports and imports are all higher but the cost is an extra £8.3 thousand million deficit on the balance of payments and an extra £6.6 thousand million on the PSBR.

In comparison with these general macro-economic policies, the effects of incomes policy and extra investment are rather small. The effects on unemployment are almost negligible, with the extra investment losing as many jobs as it creates because some of the investment inevitably replaces older capital which is much more labour intensive.

Table 2.12: An analysis of the effects of the high investment strategy, United Kingdom, 1986

Decomposition	Unemployment '000s	Consumer prices %	GDP %	Exports %	Imports %	Balance of payments £ thousand million	PSBR £ thousand million
Depreciation effect	− 271	14.3	2.1	6.2	2.7	− 0.1	2.9
Reflation effect	− 570	− 9.4	3.6	3.2	6.8	− 8.3	6.6
Total general reflation effect on present policy view	− 841	3.6	5.8	9.7	9.7	− 8.4	9.5
Incomes policy effect	− 42	− 2.1	0.3	1.0	− 0.3	+ 1.4	− 1.5
Extra investment effect	5	0.1	0.1	− 0.1	0.8	− 1.6	2.2
Total	− 878	1.5	6.2	10.6	10.2	− 8.6	11.3

Note: The 'total general reflation' effect is the combination of the depreciation and the reflation effects. The grand total is the combination of total general reflation, incomes policy and extra investment effects. Each effect is measured by successively adding components to the present policy view with real wage resistance assumed. There are percentage or absolute differences between variables projected for 1986 in the successive model runs.

In addition, a high proportion of the extra equipment is imported and therefore has no effect on domestic output and employment. Exports are hardly affected by 1986 since a two-year lag has been assumed between the extra investment and the change in export performance. By 1990 the extra investment increases exports by 5.4 per cent and reduces unemployment by 43,000.

2.6 LIMITATIONS OF THE STUDY

2.6.1 The structure of the labour market

The policy exercises reported above all assume that the labour market continues to work as it did in the past when unemployment levels were much lower. The alternative strategies envisage a return to full employment brought about by increases in the demand for labour. However, the problem is such that other measures which share out the available jobs more equitably may be necessary. For example, the promotion of part-time working would cut the numbers of full-time unemployed. Other measures reduce the supply of labour, such as lowering the age at which people retire. These measures have not been considered. Similarly, the examination of the temporary and selective job creation schemes, particularly for the young unemployed, has been excluded from the scope of the exercise. An increase in those on the temporary schemes has been left in the count of those unemployed.

A further issue which has not been investigated is the rate at which work skills are lost as people remain unemployed. Furthermore, it is assumed that the new employment opportunities offered in the alternative strategies will suit the requirements and skills of those unemployed. This may not be too much of a problem in that the new jobs are spread widely across industries, but there may well be certain locations and skills where the unemployment will persist.

2.6.2 The assessment of responses to new policies

Another limitation of the study is the use of a formal model estimated on past behaviour to asses responses to new policies. Protection is likely to result in some retaliation, the extent and character of which can only be guessed at. The new investment is intended to change the income elasticities of exports but such a relationship is tentative and imprecise. The incomes policies in the alternatives are assumed to work, yet the past incomes policies have been temporary and introduced at the last minute in response to an inflation or balance of payments crisis rather than being designed in advance as part of a package of policies for a return to full employment.

Ignorance about responses to new policies just compounds our uncertainty about how the economy works. The determination of wage inflation is particularly uncertain with unemployment at exceptionally high levels and the relationship underlying the projections is no more than considered guesswork.

2.6.3 Particular limitations of the protection alternative

There are three main qualifications and dangers in the protection strategy. First, from the experience of the 1930s, world trade is vulnerable to tariff and quota wars. Although this strategy may be undertaken in order to raise employment and although imports are very likely to continue to grow, the latter will be lower than otherwise and in some industries substantially lower. And inevitably some foreign interests will be damaged. Retaliation will be much worse than assumed if United Kingdom action sparks off a trade war between Europe and the United States.

Second, the strategy is unsound as the basis for longer-term development; the investment induced by protection is likely to be in the wrong industries, going against decades of international specialisation.

Finally, the tariff must escalate in order to keep the momentum of growth. In the present exercise a tariff on manufactures rises to 30 per cent by 1990; the main proponents of the strategy in the United Kingdom, the CEPG, expect a wider tariff to have to grow to almost 50 per cent to secure a 3.5 – 4 per cent growth rate (1983–90); and where the strategy has been widely adopted in Latin America, tariff rates have varied widely and been heavily supplemented by direct restrictions.[12] The logic of the strategy demands huge subsidies on domestic production (the reduction in VAT and national insurance are likely to have eliminated these taxes well before 1990). The strains on the economic and administrative structure are likely to be heavy, if not intolerable.

2.6.4   Particular limitations of the investment alternative

The working of a permanent incomes policy is central to this alternative because the low inflation is necessary to sustain confidence and foreign loans while there are large balance of payments deficits. In the early years the low inflation rate is largely achieved by progressive reductions in VAT and national insurance. After 1986 incomes policy is increasingly important and the success of such a permanent policy is untried.

The investment alternative also requires much higher public borrowing with the addition to the PSBR of about seven thousand million pounds by 1990 to finance the new investment. Although the PSBR/GDP ratios are lower than in the 1970s, in the present climate of financial opinion such prospects may undermine confidence and lead to high interest rates to protect the currency.

There is also the danger that the extra investment will be in the wrong projects or that the money will simply be spent on investment which would have been made in any case, and that no extra investment will materialise, let alone the planned increase in exports from the new equipment.

2.7   MAJOR POLICY CONCLUSIONS OF THE STUDY

2.7.1   The scale of the problem

The first conclusion to emerge from this study is that a major shift in policy is needed even to reverse the increase in unemployment since 1979, let alone reduce it to the 200,000 or so of the 1960s. Substantial reflation, including a 15 per cent depreciation of sterling and a reduction in VAT from 15 to 5 per cent, only reduced unemployment by 1 million from expected levels over 3 million. The numbers registered as unemployed may go down for other reasons – because benefit levels are reduced or become more difficult to claim or because particular groups are excluded from work or benefit – but the problem of people wanting employment which is not available will remain.

2.7.2   The international context

A major problem for policy is the fact that national economies have become much more open to foreign trade. The United Kingdom is no exception, with as much as 60 per cent of any increase in domestic demand being spent on imports. The attraction of the protection strategy is that it aims to contain the extra demand from domestic reflation within national boundaries. However, so strong is the demand for imports that the main feature of high tariff rates is the huge revenue they appear capable of generating.

As a result of the increased interdependence of national economies, co-ordinated reflation is more effective than ever before and the costs of unilateral reflation in the form of import expansion, balance of payments crises and unplanned depreciation are correspondingly greater. With a domestic reflation, 60 per cent of the extra final demand goes on imports; with a high investment policy the proportion is even higher. In consequence, these strategies are only sustainable for one country alone provided there is a high balance of payments surplus to begin with or provided the imports can be paid for out of reserves or by foreign loans and more exports. The United Kingdom has been in an exceptional position since 1979 of having large and growing oil revenues which could have financed a major reflation, but the opportunity has not been taken.

2.7.3   The character of the reflation

Another feature of measures to promote employment is that they vary across a wide range in their effectiveness. For example, income tax reductions in the United Kingdom are very expensive in terms of PSBR costs and per job created compared to government expenditure or reductions in national insurance contributions. This is mainly because of the different import intensities of different types of expenditure and so it is not relevant for a co-ordinated expansion, but there are also major differences between employment intensities. Both factors are worth taking into account when designing a reflationary package.

In the protection strategy as analysed, it turned out that it was not protection *per se* which reduced unemployment (because any favourable effects were outweighed by unfavourable ones from retaliation by other countries and the response of wages to higher inflation) but the spending of tariff revenues on government services which are particularly employment intensive.

2.7.4   The sources of new work

Another feature of the different strategies for full employment is that manufacturing, agriculture and public utilities are not likely to provide many new jobs. Employment in these sectors tends to decline more slowly in the alternatives than it does under present policies and there is no sign of any absolute increase. The sectors which show the greatest capacity for extra employment are construction and services, both private and public.

In the high investment alternative with the highest growth rate and the highest level of non-government employment, employment in manufacturing is lower than in the protection strategy and in services much higher. This is a result of a characteristic of the British economy which makes job creation by macro-economic policies very difficult; general measures to increase economic growth have the effect of stimulating replacement investment in manufacturing. Since this new capital equipment uses much less labour per unit of output than the old equipment it replaces, employment in manufacturing tends to fall further. Thus new employment in the service industries has to compensate for losses in manufacturing before it can make any contribution to the reduction of unemployment.

2.7.5   The resurgence of inflation

A crucial issue in the debate about reflation and a return to full employment is whether inflation will become a problem once again. Although the United Kingdom monetary targets have been repeatedly missed with measures of the money supply growing well above the target ranges (at present 8–12 per cent), the rate of inflation has fallen sharply from 16 per cent in 1980 to about 6.7 per cent in 1983. In that this is due to the increase in unemployment and fear of redundancy, we might expect that as unemployment levels stabilise and then fall, wage rates would start to rise again.

Both the alternatives to present policies discussed in this paper rely on some form of incomes policy to restrain the growth of money wages as unemployment comes down. In the protection strategy it is assumed that the tariffs and quotas will be introduced by a Labour government which would be able to rely on informal co-operation from trade unions rather than a formal incomes policy. But without such co-operation, inflation is liable to rise to 17 per cent a year and higher. In the high investment strategy some form of permanent incomes policy is assumed which will increase in strength as unemployment drops.

The lesson from the modelling work is that without restraint on wage claims in the form of high or rising unemployment, voluntary co-operation from the trade unions or an effective incomes policy, it will be difficult, if not impossible, to keep long-term inflation below 10 per cent a year.

2.7.6   A concluding remark

Attempts by the United Kingdom, on its own, to reflate are likely to fail
through balance of payment crises or inflation, or likely to lead to trade
wars. There is a major opportunity here for internationally co-ordinated
policies to succeed in substantially reducing national unemployment.

NOTES

1. The Cambridge Growth Project was financed by the United Kingdom Social
   and Economic Research Council and Cambridge Econometrics (1985) Ltd.
   and this support is gratefully acknowledged. I am grateful to members of the
   project for comments, particularly to Michael Landesmann for discussion of
   the investment policy alternative and to Tony Lawson for discussion of the
   explanation of wage inflation. I should also like to thank Cambridge
   Econometrics for the use of the forecast 82/3 as a basis for the alternatives
   reported in this chapter.
2. The Cambridge Multisectoral Dynamic Model (MDM) as a method for projecting and forecasting economic developments is described for a non-technical
   readership in Barker (1981a). A more detailed description of version 4 of
   MDM operational over the years 1980–82 is given in Barker *et al.* (1980). A
   book on version 6 (Barker and Peterson, 1988) serves as the main reference
   to the dynamic model replacing Barker (1976) which consolidated the
   research on the static version of the model. The software used to estimate
   and solve the model is described in Peterson *et al.* (1983). Version 7 of the
   model (MOM7) is maintained by Cambridge Econometrics (1985) Ltd.
3. Corden himself has some sympathy with this view: 'If one wants to know
   how a complicated protective structure will affect resource allocation and
   factor prices there is no point in pausing halfway to the complete answer.
   One needs to know, or estimate, the relevant elasticities, production functions, demand functions and so on, and . . . one can then work out how
   changes in . . . nominal tariffs affect the whole system'. (Corden, 1971: p.
   241.)
4. Allsopp and Joshi (1980) provide a mainly non-quantitative comparison of
   the London Business School (LBS), the Cambridge Economic Policy Group
   (CEPG) and the National Institute views on appropriate policies for the
   economy of the United Kingdom.
5. The Cambridge Growth Project and the CEPG were separate and independent groups in the Department of Applied Economics, University of Cambridge. The protection strategy is discussed in the April issues of the CEPG
   Cambridge Economic Policy Review. The 1980 issue contains a description
   of the main academic criticism of the strategy. The arguments against protection are set out in Corden, Little and Scott (1975) and Scott, Corden and
   Little (1980).
6. A recent comprehensive review of the United Kingdom labour market and
   its prospects is given in the Institute of Employment Research *Review of the
   Economy and Employment*, Summer 1983. The Cambridge Economic Policy
   Group *Economic Policy Review*, December 1982, discusses projections of
   regional employment and unemployment. Barker (1982) looks at the trends
   and structure underlying the unemployment and the prospects for a return
   to full employment.
7. Cambridge Econometrics provides a commercial forecasting and analysis
   service based on the Cambridge MDM. It produces three forecasts a year with

the main reports circulated to the subscribers to the service.

8. An investment strategy for the United Kingdom involving a North Sea oil investment fund has been discussed in Barker (1981b). The strategy reported above with its emphasis on an incomes policy has been described in Cunningham and Landesmann (1982) and a further version of this research appears in Landesmann (1983).

9. This policy has been followed in many countries, most notably France and Japan. For overviews see Petit (1982).

10. Inflation for 1983 is presently forecast to be about 6.7 per cent, about two percentage points below those shown in the graph. Persistently high unemployment appears to be depressing money wage inflation more than expected. The projections would then be reduced by about two percentage points from 1983 onwards, although the difference between the strategies would remain unchanged.

11. These results are found scaling the fiscal effect by four so that the net effect of protection, retaliation and special reflation is zero for the balance of payments.

12. The Latin American experience offers cold comfort to the protection strategy. The tariff rates have been highly selective and supplemented by strong direct restrictions; average tariffs reached only 21 per cent in 1965 with a strong protectionist policy in Peru (Fitzgerald, 1979: 201). Industrialisation through import substitution tends to come to an end, once all the easily produced imports have been squeezed out (Hirschman, 1971). Recent years have seen the protective measures swept away throughout Latin America, imposing high economic costs from sudden adjustment. British protection will also be subject to the same dangers of sudden reversal.

BIBLIOGRAPHY

Allsop, C. and Joshi V. 'Alternative strategies for the United Kingdom', in *National Institute Economic Review*, London, February, **91**, pp. 86–103 (1980).

Barker, T.S. (ed.) 'Economic Structure and Policy' in *Cambridge Studies in Applied Econometrics*, London, Chapman and Hall (1976).

Barker, T.S. 'Projecting economic structure with a large-scale econometric model', in *Futures*, Guildford, December pp. 458–67 (1981a).

Barker, T.S. 'De-industrialisation, North Sea oil and an investment strategy for the United Kingdom' in Barker, Terry and Brailovsky, V. (eds.), *Oil or Industry?*, London, Academic Press (1981b).

Barker, T.S. 'Long-term recovery: A return to full employment', in *Lloyds Bank Review*, 143, pp. 19–35 (1982).

Barker, Terry, Borooah, Vani, van der Ploeg, Frederick and Winters, Alan 'The Cambridge multisectoral dynamic model: An instrument for national economic policy analysis' in *Journal of Policy Modelling*, New York, 2.

Barker, Terry, Peterson, William (eds.) *The Cambridge Multisectoral Dynamic Model*, Cambridge University Press (1988).

Barker, Terry, van der Ploeg, Frederick and Weale, Martin, *A balanced system of national accounts for the United Kingdom*, Cambridge Growth Project, GPP 539 (1983).

Blackaby, Frank (ed.) *De-industrialisation*, London, Heinemann (1979).

Budd, Alan, Dicks, Geoffrey, Gosling, Tony and Robinson, Bill, 'The recession of 1981 and its causes', in *Economic Outlook*, 6, 1 (1981).

Cambridge Economic Policy Group, *Economic Policy Review*, 1–8 (1982).

Corden, W.M. *The Theory of Protection*, London, Oxford University Press (1971).

Corden, W.M., Little, I.D.M. and Scott, M.F.G., *Import controls versus devaluation and Britain's economic prospects*, London, Trade Policy Research Centre Guest Paper, 2 (1975).

Cunningham, J. and Landesmann, M., *Higher employment through investment and incomes policies*, Paper given to Conference on Alternative Strategies for Industry and the Economy, Cambridge, June (1982).

Fitzgerald, E.V.K. *The Political Economy of Peru 1956–78*, Cambridge, Cambridge University Press (1979).

Hirschman, A.O. *A Bias for Hope*, New Haven, Connecticut, Yale University Press (1971).

Institute of Employment Research, *Review of the Economy and Employment*, Warwick, University of Warwick (1983).

Jones, J.M. *Tariff Retaliation*, London, Oxford University Press (1934).

Landesmann, M. *Investment and incomes policies: Results from simulation on a multisectoral dynamic model*, Cambridge, Department of Applied Economics (1983).

Lawson, T. 'Keynesian model building and the rational expectations critique' in *Cambridge Journal of Economics*, December, 5, pp. 311–26 (1981).

Lawson, T. *Incomes policy and the real wage resistance hypothesis: Econometric evidence for the United Kingdom 1955–79*, Faculty of Economics, University of Cambridge, January (1982).

National Institute Economic Review: 'The British economy in the medium term' in *National Institute Economic Review*, November, 98 (1981)

Peston, M. 'Monetary policy and incomes policy: complements or substitutes? in *Applied Economics,* pp. 443–54 (1980).

Peterson, William, Barker, Terry, van der Ploeg, Rick, 'Software support for multisectoral dynamic models' in *Journal of Economic Dynamics and Control* 5, pp. 109–30 (1983).

Petit, Pascal 'Reflation and industrial policy in France' in *Cambridge Economic Policy Review*, April 8, 1 (1982).

Scott, M.F.G., Corden W.M. and Little, I.D.M., *The case against general import restrictions*, London, Trade Policy Research Centre, Thames Essay 24 (1980).

Singh, Ajit 'United Kingdom industry and the world economy: A case of de-industrialisation' in *Cambridge Journal of Economics*, June, 1, pp. 113–36 (1977).

Trade Union Congress *Program for Recovery*, London (1982).

United Kingdom NEDO *Industrial policies in Europe*, London, National Economic Development Office (1981).

United Kingdom Treasury *Financial Statement and Budget Report 1980–81*, London, HMSO (1980).

United Nations 'A System of National Accounts', *Studies in Methods*, New York Series F, 2, Rev. 3 (1968)

Winters, L.A. 'An econometric model of the export sector', in *Cambridge Studies in Applied Econometrics*, Cambridge University Press, 4 (1981).

Chapter Three

The forecasting of employment and unemployment using the French model DMS

Jean-Pierre Puig, Head of Department, INSEE, Paris, France

3.1 INTRODUCTION

This chapter outlines the functioning of the labour market in the French multisectoral dynamic model (DMS), presents some of the projection results obtained with the model and points out its principal short-comings.

The first part of the chapter contains a brief description of the model's architecture. The second part explains how the labour demand was formalised, with particular emphasis on industrial demand as the main focus of the model. The third part examines the projection of labour supply and the determination of unemployment, the former being established upstream of the model whereas the latter is part and parcel of the model and is based on the principle of the conjunctural shift of the activity rate. The fourth part deals with trends in employment and unemployment in France and with medium-term prospects as suggested by research conducted with the DMS model, in 1982 and 1983 during the preparation of the Ninth Plan.

3.2 THE DMS MODEL

For its medium-term projections of employment and unemployment, France's National Institute of Statistics and Economic Studies (INSEE) uses a macro-econometric multi-sectoral dynamic model known as the DMS, whose principal features and uses are outlined below.

3.2.1 Principal features of the DMS model

The DMS is a macro-econometric multisectoral model of the French economy progressing annually, whose projection horizon is the medium term (up to ten years). It was designed by INSEE's Programmes Department between 1974 and 1976 and replaced the FIFI model. Based on France's national accounts data, it has been re-estimated three times since it first came into use. The early 1985 version (DMS4) was based on the chronological series for the period 1959-82. The model contained approximately 3,000 equations, 500 of which were genuine behavioural equations. The exogenous variables (approximately 400) concern the international environment, budget, fiscal and monetary policies, demographic variables and production and prices in agriculture and energy.

The DMS is unlike other macro-econometric models in that it breaks down the national economy into 13 branches, hence its size. The breakdown is as follows: agriculture, agricultural and food industries, energy, intermediate goods, capital goods, consumer goods, construction and public works (including agricultural), transport and telecommunications, housing, other non-financial commercial services, commerce, financial services and insurance, non-market services.

- In the short term, the DMS is built along neo-Keynesian lines: production depends on demand. The level of production then determines prices and incomes through non-static variables affecting the labour market and the market for goods and services. Incomes in turn determine demand in accordance with the Keynesian multiplier principle.
- In the long term, the DMS is a supply model.
- The short/medium term dynamic of the model is a multiplier-accelerator mechanism, adjusted to allow for the income formation time-lag (employment cycle, price-quantity adjustment lag, fiscal cycles).

Alongside these typically neo-Keynesian features, the DMS comprises two innovations:

- the capital accumulation process combines the traditional multiplier-accelerator interaction with the profits-accumulation-price mechanism of the Cambridge School models, thus giving what can be called the 'double capital accumulation dynamics';
- the sharing of the market between importers and national producers has a non-linear relationship to the utilisation rate of production capacity.

3.2.2   General outline

The equations used in the DMS model have already been amply described elsewhere;[1,2,13] its principal behavioural functions do, however, need to be clarified here in order for what follows to be understood.

Overall consumption is determined on the basis of the real income by a savings relationship that reflects the relative inertia of consumption in response to short-run fluctuations in income, as per the permanent income theory. Two other effects stimulate saving in the model: inflation (real balance effect) and unemployment (caution saving). This overall consumption is then broken down by product by means of 21 relationships derived from the Houthakker and Taylor model, with the addition of a relative price factor.

The investment functions determine capital investment (equipment) and investment in construction separately. In industrial branches, investment in equipment is dependent on the return on capital and on a flexible accelerator. In non-industrial branches, investment is dependent mainly on the return of capital.

Lastly, investment in construction is dependent on capital investment with geometric adjustment lags. Investment in housing derives from the desired housing inventory in accordance with a geometric adjustment relationship determined mainly by the duration of loans. The desired housing capital is dependent on the real household income (spread over five years) and demographic growth.

Imports and exports are determined by three types of factors:

- a demand factor represented by domestic demand for imports and external demand for exports;
- a competitiveness factor, which is the ratio of external domestic prices expressed in francs to French prices;
- a supply of availability factor represented by the rate of utilisation of production capacity.

The relationships between production, employment and installed capacity are defined by production functions. Their role in the model is to determine production capacity in terms of previous investment (industrial branches) and to determine employment in terms of production (in all branches). Effective employment can be calculated by means of a standard geometric distribution relationship. Unemployment can then be determined by comparing effective employment with exogenous manpower availability, with due allowance for the tendency of the activity rate to adjust. This set of production-employment-unemployment ratios is examined in detail below.

The price of each product is determined on the basis of the wage cost per unit produced, the price of imports, the pressure of demand (capacity utilisation rate) and the previous year's profit rate, a negative factor that represents the firms' tendency to seek a 'normal' profit rate. The wage rates are calculated for each branch by means of a Phillips-Lipsey relationship, ie they are explained essentially by the increase in consumer prices and an indicator of tension on the labour market.

3.2.3 Principal uses for the model

Since 1977 the DMS model has been making medium-term projections in preparation for the government's economic plans. It has thus been used for the mid-term review of the seventh plan and for preparing the eighth plan, the 1982–83 interim plan and the ninth plan.

As from 1979, the model has been used to define the macro-economic framework for the 'detailed sliding forecasts' produced by INSEE in association with the Economic Information and Forecasting Bureau (BIPE), a private research institution specialising in business economics. The purpose of this operation is to interconnect macro-economic projections (DMS), sectoral projections (the INSEE's PROPAGE model in 40 branches) and product projections (BIPE projections of the demand-supply equilibrium for 215 products) so as to serve as a 'bridge' between macro-economics and business economics.

The DMS model is also used each year to establish forecasts on behalf of the French Senate.

Finally, the model has been used to investigate a number of economic issues such as the effects of shorter working hours, the decline in labour productivity since 1974, the consequence of an increase in the equipment utilisation time and the effects of a more flexible functioning of the labour market.

3.3   THE FORMALISATION OF LABOUR DEMAND IN THE DMS MODEL

From the Keynesian standpoint of the supply of goods and services being governed by demand, determining the demand of firms for labour entails as a general rule reversing a production function for a given volume of goods. However, because of the sectoral breakdown of the model, the specifications derived from this general principle are more or less reliable. The formalisation is most detailed – and therefore most reliable – in the industrial branches, where, in addition to labour, one of the factors of production explicitly incorporated in the clay-clay specification of the production function is a capital stock composed of differing vintages. This is explained in Section 3.3.1 below. In other branches, formalisation is more rudimentary since the demand for labour is the combined outcome of a labour productivity trend and the lagged adjustment of actual to desired employment. These specifications are set out in Section 3.3.2. Finally, there are certain branches where the link between production and employment seems very tenuous and where employment is an exogenous variable (agriculture, financial services and insurance, and non-market services, for example).

3.3.1   Labour demand in the industrial branches

In the three manufacturing branches (intermediate goods, capital goods and consumer goods), in the agro-food industries and in construction and public works (including agricultural), the DMS model represents a capital vintage production function with strict complimentarity between labour and capital for each generation of equipment.

The clay-clay production function. The contribution of each capital vintage, ie the total equipment installed during a given year (date v), to production during the period (year t) is described by a conventional complementary factor production function:

$$Q(t, v) = \lambda(t, v) \, DHC(t) \, E(v)$$
$$Q(t, v) = \mu(t, v) \, DH(t) \, N^*(t, v)$$

in which:

$Q(t, v)$ represents production during period t with equipment installed in year v;
$N^*(t, v)$ the labour required for this production;
$E(v)$ the volume of investment in equipment in year v;
$DH(t)$ the weekly hours of work during period v;
$DHC(t)$ the equipment utilisation time during period t.

The variables λ and μ represent, respectively, the hourly productivity of the equipment and labour at date t and for generation v.

The specification used for these productivity values is particularly simple since it is assumed that the two effects (that of the date of installation and that of the date of utilisation) are separable and can be expressed as constant growth rates:

$$\lambda(t, v) = \alpha(1 + a)^t (1 + b)^v$$
$$\mu(t, v) = \alpha'(1 + a')^t (1 + b')^v$$

These coefficients can be simply interpreted in the light of technical progress. Assuming that equipment suffers no physical wear, a and a' are the productivity growth rates for a given vintage over a period of time. The time trend parameters $(1 + a)$ and $(1 + a')$ are attributed to 'technical progress not incorporated' in the vintages.

On the other hand, if $t = v$ is incorporated into these relationships, $a + b$ and $a' + b'$ represent the rate at which overall technical progress improves the efficiency of the capital and of the labour with new equipment. By differentiation, b and b' measure the effect of the technical progress incorporated in the various vintages. α and α' are positive scale constants.

Before we can move on from this representation to an overall production function, the actual equipment utilised in the production process has to be specified. Two assumptions are accordingly made:

● the hourly productivity; in other words, b' is positive or nil. This means that where a firm has the option – and leaving aside the effect of other variable costs not taken into account here – it will always be to its advantage to use the most recent equipment available;

● if the total equipment actually utilised or constituting the production capacity includes a vintage v piece of equipment, then it also includes all the more recent pieces of equipment. This somewhat more risky assumption implies a certain homogeneity in the way in which fluctuations in overall demand in a branch of industry affect the activity of firms in that branch.

This latter assumption enables the equipment utilised (or constituting the production capacity) to be defined by a single value: the age of the oldest piece of equipment utilised, known as the effective margin m_t (or, alternatively, the capacity margin m_t^*).

If the hours of work and the degree of utilisation of the equipment are known, the various possible combinations of production and employment can be fairly represented on a graph, in which employment broken down by generation of equipment is measured horizontally and labour productivity is measured vertically. The generations are classified by increasing age, ie by decreasing productivity. Each generation is represented by a rectangle whose base is the volume of employment required to operate the equipment and whose height is the labour productivity. The area of the rectangle is thus the potential output of the equipment (see Figure 3.1)

For a total given production, determined by demand, a firm operates its equipment by increasing age, until the sum of the areas of the rectangles is equal to production, which is assumed to be pre-established. This gives us the effective margin and, hence, total efficient

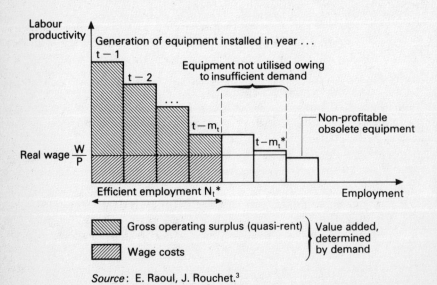

Figure 3.1: Solow's diagram

employment. Potential production is determined by the capacity margin. Lastly, the real wage rate $\dfrac{w}{p}$ enables us to determine which pieces of equipment are profitable, ie show a positive gross operating surplus and thus offer a profitability margin.

If the profitability margin determines obsolescence, in so far as no piece of equipment is used with a labour productivity lower than the real wage, then profitability margin and capacity margin should be identical. However, such information as is available would not as a general rule seem to bear out this assumption. Moreover, the fact that the model operates along Keynesian lines means that the effective margin is invariably lower than the profitability margin (implying rationing of the supply of goods and services).

From the formalisation of production to the determination of employment. It can be assumed that, given the cost of recruitment, training and dismissal and the rigidity of the employment market, there is a time lag in the adjustment of effective employment N_t to efficient employment N_t^*. This inertia of employment can be described by a constant elasticity adjustment relationship:

$$N_t/N_{t-1} = (N_t^*/N_{t-1})^\lambda$$

If we eliminate N^* – not directly observed – from the equations determining total production, if we assume that investment is incorporated in the capital only the following year and if we then express these equations in logarithmic form, then we obtain the deterministic component of the relationships to be estimated as follows:

Hourly production equation

$$\text{Log}\left(\frac{Q_t}{DHC_t \cdot R_t(m_t)}\right) = \text{Log } \alpha + t \text{ Log } (1 + a)$$

Employment equation

$$\frac{N_t}{DHC_t \cdot S_t(m_t)} = (1 - \lambda) \text{ Log}\left(\frac{N_{t-1}}{\frac{DHC_t}{DH_t} \cdot S_t(m_t)}\right) + t\lambda \text{ Log } \frac{\alpha}{\alpha'} + \lambda \text{ Log } \frac{1 + a}{1 + a'}$$

in which

$$R_t(m_t) = \sum_{v=t-m_t}^{t-1} (1 + b)^v E_v \text{ and } S_t(m_t) = \sum_{v=t-m_t}^{t-1} \left(\frac{1 + b}{1 + b'}\right)^v E_v$$

The two latter values, which are the sums invested weighted according to the rate of incorporated technical progress, may be interpreted as two measurements of the capital stock actually utilised in the production process, as they appear separately in each of the two equations.

The two relationships to be estimated can indeed be used to determine employment in terms of production. The first serves to calculate effective margin m_t for a given output Q_t and the second determines the level of employment N_t once the effective margin is known.

Because of the non-linear relationship to the parameters to be estimated and to the number of parameters, the estimation derived from this simple model's behavioural assumptions poses a number of serious problems.

Shift work and equipment utilisation time. Before commenting on the results of these econometric estimations, we should point out that the relationships to be estimated comprise an equipment utilisation time (*DHC*) that is not directly observable but based on the findings of surveys on weekly hours of work and on the development of shift work. Exactly how this DHC series is established calls for some explanation, and the following paragraphs are based on a published article on the subject.[3]

From the Ministry of Labour's surveys on manpower activity and conditions of employment, it is possible to measure how shift work has developed over the years. The surveys' findings can, moreover, be used to build up an indicator of equipment utilisation time that can be compared with weekly hours of work.

The average utilisation time (per shift) is equal to the average of the various operating periods (DHC_i variables) permitted by the successive use of i shifts at the same work unit, weighted by the relative shares of the pieces of equipment operating with one, two, i teams, ie:

$$DHC = \frac{\Sigma \alpha_i DHC_i}{\Sigma \alpha_i}$$

The weights (α_i) of the pieces of equipment according to the number of shifts derive directly from the replies to the survey, ie from the percentages of workers (variable P_i) employed in i shifts on the same piece of equipment. Hence, if the size of the shifts is constant, then $\alpha_i = P_i/i$.

The permitted utilisation time (DHC_i) is calculated along basically conventional lines, though in practice the order of shifts and arrangements for changing shifts vary enormously, may be more or less complicated and depend on a large number of parameters: production requirements, laws, regulations and agreements, standard practice in the branch. Simplifying somewhat, therefore, we find:

● the two-shift system, with a break at night and during the weekend;

Table 3.1: Calculation of permitted utilisation rate

	One-shift or no shift	Two-shift system	Semi-continuous three-shift system*	Continuous four-shift system
Daily utilisation time (in hours)	$DH/5$	$\frac{2}{5} \times DH$	$\frac{3}{5}\text{Inf}\,(DH,40)$	24
Number of days in operation during the year	231	231	231	337
Weekly equivalent calculated on the basis of 1 shift = DHC_i (in hours)	DH	$2 \times DH$	$3 \times \text{Inf}$ $(DH,40)$	$24 \times 5\,\frac{337}{231}$ ie 175

* Bearing in mind that three shifts can maintain continuous production five days a week – ie 120 hours of work – only if the working week is over 40 hours. Conversely, if the working week is over 40 hours, the utilisation period is still restricted to 120 hours (5×24) per week.

Source: E. Raoul and J. Rouchet: "Utilisation des équipements et fléchissement de la productivité depuis 1974", in *Economie et Statistique* (Paris, INSEE), Nov. 1980, pp. 39–53.

- the semi-continuous three-shift system, with a break at the weekend only;
- the continuous shift system where production is uninterrupted 24 hours a day and every day of the week including public holidays.

It may be assumed that equipment operating with four or more shifts can maintain continuous production throughout the year, apart from holidays. For an average year comprising four weeks of holiday, ten public holidays and 96 Saturdays and Sundays (excluding holidays) (ie 231 days of activity for the one, two and three shifts as against 337 days for four or more shifts), if DH is the length of the working week, the DHC_i rates, calculated in terms of single-shift equivalent, are as follows:

If P_1, P_2, P_3 and P_4 are the share of the workforce working respectively in one, two, three and four or more shifts, then:

$$DHC = \frac{P_1 \times DH + P_2 \times DH + P_3 \times \text{Inf}(DH,40) + P_4 \times 175/4}{P_1 + P_2/2 + P_3/3 + P_4/4}$$

The values for shares P_i are known only for the surveys of 1957, 1959, 1963, 1970, 1974, 1977, 1981 and 1982. In order to have annual series covering the period 1957–79, the corresponding values have been interpolated linearly.

Furthermore, these indicators have been calculated only for the industrial sector as such, ie intermediate goods, capital goods and consumer goods, and for the agro-food industries. In the construction industry (with 1.4 per cent of the workforce working in shifts in 1974) shift work is on too small a scale to have any significant impact. Consequently, utilisation time in this sector is conventionally taken as equal to working time.

Calculated in this way, utilisation time is largely dependent on, if not directly proportional to, weekly hours of work. Yet the increase in utilisation time between 1957 and 1974 coincided with a levelling off and, as from 1966, a sharp reduction in the working week. The fact is that there was a major structural adjustment corresponding to the displacement of the weights towards an increasingly large number of shifts. Conversely, the reduction in utilisation time since 1974, which was more rapid than the reduction in the working week, reflects a diametrically opposite phenomenon and hence a break in the trend towards shift work.

The estimation results. Table 3.2 contains the coefficient estimations of the two equations of the model and of the structural parameters.

The estimation results and the structural parameters vary considerably from branch to branch. Whereas the life of the equipment is comparable in the industrial branches (roughly ten years) and the difference in rate of technical progress fairly small (5.5 per cent for labour and − 2.2 per cent for capital), the short-term responsiveness of employment to demand varies enormously: the average adjustment lag ranges from one year for consumer goods to six and a half years in the agro-food industries. Similarly, whereas the total technical progress rates are comparable from one branch to the other, the distribution between incorporated and non-incorporated progress is very different; it is particularly asymmetrical in the construction and intermediate goods branches. The inclusion of construction in this type of estimation leads to highly specific results, as the technical progress rates are much lower (roughly one point per year) than in the strictly industrial branches – not surprising for a branch that is protected from international competition. In this relatively non-capital-intensive branch, however, the estimation is considerably less accurate than for industry, and the proposed model, which emphasises the use of capital as a factor of production, is not ideally suited to this sector.

These estimations, which cover a fairly long period (1959–80) which includes seven years subsequent to the energy crisis, outline the annual trends for the whole period.

3.3.2   Demand for labour in non-industrial branches

Principles

The model used here is much simpler than for the manufacturing

Table 3.2: Results of the estimations for the period 1959–80

	Intermediate goods[3]	Capital goods	Consumer goods	Construction and public works (including agricultural)	Agro-food industries
Hourly production equation:					
Time coefficient (%)[1]	−1.70 (−69)	−2.28 (−114)	−2.20 (−159)	−3.25 (−117)	−3.07 (−147)
Constant	−2.28	−1.28	−1.18	−0.21	−0.27
Standard error (%)[2]	−0.73	0.45	0.41	0.81	0.46
Employment equation:[1]					
Time coefficient (%)[1]	−0.28 (−6.7)	−2.07 (−14.4)	−1.91 (−16.1)	−0.77 (−6.0)	−0.55 (−3.5)
Coefficient of log $(N - 1/S \times \frac{DHC}{DH})$ (%)[1]	78.5 (20.5)	51.1 (14.4)	50.6 (16.2)	61.1 (7.2)	87.0 (19.7)
Constant	0.12	1.03	1.05	1.01	0.22
Standard error (%)[2]	1.0	0.62	0.52	1.1	0.57
Average effective margin (years)	10	10	10	8	10
Productivity cycle elasticity (%)[4]	21.5	48.9	49.4	38.9	13.0
Rate of technical progress (%) with regard to:					
Capital (not incorporated (a))	−1.80	−2.3	−2.2	−3.2	−3.0
(incorporated (by hypothesis (b))	0	0	0	0	0
Labour (not incorporated (a'))	−0.36	2.0	1.7	−1.3	1.2
(incorporated (b'))	6.0	4.0	4.0	6.0	4.0
(total (a' + b'))	5.64	6.0	5.7	4.7	5.2

1. The figures in brackets are the t of Student.
2. This standard error should be interpreted as the relative error of each adjustment.
3. The estimation period is 1954–79 for capital goods and 1963–80 for the agro-food industries.
4. An elasticity of 33 per cent, for example, means that a third of the lag between desired employment and actual employment is absorbed in the course of the year.

Source: INSEE.

branches. Although the assumptions are the same (complementarity between factors, a constant rate of technical progress and the existence of a productivity cycle), measuring production capacity and its underutilisation raises both conceptual and statistical problems. Consequently, the model is restricted here to the overlaying of two behavioural patterns:

1. A (medium-term) trend projection of apparent labour productivity, thus:

$$\mathrm{Ln}\left(\frac{Q_t}{N_t^*DH_t}\right) = \alpha t + \beta + \epsilon t$$

(Q_t = value added at constant prices, N_t^* = total desired or efficient manpower, DH_t = weekly hours of work).

2. A short-run adjustment relationship between the actual workforce and the desired workforce (current productivity cycle) which takes the standard Brechling form that has already been used for the industrial branches:

$$\frac{N_t}{N_{t-1}} = \left(\frac{N_t^*}{N_{t-1}}\right)^\lambda \text{ with } 0 < \lambda < 1$$

(N_t = actual workforçe, λ = productivity cycle elasticity).

As regards the econometric estimation, only one equation is estimated after elimination of N_t^* not observed between the two equations considered.

A few general remarks may be in order concerning the application of this fairly simple model to the various branches concerned: energy, transport and communications, commerce and commercial services.

1. This model does not give significant results for all branches. Where such is the case, a partial, more restrictive model will have to suffice.
2. For purposes of consistency with the rest of the DMS model, especially the wage rates equations, the model is normally tested with apparent hourly labour productivities. However, measuring the working week may pose a problem and/or the branch may comprise a large number of non-wage-earners whose hours of work are not measured. In this case, the model is expressed in terms of per capita productivity.
3. The model is enriched by the introduction of a break in the labour productivity trend over the recent periods, particularly following the first petroleum crisis.

Although they improve the descriptive potential of the model, these breaks cannot provide an explanation. We are therefore faced with an apparent effect that explains neither the form nor the cause of these real trend breaks: changes in the rate of capital accumulation, in the pace of technical progress, in the organisation of work and in the type of production (changes in the weight structure of various by-products, etc).

Moreover, it is somewhat risky to interpret these breaks directly as institutional changes, with the notable exception of the trade sector which, in 1974, was directly affected by the adoption of the Royer Act. This Act considerably slowed down the creation of hypermarkets and, consequently, the dissemination of productivity gains (average apparent productivity of the branch).

4. The model estimated is that obtained by eliminating the desired employment variable N_t^* between the equation for determining the labour productivity trend and the equation for adjusting the employed workforce to the theoretical workforce. Hence:

$$\log \frac{N_t}{N_{t-1}} = \lambda \log \frac{Q_t}{N_{t-1}DH_t} - \beta\lambda - \alpha\lambda t + \alpha'\lambda \operatorname{Max}(t, \text{date}) + E_t$$

in which 'date' represents the date of any break in the labour productivity trend.

3.3.2.1 *Energy*

For reasons of behavioural homogeneity, the energy branch is divided into two sub-branches: solid mineral fuels (CMS) and non-coal energy. No productivity cycle has been found for either of these components and the relationships used correspond to productivity tendencies with a break in 1970 in the case of solid mineral fuels and a break in 1973 in the case of non-coal energy.

(a) CMS:

$$\log \frac{Q_t}{N_t DH_t} = \underset{(0.1)}{-0.027} + \underset{(12.1)}{0.03\,t} - \underset{(7.8)}{0.04 \operatorname{Max}(t, \text{date})} \quad \begin{array}{l} R^2 = 0.908 \\ DW = 1.71 \\ \sigma\,(\%) = 3.39 \end{array}$$

(estimated period 1959–79)

(b) non-coal energy:

$$\log \frac{Q_t}{N_t DH_t} = -0.535 + 0.08\,t - 0.06\,\mathrm{Max}(t,\,\mathrm{date}) \quad R^2 = 0.996$$
$$(1.9)\quad(51.1)\quad(11.7)\qquad DW = 1.07$$
$$\sigma\,(\%) = 3.06$$

(estimated period 1959–80)

3.3.2.2   *Commerce*

The model used for this branch combines a trend projection of per capita labour productivity and a short-term adjustment cycle. Once desired employment has been eliminated from the two relationships and a break in the productivity trend in 1974 has been taken into account, the estimated relationship is as follows:

$$\log \frac{N_t}{N_{t-1}} = 0.261 \log \frac{Q_t}{N_{t-1}} - 0.625 - 0.01\,t + 0.006\,\mathrm{Max}(t,\,\mathrm{date})$$
$$(3.2)(2.8)\quad(3.4)\quad(2.8)$$
$$R^2 = 0.569$$
$$DW = 1.89$$
$$\sigma\,(\%) = 0.54$$

(estimated period 1959–80).

3.3.2.3   *Transport and telecommunications*

The model used combines an hourly productivity trend without a break and a productivity cycle:

$$\log \frac{N_t}{N_{t-1}} = 0.117 \log \frac{Q_t}{N_{t-1}DH_t} - 0.006\,t + 0.461$$
$$(2.6)(2.7)\quad(2.8)$$
$$R^2 = 0.329$$
$$DW = 1.71$$
$$\sigma\,(\%) = 0.69$$

(estimation period 1959–80)

3.3.2.4   *Private services*

The model combines productivity trend and productivity cycle. The productivity trend differs in this case in that it is calculated on the basis of real output and not value added, is expressed in per capita terms and does not allow for any break.

$$\log \frac{N_t}{N_{t-1}} = \underset{(3.1)}{0.243} \log \frac{Q_t}{N_{t-1}DH_t} - \underset{(2.8)}{0.004} \, t - \underset{(3.0)}{0.683}$$

$$R^2 = 0.35$$
$$DW = 1.14$$
$$\sigma \, (\%) = 0.94$$

(estimation period 1959-80).

If we look at all the branches where the existence of a productivity cycle has been established, the extent of the lag in recruitment is extremely variable. The average lag is particularly long in the agro-food industries (6.5 years) and in transport and telecommunications (7.5 years). Generally speaking, the lag is also long in the tertiary sector (2.8 years in commerce, 3.1 years in commercial services) but shorter than 1 year in the capital goods and consumer goods sectors. The intermediate goods sector is the only industrial branch where the recruitment lag (3.7 years) is comparable to that of the service sector. In building, engineering and agriculture the average lag is 1.6 years.

3.4 LABOUR SUPPLY AND THE DETERMINATION OF UNEMPLOYMENT IN THE DMS MODEL

For accounting purposes, the active population or labour force is the sum of total employment and unemployment. Using this concept, it should be possible to model the functioning of the labour market as follows: the labour demand of firms determines total employment, as per the formalisation outlined in the previous section; the labour supply of households determines the active population, this being established outside the model in accordance with demographic considerations (age pyramid) and sociological considerations (activity behaviour of the population by sex and age); unemployment is then the surplus of supply over demand so established.

In practice, although the firms' labour demand does indeed determine the level of employment, it is not possible to assimilate labour supply to active population, since the *ex post* activity rate also depends on economic phenomena and, above all, on the employment supply of the firms. Thus, the formalisation of the functioning of the labour market in the DMS model may be outlined as follows: an *ex ante* labour supply is established exogenously in accordance with demographic and sociological considerations; unemployment is determined by setting this supply against the volume and composition of the labour demand of the firms; the active population is deduced from the working equation: active population = employment + unemployment.

The distinction made between the factors that affect the volume of the potential active population, which is assumed to be independent of the economic situation, and the strictly economic factors responsible for the gap between the potential active population and the *ex post* active population is somewhat conventional. Since the demographic factors depend in part on economic phenomena, especially inflow and outflow of active migrants, how can an activity behaviour trend distinguish a ground swell from a reaction to a specific economic situation? Consequently, this part of our analysis deals with the determination both of the potential active population and of unemployment. The determination of the potential active population is described in the Sections 3.4.1 and 3.4.2, the first of which outlines the method employed to project the availability of manpower in the light of the demographic and sociological characteristics of the French population, while the second explains how this initial assessment was modified in the course of preparations for the ninth plan to make allowance for measures specifically aimed at the labour market that were taken as part of the economic policy to combat unemployment (advancement of the age of retirement, training programmes, etc.). Section 3.4.3 describes the method of formalisation used to determine unemployment.

3.4.1   Determination of the potential active population

Principal assumptions and projection results

The beginning of the 1960s saw the start of a new and highly distinctive phase in France's demographic evolution, with an exceptional increase both in the working-age population and in the adult female activity rate and a sharp decline in activity among those in the higher and lower age brackets. The projection conforms to this general framework, with the assumptions that these broad trends will continue. This introduces a major element of uncertainty, as the activity trend, especially among women, may fluctuate widely.

Appropriate adjustments are, however, made here and there to make allowance for factors which can be confirmed, such as the evolution of the working-age population, or which derive from new assumptions, such as a decline in the net inflow of migrants or the female activity growth rate as it approaches a 'ceiling'.

The projection of the total population on which that of the active population is based derives from a specific survey. This projection, however, includes one highly uncertain element, namely the number of births in future years, though this has only a limited impact on the active population since children born in 1979 will not reach active age before 1995 (the difference between the projections made with the two fertility assumptions as they relate to the working-age population is about 370,000 for the year 2000). Of course the number of dependent children does have a bearing on the female activity rate but, as we shall see, only to a limited extent. The projection was based on the assumption of 2.1 children per woman.

The fact that little is known of the net inflow of active migrants is rather more serious. The assumption made is that the net flow will be nil, which corresponds to the current situation – though in the early years of the crisis the number of active foreigners may have declined, which would mean a negative inflow. Lastly, the margin of error in the forecasting of deaths is certainly minimal.

Table 3.3 shows the results of the projection up to 1990, broken down into the various components of the potential active population trend (net natural growth, net inflow of migrants, activity rate trend).

Table 3.3: Results of projections to 1990

	Observations			Projections		
	1954–62[1]	1962–68[1]	1968–75[1]	1975–80	1980–85	1985–90
1. Impact of demographic trend (not including net migration inflow)	99	658	849	1,002	912	612
2. Net inflow of active migrants	329[2]	679[2]	290	20[3]	0	0
3. Impact of the variation in the male activity rate:						
(a) under 25	– 88	– 218	– 254	– 73	– 36	– 36
(b) 25–54 years old	– 13	– 26	11	– 6	– 4	– 4
(c) 55 years old or over	– 107	– 285	– 216	– 218	– 162	– 115
4. Impact of the variation in the female activity rate:						
(a) under 25	– 8	– 102	– 97	– 31	53	50
(b) 25–54 years old	– 16	126	568	515	471	220
(c) 55 years old or over	– 54	– 134	– 134	– 68	– 85	– 62
5. Total variation in the active population (= 1 + 2 + 3 + 4) of which:	142	698	972	1,203	1,149	665
men	171	301	250	373	370	221
women	– 29	397	722	830	779	444

1. The figures have been adjusted to indicate the variation over five years: ie the variations during the period 1954–62 have been multiplied by 5/8ths, those for 1962–68 by 5/6ths and those for 1968–75 by 5/7ths.
2. Including persons repatriated from Algeria.
3. Estimated net inflow of migrants for 1975; thereafter, it is assumed to be nil.

Source: INSEE: *Economie et statistique.*[4]

Activity rate projection methodology

The activity rate projections are dissaggregated by sex and age; for the female population in the 25–54 age bracket, the projection allows for the number of dependent children, since the female activity rate tends to decline with the number of children. The method of projecting the activity rate varies according to the population considered: for example, an *ad hoc* assumption for a segment of the population covered by a specific law or regulation (raising of compulsory school age from 14 to 16), the projection of observed behaviour by generation or the use of a logistic curve to project the female activity rate. Because the projection of the female activity rate is particularly relevant to the projection results and because of the original manner in which the projections are made, this latter aspect merits some further explanation.

The method as described here takes the form of women in the 30–34 bracket. In this group, a distinction is made between women who are spouses of the head of the family and the other women (children of the head of the family or themselves heads of families), a distinction which is not quite the same as married/unmarried. A second distinction, which concerns spouses only, is made as to the number of children in the family under the age of 16: 0, 1, 2, 3 or more. The activity rate of 'non-spouses' and of childless 'spouses' increased only very slowly over the earlier years and, in this projection, were stabilised at their 1975 level. For 'spouses' with one to three or more children, on the other hand, a logistic curve was applied to the earlier trend. The equation of the logistic curve is:

$$\log \frac{y - y_0}{y_1 - y} = at - b$$

in which

- y represents the activity rate;
- t the time;
- a, b, y_0, y_1 the parameters of the curve;
- y_1 is the upper limit or 'ceiling' of the activity rate towards which y tends when $t \to +\infty$;
- y_0 is the rate towards which y tends when $t \to -\infty$.

The logistic curve climbs continuously from y_0 to y_1, at first gradually and then more rapidly, the sharpest occurring when:

$$y = \frac{y_0 + y_1}{2};$$

it then climbs more and more slowly as y approaches y_1.

The higher the parameter, the sharper the rate of climb, ie the less time y_0 takes to reach y_1.

The y_0 and y_1 rates were established in the light of the following considerations. For the 30–40 age group, the rates were set as follows:

women with one child: $y_0 = 40$, $y_1 = 75$;
women with two children: $y_0 = 20$, $y_1 = 60$;
women with three or more children: $y_0 = 10$, $y_1 = 50$.

Parameters a and b were then estimated and adjusted by the ordinary least squares of:

$$\log \frac{y - y_0}{y_1 - y} \text{ over time } t.$$

Table 3.4: Estimation of parameters a and b

	Coefficient a (estimated)	Coefficient b (estimated)
1 child	0.26 (0.02)	– 2.7 (0.2)
2 children	0.23 (0.01)	– 2.7 (0.2)
3 or more children	0.16 (0.01)	– 3.0 (0.1)

Note: The standard error of each estimation is shown in brackets.

Source: Eymard-Duvernay, F. 'Combien d'actifs d'ici l'an 2000?', *Economie et Statistiques*, Oct. 33–46 (1979).

The y_0 values were selected by trial and error. The quality of the fit is very sensitive to y_0; according to the value of y_0, the fit may or may not accurately reflect the inflexion of the curve at the beginning of the period (from a slow growth rate between 1962 and 1968 to a more rapid growth rate thereafter).

For women in the 30–34 age group, the activity rate's upper limit y_1 was set at 75 per cent for women with one child, 60 per cent for women with two children, 50 per cent for women with three or more children. For women with one child, the upper limit is the projected rate for childless women (80 per cent for women in the 30–40 age group) reduced by 5 points. In 1975, the gap between the activity rate of women with one child and that of women with two is 20 points (in the 30–34 age bracket). It was assumed that it would drop to 15 points in the long run (upper limit 60 per cent). It was further assumed that the gap between the activity rate of women with two children and that of women with three or more children would decline from 24 points in 1975 to 10 points in the long run (upper limit 50 per cent).

Setting an upper limit is very much a matter of guesswork. Usually, the point at which the ascending curve to level off (as it approaches the upper limit) has not yet been reached and the upper limit can therefore not be gauged from observation.

3.4.2   Making allowance for economic policy measures aimed specifically at employment

So far, in assessing the potential active population, account has only been taken of the demographic characteristics of the French population and the trend in activity behaviour. However, the *ex ante* labour supply is also affected by measures aimed specifically at the labour market that the economic policy-makers take to combat unemployment.

During the preparatory work on the ninth plan, the impact of these measures was calculated and assessment of the potential active population (according to the principles outlined above) was modified accordingly. The economic policy measures taken into consideration were directed both at the older active population and the young population coming on to the labour market. In the first case, account was taken of the effect of lowering the retirement age to 60 and the impact of the solidarity contracts affecting those in the 55–59 age group. In the case of the young population, account was taken of the effect of measures designed to promote training courses for the 16–21 age group and of the enhancement of the role played by vocational training schools.

As far as the methodology is concerned, it is unnecessary here to go into the details of how the impact of the economic policy measures is calculated except to indicate that care must be taken to avoid double accounting when making the consequent downward adjustment of the potential active population. This is because the examination of earlier series already reveals a *de facto* lowering of the age of cessation of activity; moreover, training facilities for first-time jobseekers have already existed for several years. Projecting a past trend automatically implies that the trend is maintained. Consequently, allowance must be made for such economic policy measures only in so far as they modify the effects of a previous trend which, for the purposes of the projection, has been assumed to continue. This goes to show the somewhat ambiguous nature of potential active population projections that implicitly incorporate random trend factors.

3.4.3   The determination of unemployment

Once the potential active population and employment supply of firms is known, unemployment can be determined as soon as the employment demand behaviour of households has been specified.

This process derives from the assumption that activity behaviour adapts itself to the state of the labour market: when the labour market is down from a reference situation, certain potential offerers of labour are discouraged from seeking employment and spontaneously withdraw from the market. The increase in unemployment in terms of the reference situation is therefore lower than the *ex ante* accentuation of the gap between the potential active population and total employment.

Quantifying this type of situation calls for disaggregating both the potential active population and total employment. Obviously, the decline in the activity rate is going to differ considerably according to the type of worker offering his services. The labour supply of the male population between 25 and 50 will not be greatly affected by the developments in the labour market situation, whereas young persons may opt either for prolonging their studies or for entering the labour market, older workers may advance or postpone their decision to stop working and women, depending on the circumstances, may be inclined to look for work outside the home or, on the contrary, to devote themselves to domestic chores. The size of the active population may also be affected by the net inflow of active migrants which, though influenced by the labour market situation, cannot strictly speaking be assimilated to an adjustment tendency of the activity rate. A change in activity behaviour depends not only on the trend in total employment but also on its composition. It may also be affected by the composition of the potential active population, in so far as the different categories of active persons are not evenly distributed among the various branches of activity.

In practice, the quality of available employment and unemployment statistics is such that only economic activity is dissaggregated. The earliest French studies of the adjustment tendency of the activity rate were by R. Salais[5] and by F. Eymard-Duvernay and R. Salais.[6] The study by R. Salais was based partly on research conducted by T. Dernburg and K. Strand[7,8] who were the first to formalise the responsiveness of activity rates to the unemployment rate, by sex and age group, using data on the United States economy.

Traditionally, the relationship for formalising the unemployment is:

$$\Delta(C - C_0) = a\,\Delta(L_0 - C_0 - A) - \sum_i b_i\,\Delta E_i$$

in which:

Δ represents the first difference operator;
C the observed level of unemployment;
C_0 the reference level of unemployment;
L_0 the potential manpower resources;
A the agricultural active population;
E_i employment in branch i;

$\sum_{i=1}^{n} E_i$ total non-agricultural employment.

The reference unemployment level C_0 serves to determine that part of the unemployment trend that is due to demographic factors irrespective of economic considerations.

This is the specification used in the DMS model, with non-agricultural employment broken down further into industrial employment (manufacturing, energy, agro-food industries, construction and public works) and employment in the tertiary sector.

The values of the coefficiencies, estimated by the non-linear least squares methods on the basis of annual data for 1962–80, are as follows:

$$a = 0.42 \qquad b_1 = -0.62 \qquad b_2 = -0.27$$
$$(7.1) \qquad\qquad (-14.8) \qquad\qquad (-3.1)$$

This relationship signifies that either 1.6 industrial jobs or 3.7 jobs in the tertiary sector must be created to reduce the number of unemployed by 1. Furthermore, all other things being equal, 2.4 additional potential active persons will entail an increase of 1 in the number of unemployed.

The values of coefficients a and b_1 are close to those obtained with INSEE's quarterly model, METRIC; the difference between the two models is greater in the case of the tertiary employment coefficient, but the coefficient estimates for tertiary employment are very much less accurate in both cases.

Some shortcomings of the data used

A. Unemployment. The quantitative assessment of unemployment is derived directly from the conventional distinction between unemployment and inactivity and from the method employed to measure this factor (survey, voluntary statements, etc.).

Three alternative indicators are generally used in France; unemployed population seeking employment (PSERE), unemployment as defined by the International Labour Office (ILO), and end-of-month jobseekers (DEFM). It is unnecessary here to recall the definition and precise content of each of these measurements; it will suffice to indicate why one indicator might be preferable to another.

The DEFM series (which covers jobseekers registered with the national employment agency, the ANPE) is generally considered to be a fairly unreliable indicator of the trend of unemployment. It is in fact an administrative measurement that reacts to any change in legislation, regulations or institutions. For example, the employment ordinances of 1967 that afforded greater social protection for the unemployed and the introduction in 1978 of a procedure whereby an unemployed person was struck off the register after one failure to register instead of after two, have had a definite impact on the volume of registered end-of-month jobseekers without signifying any real change in the labour market situation. The gradual spread of ANPE offices, moreover, has caused something of a 'drift' in the monthly increase in jobseekers.

The PSERE series and ILO-type unemployment series are based on data obtained from population surveys and opinion polls that have so far been carried out each year in March among a representative random sample of 60,000 households. The PSERE measurement derives directly from one of the questions asked of the household in the employment survey. On the other hand, unemployment as defined by the ILO, which is obtained by combining the replies to various employment survey questions, is more suitable for international comparisons.

Which of these three yardsticks is chosen to estimate an activity decline relationship can, because of the observed differences between the series, have a considerable bearing on the results. Although the changes in the way the concepts are defined and in the administrative handling of registration with the national employment agency make it difficult to make any valid comparisons since 1982, Table 3.5 shows that between October 1980 and October 1981 the assessment of the increase in unemployment still differs substantially according to the source.

Table 3.5: Assessments of the increase in unemployment

	Available population seeking employment*	Unemployment as defined by the ILO	Registered end-of-month jobseekers
October 1980	1,642,000	1,589,100	1,540,300
October 1981	1,921,700	1,895,100	1,933,000
Growth rate 1981/1980 (%)	17	19	26

* The equivalent of the PSERE prior to 1982.

Source: N. Coëffic[9]

The unemployment determination relationship in the DMS model uses the ILO-type unemployment series.

B. The measurement of employment. Employment is measured in national accounts on the basis of the annual data supplied by UNEDIC and covering wage earners only (in *Photographie* on 31 December each year) and of information derived from surveys on labour force activity and employment conditions (ACEMO) conducted by the Ministry of Labour.

The ACEMO survey covers all establishments with ten or more wage earners, except for agriculture, public administration and certain scheduled undertakings. The questionnaires used are sent to all establishments with 50 or more wage earners and to a third of the establishments with 10 to 49 wage earners.

Given the statistical sources utilised, the employment measurement is somewhat imperfect for the construction and public works sector, the non-commercial tertiary sector and the health services. Moreover, it naturally makes no allowance for clandestine work.

Lastly, temporary workers (of which there were 122,000 in April 1982 according to the employment survey) are included in the commercial services sector.

Despite these shortcomings, the employment measurement seems to be very much more reliable than the measurement of the variables outlined above.

3.5   RECENT TRENDS IN EMPLOYMENT AND UNEMPLOYMENT AND MEDIUM-TERM PROSPECTS

Before considering the medium-term employment and unemployment prospects as determined by the projections made with the DMS model, it would be well to consider the labour market in France in 1982, the last year on which information was available at the time of preparing this chapter and one in which important policy measures were taken to improve the labour market situation.

3.5.1   The labour market in France in 1982

In 1982 the labour force employed in the non-agricultural commercial sectors declined slightly (– 0.2 per cent). By sector, the trend varies considerably. Industrial employment, including construction and public works, dropped by 2.1 per cent, thus pursuing the observed trend since the first petroleum crisis (employment in the industrial sector has declined by 1.1 million since 1973).

It is the increase in manpower in the service sector that accounts for the overall growth in the employment of wage earners since 1975 – though there has been a tendency for the annual increase to fall off somewhat from 2.3 per cent per year from 1976 to 1979 to 1.3 per cent in 1980–81 and 1.5 per cent in 1982.

The annual average unemployment rate, as defined by the ILO, was 8 per cent. However, in 1982 the number of end-of-month jobseekers levelled off at slightly over 2 million, after rising very sharply since the middle of 1980: the growth rate was 5.8 per cent in 1982 as against 23.4 per cent in 1981. The main reasons for this levelling off were the recruitment campaigns that resulted from the solidarity contracts and the steps that were taken to incorporate young workers into the labour market and on behalf of the long-term unemployed. Finally, labour market activity was more sustained in 1982 than in 1981, with the number of unemployed returning to work on the increase.

For several years the active population trend, that is, all persons employed and unemployed, had been substantially different from the trend in manpower resources: the potential increase in the active population had been roughly 250,000 persons a year. The bulk of this increase (about 180,000 persons) was attributable to population growth (given the same activity rate) but the figure also allowed for medium-term variations in the activity rate: the activity rate at both ends of the age scale declined, while that of women continued to rise at the same pace as before 1975. Since 1977 the effective increase in the active population (employed plus unemployed) had always been less than the potential increase. In 1982 alone, the difference between the two was 140,000 persons, indicating a significant decline in the activity rate, and for the past five years the accumulated effect of the decline amounted to 400,000 persons. This relative drop in the activity rate derived partly from fluctuations in the average age at which young people entered the labour market but also from a much faster decline in the activity rate of older workers, very much encouraged by government policy. The activity rate trend may also have been affected by migration between France and the rest of the world, about which very little is known outside the inter-census periods. The decline in activity may thus have been overestimated if the deteriorating labour market situation provoked a net outflow of migrants that was not recorded.

3.5.2 Consequences of the reduction in working hours

The government has taken a number of measures to combat unemployment. The January 1982 ordinance contains four main points: a shorter official working week (reduced from 40 to 39 hours); general introduction of a fifth week of paid leave; possibility of adjusting hours of work according to the season; adoption of steps to discourage overtime.

Little information is to be had on the consequences of standardising the practice of a fifth week of paid leave. By contrast, shortening the official working week to 39 hours has had a considerable effect on actual hours of work: the Ministry of Labour's quarterly survey shows a drop of almost one hour in the average working week during the first three months of 1982, and of 1.2 hours between October 1981 and October 1982. This very significant reduction has been virtually across the board and has affected both manual and white-collar workers. In almost every sector, the average working week has dropped below 40 hours. In other words, enterprises have to a very large extent responded to the reduction in the official working week by reducing the number ' of hours worked.

In September 1982 INSEE conducted a special survey in the industrial and trade sectors on the shorter working week and its repercussions.[10] One-fifth of the firms in the industrial sector and one-sixth in the trade sector stated that they had taken on extra permanent staff. These findings were then used to calculate the impact of the shorter working week on employment, though the result may not be altogether reliable. However, judging from the statements of the firms in these two sectors, which employ half the wage earners engaged in commercial activities, the number of new jobs created can be estimated at between 0.2 and

0.4 per cent of the total workforce, that is, 15,000 to 30,000 jobs.

Since the impact on employment was relatively limited, the shorter working week was probably mainly reflected in productivity gains; 53 per cent of the firms, especially the larger companies, said that they had made changes in the organisation of work. There may also well have been repercussions on production, and 62 per cent of the undertakings did indeed claim that they had had to reduce output – though this would not seem to be borne by other sources and, at most, may have been only a temporary phenomenon. On the other hand, there is in certain branches a substantial gap between the margin of capacity if more workers were taken on, as declared by the firms replying to the short-term surveys, and the trend in installed capacity, which may mean that production capacity was reduced in the wake of the shorter working week.

Reducing the working week was not the only government measure to improve the employment situation, and several steps have been taken in recent years to encourage older workers to retire. In 1982, for example, the system of solidarity contracts was introduced, with an early retirement pension paid by the National Employment Fund. Some 98 per cent of the 30,000 contracts signed in 1982 were of this type and the beneficiaries numbered around 300,000, 80,000 of whom had already taken advantage of the scheme by December 1982. As a result, the age of cessation of activity has dropped considerably. Early retirement has become more common than retirement at the official age, and in fact lowering the official retirement age to 60 in April 1983 had done little more than give official sanction to a situation that already existed. There had also been a sharp drop in the activity rate in the 55–59 age group, which is increasingly concerned by early retirement schemes.

3.5.3   Scenarios for the preparation of the ninth plan

To facilitate the preparatory work for the ninth plan, the general Commissariat for the Plan defined a number of scenarios leading up to the year 1988 and asked INSEE to simulate them with the DMS model. The conclusions drawn from this exercise are described briefly below, with particular emphasis on the aspects relating more specifically to the labour market (see also Raoul *et al*).[11]

3.5.3.1   *The assumptions*

A scenario is a set of assumptions relating to the international environment and to domestic economic and social policy.

Scenarios relating to the international environment. Three scenarios identified by the letters X, Y and Z were devised which can be summarised as follows:

- Scenario Z excludes both the assumption that the crisis will end and the assumption that it will become more acute. It assumes that the world economy will slowly recover and that the trends that were apparent during the period 1975–80 between the two petroleum shocks will resume. The annual average growth rate of production of France's main trading partners would thus be 2.7 per cent and their rate of inflation 7.1 per cent during the five years of the plan (1984–88).
- Scenario Y assumes that the prevailing situation of the past few years will continue and that there will be persistent economic stagnation leading to a deflationary spiral and to increasing compartmentalisation of the world economy. In this case the annual average growth rate of France's partners would be 1.5 per cent between 1984 and 1988 and the inflation rate 5.4 per cent.
- Scenario X makes the assumption that the United States policy of disinflation and stabilisation will be successful, thus giving a new boost to world economic growth led by the most advanced countries (United States and Japan). The growth rate of France's principal partners would be 2.8 per cent, much as in scenario Z, but inflation would be much lower at 4.5 per cent.

Domestic economic and social policy assumptions. Seven sets of assumptions identified by the letters A to G were initially set up, but only five (scenarios A, B, E, F and G) were actually used for projection purposes.

- Scenario A assumes a steady increase in public spending and a fairly rapid growth of the per capita purchasing power of the average wage (1.5 per cent per year). The purchasing power of social security benefits continues to rise faster than the gross domestic product, though much more slowly than in the past. The official working week is reduced to 35 hours by the end of 1985 and thereafter continues the downward trend observed over recent years (– 0.4 per cent). Thanks to a more extensive use of shift work and the consequent easing of the physical strain on the production apparatus, the shorter working hours entail only a fairly small reduction in the utilisation time of equipment.
- Scenario B differs from scenario A in that it assumes tighter control over public spending and a more moderate increase in the purchasing power of social security benefits. The extra resources needed to balance the social security accounts would derive not from indirect taxes, as in scenario A, but directly from household income.
- Scenario E is identical to scenario A except that the per capita purchasing power of the average wage increases by 0.5 per cent per year instead of 1.5 per cent.
- Scenario F assumes a more rapid modernisation of the industrial

production apparatus, led by the public sector. Total investment is 4.6 per cent higher than in scenario E, the aim being to reduce the external dependency of the French economy more rapidly and more effectively. It is assumed that investment will be in areas currently unexploited by national producers who can thus win over the domestic market. Wages rise at the same rate as in scenario E.

- Scenario G examines the consequences of decentralising the programming of hours and organisation of work, encouraged by state incentives. The reduction in the working week takes place more gradually than in the previous scenarios which assume as 35-hour week by the end of 1985. In scenario G, however, the process continues at the same pace after 1985, so that by 1990 the working week is the same as in the other scenarios. Moreover, this slower and concerted reduction in the hours of work is assumed to be conducive to a more efficient reorganisation of working conditions that would cause a smaller drop in the utilisation time of industrial equipment than in the other scenarios. Wages are as in scenario E.

3.5.3.2   *The results.*

Altogether projections were made on the basis of seven scenarios combining various assumptions relating to the international environment and to domestic economic and social policy, namely scenarios EX, EY, EZ, AZ, BZ, FZ and GZ. Although the projection results progress annually, those given in Table 3.6 relate only to the averages for the whole of the ninth plan (1984–88) or for the last year of the plan (1988). This is because the scenario assumptions were made during the first half of 1982 and therefore do not take into account the economic policy measures adopted in France over the ensuing 15 months.

The table illustrates for each scenario the repercussions on employment and unemployment and on the principal macro-economic variables: growth, inflation, and the balance of public expenditure and balance of trade.

As far as the effectiveness of domestic economic and social policy is concerned (from a comparison of scenarios AZ, BZ, EZ, FZ and GZ), scenario AZ is the most successful in terms of employment and unemployment thanks to the economic boost provided by the high level of public spending and the increase in earnings. This, however, is at the cost of a rate of inflation that is 3.6 points per year higher than that of France's trading partners and of a persistently large public spending expenditure and balance-of-trade deficit.

Scenarios BZ and EZ are designed to curb these unfavourable repercussions, the former by means of a tighter control on public finances and the latter by means of a much less rapid increase in the per capita purchasing power of the average wage. As regards France's financing capability, the improvements achieved in 1988 are identical in both

Table 3.6: Projection results of various scenarios covering the period of the ninth plan

Scenarios	EZ	EY	EX	AZ	BZ	FZ	GZ	PGD
Rest of world GDP (%)	2.7	1.5	2.8	2.7	2.7	2.7	2.7	2.3
Rest of world GDP prices (%)	7.1	5.4	4.5	7.1	7.1	7.1	7.1	5.8
French GDP (%)	2.5	2.1	2.4	2.9	2.5	2.7	2.8	1.8
Consumer prices (%)	8.9	6.5	6.3	10.7	5.8	8.8	4.9	5.1
Variation in total employment between 1983 and 1988 ('000s)	+ 289	+ 64	+ 195	+ 447	+ 95	+ 361	+ 194	− 415
Unemployment rate as defined by the ILO in 1988 (percentage of active population)	9.5	10.1	9.8	9.2	9.9	9.3	9.8	12.0
Central government financing capability in 1988 (percentage of GDP)[1]	− 2.0	− 2.8	− 2.1	− 2.6	− 1.4	− 1.5	− 1.9	− 3.2
General government financing capability (percentage of GDP)[2]	− 0.5	− 1.2	− 0.3	− 1.3	− 0.5	− 0.4	− 0.6	− 0.1

1. Proxy for public deficit.
2. Proxy for current balance deficit.

Source: INSEE.

cases, leaving a slight financing shortfall corresponding approximately to the balance-of-payments deficit on current account.

From the standpoint of employment and unemployment, on the other hand, the slower increase in wages (scenario EZ) has a much less unfavourable effect than the reduction in public expenditure (scenario BZ).

Scenarios B and E do not offer any lasting solution to the problem of the external deficit. What is fundamentally at stake here is the competitivity of the production apparatus. Scenario F assumes that investment will be substantially higher from 1983 onwards and continues through the first years of the plan so as eventually to ease the pressure on the balance of payments. This scenario seems better than scenario E in so far as, for much the same results in terms of external deficit in 1988 and rate of inflation throughout the ninth plan, scenario F is much more conducive to economic growth and, consequently, to employment. The public expenditure deficit in 1988 is also lower. The only drawback to this scenario is the increase in the balance of payments deficit during the period of intensive investment, owing to the high import component of the capital goods.

Scenario G offers similar results to scenario E as far as the public expenditure and balance of payments deficits are concerned. It is considerably more attractive from the standpoint of economic growth and inflation, thanks to the volume of investment induced by the assumed reorganisation of working conditions. However, despite the more rapid growth, the employment and unemployment situation is much less satisfactory during the ninth plan than in scenario E. The difference between the two scenarios stems from the different rate of reduction of the working week.

Unlike scenario EZ, scenarios EY and EX can be used to assess the effect on the French economy of a change in the international environment.

In scenario EY the deterioration in the international environment is directly reflected in poor performance as far as growth, employment, unemployment and public expenditure deficit are concerned, as well as in the worsening balance of payments situation. Consequently, the foreign trade balance achieved in scenario EZ would be possible only at the expense of a further deterioration in economic growth and the labour market situation.

Scenario EX shows a France handicapped by its own tendency towards inflation and therefore unable to take full advantage of the United States economic recovery in a disinflationary situation. Whereas the growth rate of France's principal partners is on average higher by 0.1 point per year than in scenario EZ, the growth of the French economy in scenario EX is lower by 0.1 point than in scenario EZ, owing to the difficulty for French firms to compete in a situation of rapid disinflation.

In the light of these projections the macro-economic strategy of the ninth plan was defined on the principle of intensive investment in order to ease the pressure on the balance of payments in the medium term (scenario F). However, to limit the short-term foreign trade deficit the investment effort will have to go hand in hand with a tight budget policy (scenario B) and a slower increase in wages (scenario E). The reduction in working hours would be greater in the industrial sector than in the services sector (mid-way between scenarios A and G).

3.5.4   The consequences of a rapid return to an equilibrium of the balance of payments

The projections made for the ninth plan were intended in no way as forecasts but merely as an assessment of the medium-term macro-economic effects of certain very clearly defined economic policies. Moreover, since they were established around the middle of 1982 they do not reflect very closely the early years of the projection period. The INSEE'S Programmes service followed up this exercise with further projections as part of an operation known as 'detailed sliding forecasts' (PGD) which is carried out each year in conjunction with a private institution, the Economic Information and Forecasting Bureau (BIPE). This operation, which was conducted under the latter's auspices and with BIPE assumptions, involves a macro-economic projection by INSEE using the DMS model. The purpose of the projection is to provide a benchmark for French firms. The most recent projection, at the time this chapter was written, carried out in the first half of 1983, covers the period 1982–88[12] and incorporates data for 1982 and the beginning of 1983, including the March 1983 exchange rate adjustment and accompanying measures.

One of the factors of this projection is the attempt to establish an equilibrium of the balance of payments on current account as from 1985; this was the government's stated objective and was the basis on which the projection exercise proceeded. This preordained requirement has major implications for the French economy, as can be seen from the projection results listed in the last column of Table 3.6 (PGD). The results are not directly comparable to those obtained for the Plan as these projections were made one year later and have a quite different status. Nevertheless, balancing the current transactions account as from 1985 means that France has an average negative growth differential with its principal trading partners of half a point during the period 1984–88. This relatively slow growth of production (an average of 1.8 per cent per year) results in a significant deterioration in the labour market situation in the medium term: the loss of 415,000 jobs and an unemployment rate of 12 per cent in 1988.[12] The deterioration is particularly serious because in the assumptions used for this projection BIPE set a lower rate of decline in the weekly hours of work than that normally used in projections made for the plan: here the official working week does not reach 35 hours until 1990.

3.5.5 Shortcomings in the projection of employment and unemployment

Like any macro-economic projection those described above may be unreliable to the extent that they include errors of appreciation of the future values of exogenous variables describing the international environment and domestic economic and social policy. The behaviour relationships used in the model are a further source of possible error. In the latter case the explanation may be that a given relationship is statistically speaking of poor quality, because there has been a change in behaviour or because the data for past years do not really help to decide between two alternative formulations. As regards the description of the functioning of the labour market, the projections made may compromise major shortcomings.

The future trend of employment is bound to depend very much on that of labour productivity. The latter, however, is liable to vary considerably both temporarily and geographically, as illustrated in the following table taken from OECD data.

Consequently, it is essential that the labour productivity trend should

Table 3.7: Labour productivity (GDP/total employment)

Geographic area	1960–73	1973–81
Nine-member EEC	4.4	2.0
United States	2.0	0.2
Japan	9.1	2.9

Source: OECD.

be analysed on the basis of previous years. In the DMS model the situation differs widely according to the branches considered: productivity is roughly formalised for the service sector (broken down into a productivity trend and a cycle generated by the inertia of effective employment) and more complex in the industrial branches (see above). In the latter case, in addition to the effect of the productivity cycle the productivity trend is positively dependent on the trend in incorporated and non-incorporated technical progress, on the rate of investment and on capital utilisation rate (the higher the rate the less call there will be to use old equipment) and negatively dependent on the extensive margin (the greater the margin the higher the average age of the equipment). In fact, neither the equipment utilisation time nor the extensive margin is observed directly, which means that any interpretation of the labour productivity trend in the past may be unreliable.

Sophisticated though it is, the DMS model's formalisation of the production function in industry does not explicitly take into account the capital-labour substitution phenomenon, and a change in the ratio of labour cost to capital utilisation cost during the projection period is liable to modify the per capita capital and, hence, labour productivity.

Whereas the DMS model opts for a clay-clay production function, France's quarterly METRIC model assumes that, in the case of new equipment, the choice of the production technique is influenced by the relative price of the factors of production. Yet both models have been estimated over the same period and provide equally satisfactory representation of recent economic trends despite the fact that, on this important capital-labour substitution assumption, they differ. If the METRIC model affords a good econometric representation of capital-labour substitution in terms of the relative price of the factors of production, then the price of labour relative to the capital utilisation cost must drop considerably for there to be any significant improvement in the employment situation. This raises the question of whether it is realistic to assume that such major shocks do not cause distortions that are ignored by the model. The question is particularly relevant because the extent of capital-labour substitutions at relative factor prices is still a controversial issue and because the truth may well lie somewhere between the zero effect assumed in the DMS model and the effect estimated in the METRIC model.

To turn from employment to unemployment, the projection of the latter is centrally dependent on the adjustment tendency of the activity. There is nothing to indicate that, in a rising unemployment situation, the tendencies identified in the past will hold true in the future. On the one hand, there may be a limit to the decline in activity of people in the highest and lowest age brackets that has accounted for the downward trend observed in the past; on the other hand, the steady tendency for female labour to increase may, contrary to what has happened for the past ten years, be affected by the persistence of the crisis, though it may not be possible to be sure what direction the change will take (discouraging women from seeking employment or, on the contrary, encouraging them to do so because their spouse's job may be threatened).

CONCLUSION

The DMS model is an illustration of the development of macro-economic formalisation and, specifically, of the formalisation of France's labour market over the past fifteen years. The progress made in these projections should help governments to assess the future medium-term trend in the labour market situation and, thus, to take appropriate corrective measures to forestall any favourable developments that may be anticipated. The DMS model, for example, was first used in 1978 for the mid-term appraisal of the seventh plan. (The seventh plan covered the years 1975–80 inclusive. The eighth plan, which should have covered the years 1981–85, was never voted by Parliament. Following the advent of the left-wing government in France in spring 1981, an interim two-year plan for 1982 and 1983 was drawn up. The ninth plan covers the five-year period 1984–88.) The projection at that time covered the period 1976–83 and forecast a very much slower increase in total employment than in the past: total employment was expected to increase by 288,000 as against 1,278,000 during the previous eight-year period. Because of the lag between the employment trend and the trend in the potential active population, the number of unemployed was expected to rise by 600,000 persons during the same period.

Without wishing to attempt a comparison between projection and reality, let alone identify the reasons for any discrepancy, it is fair to say that between 1976 and 1982, the last year for which data are available when this paper was written, the trend of the French economy more than confirms the pessimistic diagnosis drawn up at the time with respect to the future labour market situation. Total employment rose by only 46,000 between 1976 and 1982 while unemployment increased by 875,000. It is therefore quite clear that anticipating the downward trend was not enough and the appropriate measures to forestall it failed to be implemented. In other words, there is a divorce between the growing sophistication of projection methods designed to anticipate downward trends more accurately and the declining capability of economic policy to prevent such trends developing. Instead of serving as scouts who can reconnoitre the pitfalls to be avoided, the forecasters find themselves cast in the role of Cassandra.

This uncomfortable situation stems from the increasing ineffectiveness of the traditional instruments of economic policy. As an article by members of the Programme Service puts it in INSEE's monthly *Economie et Statistique*, the narrow path of an employment strategy[11] and the government's room for manoeuvre in its efforts to combat unemployment are nowadays much reduced. Because the French economy is more and more open to international trade, the chances of using public expenditure to boost the economy in the Keynesian manner have been diminished both by the drop in the multiplier (from 1.5 in 1963 to 1.1 in 1982) and by the rising cost of such a policy in terms of public spending and the balance-of-trade deficit. France's attempt at economic recovery in 1981 demonstrated clearly the drawbacks to this option. Less effective, too, is the option of competitive currency devaluation in a situation where the volume of imports is less responsive to price variations and where the initial level of the deficit increases the risk of negative repercussions; in addition, this measure is not consistent with the French european commitments.

Although indirect intervention on the labour market by simulating the market in goods and services seems less feasible than in the past, it may be possible to 'disconnect' the labour market trend from the trend in goods and services by adjusting working hours and, hence, the distribution of total working time among the entire active population. But for this to be successful, the disconnection between the markets must be total; in other words, there must be not unfavourable repercussions of the reduction in hours of work on the market in goods and services. Among other things this means no wage compensation for those whose hours of work have been cut, so as not to increase the cost to the undertaking and thereby reduce their competitiveness. However, this is particularly difficult in a crisis situation where the spontaneous increase in per capita purchasing power of the average wage is already much slower than in the past. This disconnection also presupposes that the reduction in working hours does not lead to shorter equipment utilisation time.

The macro-economic strategy for the ninth plan combines a massive capital stock modernisation campaign so as to lessen the country's external dependency, with an attempt to halt the increase in the per capita purchasing power of the average wage so as to maintain the initially high balance of trade deficit within acceptable limits, especially with the extra burden generated by the stepping up of investment by undertakings. Financing this extra investment means that a special effort has to be made to increase household savings, especially as earnings will be increasing much more slowly than in the past. This 'narrow path' may have unpredictable results, as the conditions for implementing the strategy, unlike those considered above, are not basically dependent upon government decisions. Like the redistribution of income so as to benefit the poorest, reallocating resources between investment and consumption demands a consensus of all the economic partners, a consensus that government action may facilitate but cannot possibly guarantee.

NOTES

1. Fouquet, D., Charpin, J.M., Guillaume, H., Muet, P.A., and Vallet, D. *DMS - modèle dynamique multi-sectors*, Paris, Les collectionie de l'INSEE, September (1978).
2. Service des Programmes de L'INSEE: in *Revue Economique*, September, pp. 930–81 (1980).
3. Raoul, E. and Rouchet, J. 'Utilisation des équipements et fléchissement de la productivité depuis 1974', in *Economie et Statistiques*, pp. 39–53 (1980).
4. Eymard-Duvernay, F. 'Combien d'actifs d'ici l'an 2000?', in *Economie et Statistique*, October, pp. 33–46 (1979).
5. Salais, R. 'Sensibilité de l'activité par sexe at age aux variations du chômage', in *Annales de l'INSEE*, Paris, INSEE, September–December, pp. 83–139 (1971).
6. Eymard-Duvernay, F. and Salais, R. 'Une analyse des liens entre l'emploi et le chômage', in *Economie et Statistique*, July–August, pp. 19–32 (1975).
7. Dernburg, T. and Strand, K. 'Cyclical variation in civilian labour force participation, in *Review of Economics and Statistics*, November, pp. 378–91 (1964).
8. Dernburg, T.F. and Strand, K.T. 'Hidden unemployment, 1953–62: A quantitative analysis by age and sex', in *American Economic Review*, Menasha, Wisconsin, American Economic Association, March, pp. 71–95 (1966).
9. Coëffic, N. 'D'octobre 1980 à octobre 1981, l'aggravation du chômage s'est poursuivie', in *Economie et Statistique*, June, pp. 29–40 (1982).
10. Marchand, O., Rault, D. and Turpin, E. 'Des 40 heures aux 39 heures: Processus et réactions des entreprises', in *Economie et Statistique*, April, pp. 3–15 (1983).
11. Raoul, E., Caffet, J.-P., Joly, P., Piens, B. and Thave, S. 'Les voies étroites d'une stratégie pour l'emploi', ibid., June, pp. 47–59 (1983).
12. *Perspective à l'horizon 1988*, Paris, INSEE, Archives et Documents, September (1983).
13. Euipe DMS, 'DMS-7: modèle dynamique multi-sectoriel', Les Collections de l'INSEE, c 139, July (1987).

Chapter Four

Unemployment, employment and forecasting models: The Belgian experience

M. Vanden Boer, Belgian National Planning Office, Brussels, Belgium *

4.1 THE EVOLUTION OF REAL UNEMPLOYMENT IN BELGIUM, 1970–1981/82

The problem of unemployment is extremely acute in Belgian society. The official unemployment figures underestimate it because the authorities have, by all kinds of measures, succeeded in artificially keeping them beneath the real level. Table 4.1 shows the evolution of the Belgian demographic structure as represented by official figures.

Total population has been divided into an active and non-active part. The active population consists of an employed and an unemployed part. The employed population is, in its turn, divided into domestic and foreign employment. Foreign employment corresponds to the balance of working people entering and leaving the country. Domestic employment includes both the self-employed and employees working in the country. Employees have then been divided according to whether they are employed in enterprises, the government or households.

Table 4.1a shows that, according to official figures, in 1970 the number of unemployed amounted to 68,000, compared to a total of 3,751,000 employed, whereas in 1981 the unemployed numbered 433,000 compared to 3,745,00 employed. At first glance it seems that the number of people employed has remained steady whereas the number of unemployed increased by 365,000, completely absorbing the 360,000 increase in the active population. In structural terms this means that in 1981, 42.4 per cent of the total population was active compared to 39.6 per cent in 1970 (Table 4.1b). But in 1970, 38.9 per cent had a job and 0.75 per cent had not, compared to 38 per cent and 4.4 per cent in 1981.

The official figures therefore show a remarkable stability of employment during the period 1970–81; only unemployment has shown an upward trend.

Official figures, however, use restricted definitions of employment and unemployment; because of the economic crisis the content of the

---

* The view expressed in this chapter is a strictly personal one and is not officially held by the Belgian National Planning Office.

Table 4.1a: The evolution of the Belgian population per main category in absolute figures based on official sources ('000s)

	1970	1971	1972	1973	1974	1975	1976	1977	1978	1979	1980	1981
Total	9,638	9,673	9,709	9,738	9,768	9,795	9,811	9,822	9,830	9,837	9,847	9,852
A. Non-active	5,819	5,819	5,841	5,821	5,792	5,798	5,780	5,765	5,744	5,692	5,686	5,674
B. Active	3,819	3,853	3,868	3,918	3,976	3,997	4,031	4,057	4,085	4,145	4,161	4,179
1. Employed	3,751	3,787	3,783	3,828	3,879	3,819	3,792	3,783	3,785	3,829	3,825	3,745
(a) Domestic sector	3,702	3,739	3,737	3,783	3,837	3,784	3,760	3,753	3,756	3,801	3,798	3,719
(i) Self-employed	693	669	651	642	634	630	623	621	621	626	623	622
(ii) Employees	3,008	3,070	3,085	3,141	3,203	3,154	3,136	3,132	3,135	3,175	3,174	3,097
– enterprises	2,393	2,445	2,444	2,490	2,545	2,493	2,467	2,454	2,430	2,436	2,428	2,351
– public sector	491	501	516	527	536	546	558	570	600	635	646	645
– households	124	123	126	123	122	115	111	108	105	105	101	101
(b) Foreign sector (balance)	49	48	46	45	42	35	32	31	30	28	27	26
2. Unemployed	68	66	85	90	97	178	239	274	300	316	336	433

Source: Belgian National Planning Office.

Table 4.1b: The evolution of the Belgian population per main category in terms of structural data with respect to the total population based on official sources

	1970	1971	1972	1973	1974	1975	1976	1977	1978	1979	1980	1981
Total	100	100	100	100	100	100	100	100	100	100	100	100
A. Non-active	60.4	60.2	60.2	59.8	59.3	59.2	58.9	58.7	58.4	57.9	57.7	57.6
B. Active	39.6	39.8	39.8	40.2	40.7	40.8	41.1	41.3	41.6	42.1	42.3	42.4
1. Employed	38.9	39.1	39	39.3	39.7	39	38.6	38.5	38.5	38.9	38.8	38
(a) Domestic sector	38.4	38.7	38.5	38.8	39.3	38.6	38.3	38.2	38.2	38.6	38.6	37.7
(i) Self-employed	7.2	6.9	6.7	6.6	6.5	6.4	6.4	6.3	6.3	6.4	6.3	6.3
(ii) Employees	31.2	31.7	31.8	32.3	32.8	32.2	32	31.9	31.9	32.3	32.2	31.4
– enterprises	24.8	25.3	25.2	25.6	26.1	25.5	25.1	25	24.7	24.8	24.7	23.9
– public sector	5.1	5.2	5.3	5.4	5.5	5.6	5.7	5.8	6.1	6.5	6.6	6.5
– households	1.3	1.3	1.3	1.3	1.2	1.2	1.1	1.1	1.1	1.1	1	1
(b) Foreign sector (balance)	0.5	0.5	0.5	0.5	0.4	0.4	0.3	0.3	0.3	0.3	0.3	0.3
2. Unemployed	0.7	0.7	0.9	0.9	1	1.8	2.4	2.8	3.1	3.2	3.4	4.4

Source: Belgian National Planning Office.

two notions has changed and this has not been taken into account in official data.

In Table 4.1 the unemployment population is identified with the full-time unemployed, including the first four categories of Table 4.2, that is, the indemnified unemployed, the statutorily insured, the voluntary insured, and the unemployed undergoing vocational training.

Besides these four officially adopted categories, seven other categories of unemployed, all essentially resulting from the economic crisis, can be identified. The figures for unemployment in Belgium should not only include the first main category of full-time unemployed, but should also take account of the part-time unemployed (reduced to work years) and a significant number of people occupied by the public sector in special absorption programmes. Before 1975 these programmes did not exist; they were created specifically to alleviate the social consequences of the economic crisis and to brighten up the bleak image of unemployment.

The latest correction to the official unemployment data (at the time of writing) therefore relates to the actual content of the notion of unemployment; the second 'correction' relates to the measurement of the officially adopted categories of unemployed. The official statistics concerning employment and unemployment in Belgium are closed as at 30 June of the current year, whereas Table 4.2 gives annual averages for the first four categories of unemployed. This explains the difference between total unemployment as in Table 4.1 and the subtotal of full-time unemployed in Table 4.2, item A. This difference varies between 10 and 15 per cent, which means that the annual average unemployment in Belgium surpasses its 30 June level by 10–15 per cent. Indeed, in the middle of the year unemployment reaches its cyclical lowest point, so that a measurement at that time necessarily implies an underestimation. Within the framework of Belgian statistical material, however, no alternative procedure is possible, because the corresponding employment statistics cover the same period of time.

If we add up all categories for the period 1970–81, real unemployment in Belgium amounts to over 122,000 units in 1970, to 760,389 in 1981 and to 870,842 in 1982.

As demographic statistics for 1982 have not yet been published, the adjustments in Table 4.3 only relate to the period 1970–81. Table 4.3 presents a totally different picture from the one we get from Table 4.1. It also divides employees in enterprises into those employed full-time and those employed part-time. The latter figure (corresponding to part-time unemployment), together with that for full-time employed, gives the total number employed in the enterprise sector.

Although the total population remained almost unchanged over the period 1970–81, its internal composition was considerably modified. In absolute figures,[1] the non-active part of the population decreased from 5,818,000 to 5,575,000, ie a fall of almost 25,000. During the same

Table 4.2: Evolution of real unemployment in Belgium, based on 11 categories of unemployed (in units)

	1970	1971	1972	1973	1974	1975	1976	1977	1978	1979	1980	1981	1982
A. Full-time unemployed	82,607	85,558	106,704	112,968	125,755	209,954	270,195	311,569	338,099	357,267	388,249	478,786	590,069
1. Indemnified	71,271	70,876	86,822	91,702	104,720	177,367	228,537	264,284	282,164	294,416	321,895	391,784	456,577
2. Statutorily insured	5,553	8,011	11,554	13,132	13,881	21,589	26,680	30,042	34,860	38,529	40,903	57,137	97,548
3. Voluntarily insured	5,144	5,645	6,851	6,370	5,532	8,817	11,343	13,324	16,359	18,839	19,555	22,638	30,044
4. Undergoing vocational training	639	1,026	1,477	1,764	1,622	2,181	3,635	3,919	4,716	5,483	5,896	7,227	5,900
B. Part-time unemployed	33,712	39,622	36,580	34,285	41,950	82,541	58,495	68,977	69,418	69,407	66,124	93,588	90,000
C. In absorption programmes	6,347	6,812	7,660	8,139	8,457	14,739	38,941	72,078	136,361	160,813	168,334	188,015	190,773
6. Unemployed occupied in public sector	6,347	6,812	7,660	8,139	8,457	10,819	15,885	21,483	28,877	34,222	36,591	34,971	31,772
7. Pre-pension: conventional	0	0	0	0	0	3,920	8,322	15,566	22,466	28,358	34,908	46,346	60,366
8. Pre-pension: legal	0	0	0	0	0	0	5,148	18,197	26,000	31,280	36,913	41,139	45,018
9. Pre-pension: special	0	0	0	0	0	0	0	0	5,428	8,949	9,526	10,981	10,000
10. Special temporary staff	0	0	0	0	0	0	0	0	22,119	27,426	22,107	25,670	17,344
11. Trainees	0	0	0	0	0	0	9,586	16,832	31,471	30,578	28,289	28,908	26,273
D. Real shortage (A+B+C)	122,666	131,992	150,944	155,392	176,162	307,234	367,631	452,624	543,878	587,487	622,707	760,389	870,842

Source: Belgian National Planning Office.

Table 4.3: 'Adjusted' evolution of the Belgian population per main category in terms of structural data with respect to the total population

	1970	1971	1972	1973	1974	1975	1976	1977	1978	1979	1980	1981
Total	100	100	100	100	100	100	100	100	100	100	100	100
A. Non-active	60.4	60.2	60.2	59.8	59.3	59.2	58.8	58.3	57.9	57.2	56.9	56.6
B. Active	39.6	39.8	39.8	40.2	40.7	40.8	41.2	41.7	42.1	42.8	43.1	43.4
1. Employed	38.4	38.5	38.3	38.6	38.9	37.7	37.5	37	36.6	36.9	36.8	35.7
(a) Domestic sector	37.8	38	37.8	38.2	38.5	37.3	37.1	36.7	36.3	36.6	36.5	35.4
(i) Self-employed	7.2	6.9	6.7	6.6	6.5	6.4	6.4	6.3	6.3	6.4	6.3	6.3
(ii) Employees	30.6	31.1	31.1	31.6	32	30.9	30.8	30.4	30	30.2	30.2	29.1
– enterprises	24.3	24.7	24.6	25	25.3	24.3	24.2	23.8	23.4	23.4	23.3	22.2
– full-time	24.7	25.1	24.9	25.3	25.8	25.1	24.8	24.5	24.1	24.1	23.9	23.2
– part-time	0.3	0.4	0.4	0.4	0.4	0.8	0.6	0.7	0.7	0.7	0.7	0.9
– public sector	5	5.1	5.2	5.3	5.4	5.5	5.5	5.5	5.5	5.7	5.9	5.8
– households	1.3	1.3	1.3	1.3	1.2	1.2	1.1	1.1	1.1	1.1	1	1
(b) Foreign sector (balance)	0.5	0.5	0.5	0.5	0.4	0.4	0.3	0.3	0.3	0.3	0.3	0.3
2. Unemployed	1.3	1.4	1.6	1.6	1.8	3.1	3.7	4.6	5.5	6	6.3	7.7

Source: Belgian National Planning Office.

Table 4.4a: The changes in absolute figures of the Belgian adjusted categories of population (in units)

	1970–74	1974–81	1970–81
Total	130,054	84,585	214,639
A. Non-active	– 26,409	– 216,917	– 243,326
B. Active	156,463	301,502	457,965
1. Employed	102,983	– 282,701	– 179,718
(a) Domestic sector	110,797	– 267,135	– 156,338
(i) Self-employed	– 58,864	– 12,131	– 70,995
(ii) Employees	169,639	– 225,022	– 85,383
– enterprises	129,687	– 282,546	– 152,859
– full-time	137,925	– 230,908	– 92,983
– part-time	8,238	51,638	59,876
– public sector	42,490	48,802	91,292
– households	– 2,400	– 21,251	– 23,651
(b) Foreign sector (balance)	– 7,814	– 15,566	– 23,380
2. Unemployed	53,496	584,227	637,723

Source: Belgian National Planning Office.

Table 4.4b: The evolution of unemployment in Belgium explained by the evolution of its main components (in percentages)

	1970–81	1974–81
1. Active population	71.8	51.6
2. Employment	– 28.2	– 48.4
A. Domestic sector	– 24.5	– 45.7
(i) Self-employed	– 11.1	– 2.1
(ii) Employees	– 13.4	– 43.7
– enterprises	– 24	– 48.4
completely	– 14.6	– 39.5
partially	9.4	8.8
– public sector	14.3	8.4
– households	– 3.7	– 3.6
B. Foreign sector (balance)	– 3.7	– 2.7
3. Unemployment (= 1 – 2)	100	100

Source: Belgian National Planning Office.

Table 4.5: Evolution of two unemployment rates in Belgium

Unemployment as % of:	1970	1971	1972	1973	1974	1975
Active population	3.2	3.4	3.9	3.9	4.4	7.6
Employees in enterprises	5.2	5.5	6.3	6.3	7.1	12.9
Unemployment as % of:	1976	1977	1978	1979	1980	1981
Active population	9.0	11.0	13.1	13.9	14.6	17.7
Employees in enterprises	15.5	19.3	23.6	25.5	27.1	34.6

Source: Belgian National Planning Office.

period the real active population increased by almost 460,000 from 3,819,000 to 4,277,000. This can be explained in purely demographic terms by the net surplus on the balance between young people entering the labour market and those leaving at retirement age.

The adjusted structural data also clearly represent the increase in real unemployment, growing from 1.3 per cent in 1970 to 7.7 per cent in 1981. In 1981 unemployment is 3.3 points higher than the official data; in 1970 this difference only amounted to 0.45 points. In 1981 the active population stands at 43.4 per cent of the total population, ie one point higher than in the official figures. The latter do not treat the pre-pensioner as part of the active population, although in 'normal' times they would have worked until their 'normal' age of retirement.

During the period 1970–74 the demographic increase in the active population by 156,000 units was practically compensated for by the increase of employment in Belgian enterprises by 130,000 units, as shown in Table 4.4a. Total unemployment rose by 50,000 units because, the increase in the active population apart, a large number of the self-employed chose to become employees during a period in which 'only' 170,000 new jobs were created. After 1974 this trend reversed suddenly; instead of creating new jobs, enterprises destroyed 280,000 existing jobs, which means an annual rate of 40,000 during the period 1974–81. In the same period the active population continued to increase at a rate of 43,000 persons per year, adding up to 300,000 extra labour supply units by 1981.

As shown in Table 4.4b, over 51 per cent of the increase in real unemployment after 1974 is explained by the continuing growth of the active population and 48.4 per cent by the decline of employment in the enterprise sector.

It can thus be seen that the 'real' unemployment rate, given in Table 4.5, which presents unemployment in relation to the active population, rose slowly during the early 1970s from 3.21 per cent in 1970 to 4.43 per cent in 1974; in 1975 it jumped forward to 7.68 per cent and it then increased rapidly to 17.8 per cent in 1981.

The unemployment rate for employees in the enterprise sector, the only part of the labour force contributing to unemployment insurance, shows even more alarming development: growing slowly from 5.23 per cent in 1970 to 7.12 per cent in 1974, it exploded afterwards to reach 35 per cent in 1981.

The unemployment situation in Belgium is consequently very serious.

4.2 THE DEMOGRAPHIC DIMENSION OF THE UNEMPLOYMENT PROBLEM IN BELGIUM

Table 4.4 illustrates the evolution of unemployment in Belgium during the period 1970–81 in terms of two factors: first, the economic factor responsible for the loss of jobs in Belgian enterprises since 1974 and, second, the demographic factor responsible for the continuing increase in the active population.

As shown in Table 4.4b, 51 per cent of the increase in unemployment after 1974 is explained by the increase in the active population. During the period 1970–74 the active population increased by 37,500 units a year; after 1974 it grew annually by 43,000.

Is this demographic trend normal or are other factors interfering? I shall give an explanation based on my own calculations which, I repeat once again, do not conform to the traditional calculations of the Belgian Planning Office.

The fluctuations in the active population are the net result of two movements: the entry into the labour market of new, mostly young people, on the one hand, and the departure of those of pensionable age on the other. An attempt will now be made to answer the question whether the entry of large numbers of young people into the Belgian labour market during the 1970s was an exceptional phenomenon or not. The traditional approach of the Belgian Planning Office is to consider only the net changes in the active population, so that any distinction between the effects of the two different movements is lost.

Before entering the labour market, young people have to leave school. Table 4.6 shows the numbers of young people, aged 14–25, leaving school in selected years over the period 1957–2000. This period was chosen to give an idea of the movement over two generations or more.

Since the compulsory school age in Belgium is between 7 and 14 years, the number of schoolchildren is determined by the number of births 7 to 14 years earlier. Although the minimum school-leaving age is 14, the number actually leaving at that age diminished rapidly during the period 1957–77. Most young people continued their education *so that school attendance in Belgium more than doubled within 20 years*. Although this may affect the age structure of school-leavers, it does not affect the number leaving school annually (except, of course, for the years in which change occurs). This number is determined by demographic factors alone.

Table 4.6: Numbers of young people leaving school annually in Belgium, 1957–2000

Year	(a) in thousands			(b) % of 1970 figure		
	Male	Female	Total	Male	Female	Total
1957	55.7	55.1	110.8	– 23.9	– 22.2	– 23.1
1961	61.0	58.9	119.9	– 16.6	– 16.9	– 16.7
1965	68.9	67.3	136.2	– 5.8	– 5.0	– 5.4
1970	73.2	70.9	144.1	0	0	0
1976	79.6	76.8	156.4	8.7	8.3	8.5
1980	80.2	77.0	157.2	9.5	8.6	9.0
1985	74.9	71.9	146.8	2.3	1.4	1.8
1990	67.3	64.5	131.8	– 8.0	– 9.0	– 8.5
1995	61.2	58.6	119.8	– 16.3	– 17.3	– 16.8
2000	61.0	59.3	120.3	– 16.6	– 16.3	– 16.5

Source: Belgian National Planning Office.

Table 4.7: Numbers of young people entering the Belgian labour market annually, 1957–2000

Year	(a) in thousands			(b) % of 1970 figure		
	Male	Female	Total	Male	Female	Total
1957	53.2	30.6	83.9	– 25.5	– 26.6	– 25.9
1961	59.7	36.1	95.9	– 16.5	– 13.6	– 15.4
1965	66.5	40.8	107.3	– 6.9	– 2.5	– 5.3
1970	71.5	41.8	113.4	0	0	0
1976	76.5	53.8	130.4	6.9	28.6	14.9
1980	77.3	54.2	131.5	8.1	29.5	16
1985	72.0	50.0	122.2	0.7	19.6	7.7
1990	65.1	44.9	110.1	– 8.9	7.3	– 2.9
1995	58.8	40.5	99.3	– 17.7	– 3.1	– 12.3
2000	58.4	41.4	99.8	– 18.3	– 1.0	– 11.9

Source: Belgian National Planning Office.

Table 4.6 shows that since 1957 the number of young people leaving school in Belgium rose steadily, reaching its highest point during the period 1976–80 and declining rapidly after that. The baby boom of the 1950s and 1960s had its full effect in the 1970s, coinciding with a world-wide economic recession.

Leaving school is only the first condition for participation in active life, however. The second condition is that 'school-leavers' actually express their desire to participate. This second step is considered normal for boys; it is (or was) not so obvious for girls. During the 1970s, social influences stimulated young girls to enter the labour force in large numbers. Table 4.7 shows a 20 per cent increase in the number of girls entering the labour market in the years 1976–80 compared to the period 1965–70. As Table 4.6b shows, we would have expected 8 per cent more young women in 1976 and 1980. In fact, the figure was over 28 per cent, which illustrates the social dimension of the present unemployment problem in Belgium. In absolute figures, this meant an extra supply of 10,000 young women per year after 1975, adding up to 60,000 in 1981, or 8 per cent of total real unemployment in Belgium (760,000 units).

The problem for Belgium is that the continuing and accelerating increase in the active population due to these demographic and social factors during the 1970s and early 1980s coincided with a worldwide economic crisis which caused a massive loss of jobs within the Belgian enterprise sector.

4.3 THE ECONOMIC DIMENSION OF THE UNEMPLOYMENT PROBLEM IN BELGIUM

If unemployment is defined as the difference between the active population and the unemployed population, the first component is determined by social and demographic factors; the second by economic factors.

The economic production process determines the labour volume necessary for realising the annual national product. The national labour volume is expressed in terms of the number of work-hours per machine per year, whereas employment is expressed in terms of the number of people working during a year. (One should not forget that within Western market economies, only the paid labour hours are taken into account.) Between the two concepts, the following relation exists.

$$E = \frac{L}{H_p}$$

where: E = employment per year, in persons,
L = labour volume per year, in hours, and
H_p = average annual hours worked per person.

Full employment is the product of two variables: the total annual amount of hours worked in the nation and the number of hours worked per person per year. The first variable, the national labour volume, is determined by the production level realised during a certain year by the technically necessary labour input (a technical coefficient determined by the technological composition of the production factors – labour, capital and intermediary inputs – in the production process). The second variable is 'conventionally' fixed: the number of hours each person works is negotiated in regular meetings. In Belgium the conventional working week was 39 hours in 1981, 40 hours in 1977, 44 hours in 1970, 48 hours in 1960 and 51 hours in 1950.

This shows that reductions in the working week are not new in Belgium, without them the unemployment situation would have been much worse than it is. The most important thing to notice is that in the past, reductions in working time have always been granted without any loss of income by individuals. This was made possible by sustained economic growth and substantial increases in labour productivity. At the same time, enterprises continued to create new, jobs, at an annual rate of 1.2 per cent per year during the early 1970s.

This process stopped suddenly in 1974 and has been reversed since then. During the second half of the 1970s, jobs were lost at a rate of 1.4 per cent per year, leading to the unexpectedly high unemployment figures given in Table 4.3.

4.4   THE BUDGETARY 'COST' OF UNEMPLOYMENT IN BELGIUM, 1970–80

The explosive growth of unemployment in Belgium since 1974 has had an immediate and unforeseen impact on the government budget. The direct impact concerns the transfers of income to the unemployed, thus unexpectedly increasing government expenditure. On the other hand, as a result of unemployment, the government did not receive the expected revenue from taxation.

Table 4.8 gives a breakdown of total government expenditure on the unemployed, expressed in terms of percentages of GNP: the total rose from 0.49 per cent in 1970 to 0.81 per cent in 1974 but exploded after that to reach 4.47 per cent of GNP in 1981.

The 'missed' revenue was calculated assigning a different wage to unemployed men and women, respectively 75 and 50 per cent of the national average. These wage hypotheses are very conservative and probably underestimate the real situation. Table 4.9 shows that even with these moderate hypotheses, 'missed' revenues represented 0.53 per cent of GNP in 1970, rose to 0.72 per cent in 1974 and finally reached 3.33 per cent in 1981.

Without the crisis, government budgets would never have known the current deficit. Deficits in their turn generate specific costs represented by interest charges due to accumulated borrowing of additional resources. If the costs directly caused by the economic crisis are eliminated, it can be seen that the government budget would never have been in deficit over the period 1974–81.

These consecutive adjustments imply that without the crisis, economic growth would have been 2 per cent per year more than it actually was during the period 1974–81. But one of the main features of the economic crisis is slow economic growth and it is this new reality that has to be coped with.

The crisis did not only affect government budgets; it also weakened the income position of enterprises and households. From 1977 onwards national expenditure exceeded national income and foreign borrowing became inevitable. The trade balance showed growing deficits, the

Table 4.8: Government expenditure on the unemployed in Belgium (in percentages of GNP)

	1970	1971	1972	1973	1974	1975	1976	1977	1978	1979	1980	1981
Indemnities												
Full time and part time	0.49	0.51	0.67	0.68	0.8	0.59	1.73	1.98	2.03	2.14	2.15	2.7
Occupied in public sector	0	0	0.04	0.04	0.03	0.06	0.07	0.11	0.16	0.18	0.18	0.17
Special absorption programmes	0	0	0	0	0	0	0.01	0.22	0.37	0.58	0.93	0.99
Pre-pensions	0	0	0	0	0	0	0	0	0.19	0.34	0.56	0.67
Pre-pensions: legal	0	0	0	0	0	0	0	0	0.1	0.18	0.3	0.35
Unemployment indemnity	0	0	0	0	0	0	0	0	0.08	0.15	0.25	0.28
Additional indemnity	0	0	0	0	0	0	0	0	0.01	0.03	0.05	0.06
Conventional indemnity	0	0	0	0	0	0	0	0	0.09	0.16	0.25	0.31
Special temporary staff	0	0	0	0	0	0	0	0	0.11	0.32	0.37	0.32
Total unemployment	0.4	0.52	0.71	0.73	0.83	1.65	1.82	2.32	2.57	2.91	3.28	3.87
Social security contributions												
on the account of government	0	0	0	0	0.05	0.11	0.19	0.64	0.65	0.56	0.56	0.59
Pensions	0	0	0	0	0.05	0.11	0.19	0.18	0.23	0.23	0.22	0.21
Public health	0	0	0	0	0	0	0	0.27	0.24	0.19	0.2	0.22
Invalidity	0	0	0	0	0	0	0	0.18	0.16	0.13	0.14	0.15
Total budgetary charge	0.4	0.52	0.71	0.73	0.89	1.76	2.02	2.97	3.22	3.48	3.84	4.47

Source: Belgian National Planning Office.

Table 4.9: Elimination of the costs caused by the economic crisis in the Belgian government budget (in percentages of GNP)

	1970	1971	1972	1973	1974	1975	1976	1977	1978	1979	1980	1981
Current expenditure	32.76	33.76	34.59	35.62	36.16	40.93	41.42	43.23	44.7	46.33	48.32	53.13
Current revenue	34.93	35.46	35.27	36.21	37.51	40.21	39.99	41.52	42.37	43.34	43.43	44.31
Balance	2.17	1.7	0.68	0.6	1.35	-0.72	-1.43	-1.71	-2.33	-2.98	-4.88	-8.82
Additional interest charges	0.06	-0.08	-0.18	-0.26	-0.13	-0.55	-0.44	-0.22	0.02	0.47	1.34	2.73
Missed revenue	0.53	0.57	0.7	0.66	0.72	1.35	1.45	1.6	2.06	2.39	2.57	3.33
Unemployment expenses	0.45	0.47	0.66	0.66	0.81	1.64	1.95	2.78	2.99	3.18	3.62	4.38
Adjusted balance	3.21	2.66	1.85	1.66	2.75	1.72	1.53	2.45	2.75	3.06	2.65	1.62

Source: Belgian National Planning Office.

capital stock was diminishing due to the lack of investment in enterprises and rising interest rates, and households were reluctant to build
new dwellings, causing a decline of 40 per cent in dwelling construction
in the last two years.

In 1981 (as in 1975) national income was diminishing in real terms.
However, the recent national accounts showed a positive growth in
1982 – everybody was expecting another fall – and all financial
imbalances are improving.

One item remains alarming: between 1982 and 1987 unemployment
figures will rise by another 300,000 units due to the loss of 200,000 jobs
in the enterprise sector and an increase of another 100,000 units in the
active population.

A possible solution of the unemployment problem by reducing
individual working time has been examined by the Belgian National
Planning Office using a simulation model to examine alternatives. The
results obtained by simulating a policy of reductions in working time are
in the first instance determined by the economic model under which
such a policy is simulated.

In the next section a theoretical scheme will be developed.

4.5   ECONOMIC ASPECTS OF REDUCTIONS IN WORKING TIME

Every policy involving a reduction in individual working time has to
provide an answer to the following questions:

1.   What will happen to the annual individual labour cost?
2.   What will happen to production time?
3.   What will happen to labour productivity?
4.   Will personal income distribution change?

The first question relates to labour costs per hour. Three possibilities
should be examined: that the cost per hour is diminishing, constant or
increasing. This is to see things from the point of view of the employer.
The employee is only concerned with net annual income: this may
remain constant or it may be reduced in proportion to the reduction in
working time or even more. The difference between net income and the
total cost of employment consists of fiscal and parafiscal taxes and this
is what concerns the government.

The second question concerns the level of production: should the
annual production time diminish according to the reduction in
individual working time, total output will fall. If enterprises are to
maintain the annual production time, they will have to engage new
workers, thus creating additional employment. By introducing shift
work, enterprises could increase production time, and hence output.

The third question concerns labour productivity. In the recent

Belgian past, reductions in working time have always led to increases in labour productivity. This is because individual earnings have never been reduced. If individual earnings are reduced there is no guarantee that labour will not be demotivated, in which case productivity will decline. This possibility should not be overlooked.

If there is a productivity increase, then the problem of distributing the productivity gains must be dealt with. Four possibilities should be examined: an increase in the remuneration of capital; an increase in the remuneration of labour (for instance in the form of increased employment); higher levels of taxation (direct or indirect); lower prices; or of course a combination of these possibilities.

The fourth question concerns the distribution of personal income. When income restraint is asked of employees in the enterprise sector, one must also consider whether the same restraint should be asked of state employees, the self-employed or groups with other sources of income. If income distribution is to be held constant then restraint must be asked of all income earners; otherwise a redistribution of personal income takes place. Alternatively, one could ask for a lesser degree of restraint from other income earners. In any case, the exact policy will never be given by a model (see next section) and therefore has to be imposed on it.

The advantage of this theoretical scheme is that each question can be answered independently of the others. However, even if you assume only three possible answers to each question, this already yields 81 combinations.

In this economic scheme two *social restrictions* should not be overlooked. The first is that the scheme accepts the hypothesis of a homogeneous labour force, implying a perfect substitution of one employee by another or by an unemployed person. Given the different skill structure of the employed and unemployed parts of the population, this assumption may not be very realistic: the replacement of an employed person by an unemployed person may well lead to a decrease in labour productivity and hence to a decrease in total annual production.

The second social restriction concerns the possible impact of a reduction in working time on participation rates. If these rates rise, unemployment will not decrease to the same extent as employment will increase. In the case of Belgium, any reduction in working time has always positively affected the participation rates of women. But, again, in the past a shorter working week has never affected net weekly income.

4.6 THE BELGIAN MODEL SIMULATIONS OF REDUCTIONS IN WORKING TIME

The Belgian National Planning Office has made several studies of the possible effects of a policy of reducing working time.

The first study examined the Palasthy proposition, named after a Hungarian professor who proposed to reduce unemployment in Belgium by introducing a generalised non-stop two-shift production system. Each shift would work six hours a day, five days a week, implying an individual working week of 30 hours (an annual reduction of 20 per cent). Part of the capital stock would be scrapped in one go while the remaining stock would be used intensively. This proposition was tried out on the SERENA model but it did not give the expected results: too many internal mechanisms in the model had to be changed and too many questions remained unanswered.

The SERENA simulation presented here was carried out respecting the internal workings of the model; it examined the reduction of working time and individual income by 20 per cent.

Another Belgian National Planning Office study has been done with the Maribel model, simulating an accelerated individual reduction of working time by 3 per cent instead of 1 per cent per year during the period 1982–86.

The different questions of the theoretical scheme are examined in Table 4.10. Professor Palasthy wanted to keep the total wage bill constant for the enterprise sector and at the same time to incorporate all the unemployed in the generalised two-shift system so that annual labour costs per head would decrease. But if one assumes a constant net annual income for all workers, government revenue (the difference between gross labour cost and net individual income) will diminish. In the SERENA simulation labour costs per head and net income per head are reduced in proportion to the reduction in working time, thus keeping the total wage bill constant for the enterprise sector. In the Maribel

Table 4.10: Theoretical scheme: economic consequences of reductions in individual working time

	Palasthy	SERENA	Maribel
1a. Individual annual labour cost	Proportional decline	Proportional decline	Less than proportional decline
1b. Annual net income	Constant	Proportional decline	Less than proportional decline
2. Production time	Increases	Constant	Decreases
— possibility of scrapping part of capital stock	Yes	No	No
3. Labour productivity	Increases	Constant	Proportional increase
— possible distribution of productivity gains	Employment	—	— wages — profit — employment
4. Personal income distribution	Constant	Constant	More unequal

Source: Belgian National Planning Office.

simulation, individual labour costs and individual net income are reduced but not in proportion to the reduction in working time; the total wage bill decreases because enterprises are not forced to compensate for lost working time by employing additional workers.

Production time is increasing in the Palasthy proposition, constant in the SERENA simulation and decreasing in the Maribel simulation. Notice that Professor Palasthy proposes to scrap a considerable part of the existing capital stock while increasing the production time of the remaining stock.

Palasthy and Maribel assume a 'natural' increase in labour productivity. These productivity gains are distributed by Palasthy to an enlarged labour force, whereas in Maribel the profit is distributed between capital and labour. SERENA assumes no gain in productivity. Notice that no fall in prices or increase in taxation has been simulated. The possibility of a decline in labour productivity has not been taken into consideration either.

Personal income distribution is constant in the Palasthy proposition and the SERENA simulation, while in the Maribel simulation only income restraint on the part of the employees in the private sector is considered. In the SERENA simulation a 20 per cent reduction is asked of all income earners.

The Palasthy proposition as such has never been simulated in full because it assumed enormous changes in the Belgian economic system and hence required very clear and realistic answers to the different questions in the theoretical scheme. Palasthy also assumed a perfect substitution of an employed by an unemployed person – an assumption that is not obviously justifiable. If this assumption was unrealistic then a fall in total production was to be feared; Palasthy did not examine this possibility. Scrapping a considerable part of the Belgian capital stock all at once is theoretically tempting but identifying the practical indicators in order to determine which enterprises should be closed and which should survive appears to be an impossible task. And, last but not least, maintaining the total wage bill constant for enterprises and net income constant for employees would enormously reduce government tax receipts, thus aggravating the large deficits already experienced by the national treasury; on these grounds alone the whole proposition has been rejected as unrealistic.

Out of the many SERENA simulations testing the Palasthy proposition, the variation presented here, is one which Palasthy always refused to examine: redistributing both work and income. A reduction of individual working time by 20 per cent, immediately compensated for by the engagement of additional labour, would have created 600,000 new jobs in 1982. The total wage bill for enterprises is not affected because labour cost per hour is kept constant. Keeping personal income distribution unchanged implies that the same income reduction is asked of all other income earners in society. This yields extra revenue for the

Table 4.11: Effects of a redistribution of work and income in Belgium simulated by the SERENA model

	Reference		Changes with respect to reference	
	1981–85	1985	1981–85	1985
Real growth rates:				
GNP	1.45		– 1.91	
Private consumption	2.35		– 4.50	
Balances in % of GNP:				
Current public account		– 17.9		+ 17.4
Trade balance		– 5.3		+ 4.4
Saving rate, households		17.9		– 4.6
Unemployment (in 000s)	+ 200		+ 140	

Source: Belgian National Planning Office.

government (because of the way income is taxed in Belgium), which, in the simulation, is used to diminish the current deficit. Other ways of using these funds are possible, such as a reduction of labour costs for enterprises or additional subsidies for investments or a smaller reduction in personal available income. These alternatives have not been tested yet but will be in the near future.

The results of the simulation (Table 4.11) show that the redistribution of both work and income has a negative impact on growth rates by reducing domestic demand dramatically through a shift of income away from households in favour of the government. The decline in private consumption was important during the first years but was partially compensated for by an increased consumption quota. The improved trade balance was mainly due to a decrease in imports. The current public spending deficit was reduced by two-thirds of the initial transfer of extra funds, because of internal non-linearity.

Exports did not increase because of deteriorating terms of trade due to increasing inflation. The sudden fall in domestic demand accelerated the scrapping mechanisms in the model which was partially compensated for by an increased capacity utilisation rate leading to higher prices. Negative growth rates caused unemployment to rise by another 140,000 units.

These and other results of the SERENA simulations have to be examined in more detail with regard to some mechanisms in the model and some assumptions exogenous to the model. Instead of continuing, we prefer to remake a new reference projection, updating the data base and reviewing some equations, so further simulations along these lines were postponed until later.

Meanwhile the Maribel model was also used to simulate reduction in individual working time. Maribel is a national model without any sectoral or regional dimension, as opposed to SERENA (standing for

Table 4.12: Effects of an accelerated reduction in individual working time in Belgium, simulated by the Maribel model

	Reference		Changes with respect to reference	
	1982–86	1986	1982–86	1986
Real growth rates:				
GNP	1.6		– 0.1	
Private consumption	0.02		– 0.16	
Price of private consumption	6.9		+ 0.2	
Balances in % of GNP:				
Current public account		– 12		+ 0.7
Trade balance		– 4.3		+ 0.6
Unemployment (in 000s)	+ 160		+ 90	

Source: Belgian National Planning Office.

SEctoral, REgional, NAtional). Maribel distinguishes only three sectors – government, households and enterprises. SERENA distinguishes seven economic sectors and has a regional dimension, distinguishing the Flemish, Walloon and Brussels regions. Maribel is much smaller, with only 300 endogenous variables, compared to SERENA's more than 2,000 variables and 800 equations. A description of both models can be found in the reference cited at the end of the chapter.

In both models employment in the government sector is a policy variable, whereas employment in the enterprise sector is endogenous. In SERENA the latter is determined by a putty-clay production function determining demand for input factors (labour, capital, energy and others) with respect to their relative prices. In Maribel the endogenous sector is characterised by a production function with two factors, labour and capital: this function thus connects productivity to the evolution of capital intensity and an autonomous technological progression factor. Labour is expressed in terms of production hours in both models.

Although both models differ greatly in mechanism and construction, the differences in the results, shown in Tables 4.11 and 4.12, can be explained in the first place by the difference in the economic scenario they simulate. The Maribel simulation of an accelerated reduction in individual working time by another 2 per cent per year has only a small impact on economic growth, mainly due to decreasing private consumption. The decline in the available income of households is caused by a decline in annual net income per head of employees in enterprises, which is not compensated for by a corresponding increase in employment. The total cost of wages diminishes, which has a negative impact on revenue from taxation but this is more than compensated for by the reduction in expenses relating to unemployment. Production time is not maintained at its previous level, so production capacity is scrapped; this, given the stagnation of domestic demand, explains the accelerated inflation. This higher inflation is neutralised by improved terms of trade, thus explaining the improved trade balance.

The Maribel simulation results in an increase in employment by 90,000 units in 1986, whereas the SERENA model, which starts with a mechanically created additional employment of 600,000 units in 1981, then destroys another 140,000 of these jobs in 1985; this means a net surplus of 460,000 new jobs, a powerful argument in favour of the SERENA scheme of redistributing the available work. Concluding that this is the best course to follow is premature, however; other alternatives have to be tested and further analysis has to be done.

Interesting as it is to detect the direct and indirect effects of a policy by means of a model, it is very difficult when simulating different economic scenarios to obtain a clear view of the relative importance of the numerous effects. That is why a simplified multisectoral employment model for Belgium has been constructed. This is discussed next.

4.7   SECTORAL EMPLOYMENT FORECASTS FOR BELGIUM, 1982–90

In order to obtain more detailed employment forecasts for Belgium covering a longer period, a simplified sectoral employment model has been developed, distinguishing 17 subsectors in the enterprise sector. Employment in the government sector is considered as a policy variable whereas employment in the enterprise sector depends on output and productivity. Notice that the employment figures are the official ones given in Table 4.1.

Table 4.13 gives a breakdown of the average annual growth rates of sectoral employment for the period 1953–81 into three sub periods. During the whole period, employment was decreasing in agriculture (1), mining (coal and others, 2 and 3 respectively), textiles (5), clothing (6), and wood (7). The other industrial sectors (4, 8–13) already showed declining growth rates in the 1960s and early 1970s, so that industry as a whole can be considered as a declining sector long before the economic crisis. Only two sectors realised positive growth rates during the period 1974–81: transport (17) and distribution/services (16). The latter, representing 35 per cent of total employment in Belgium in 1981, has become more important than industry (28 per cent).

The evolution of sectoral employment is in the first place determined by the evolution of labour productivity. Table 4.14, showing the breakdown of annual growth rates of labour productivity per hour, indicates that after 1974 productivity growth was slowing down in all sectors but three (textiles, paper and steel).

Increases in labour productivity per hour are seen as the result of increasing capital intensity per production hour and an autonomous

Table 4.13: The average growth rates of sectoral employment in Belgium (self-employed and employees in enterprises)

		1953–64	1964–74	1974–81	1953–81
1.	Agriculture	– 3.9	– 5.5	– 3.5	– 4.6
2.	Mining – coal	– 5.8	– 9.8	– 4.5	– 6.9
3.	Mining – others	– 3.3	– 2.5	– 4.1	– 3.1
4.	Food	0.1	– 1.4	– 2.2	– 1.0
5.	Textiles	– 1.3	– 3.6	– 6.7	– 3.2
6.	Clothing	– 1.1	– 1.5	– 8.3	– 2.7
7.	Wood	– 0.5	– 0.2	– 4.4	– 1.0
8.	Paper	1.8	0.3	– 3.5	0.2
9.	Chemical industry	2.1	0.9	– 0.7	1.0
10.	Glass	1.5	– 1.9	– 6.1	– 1.2
11.	Iron, steel	1.0	– 0.2	– 5.6	– 0.8
12.	Metal construction	2.4	1.2	– 2.7	0.9
13.	Diverse	4.5	1.4	– 2.4	1.8
14.	Construction	1.8	0.4	– 1.6	0.4
15.	Energy	0.1	1.1	0.1	0.5
16.	Distribution	0.9	2.3	1.8	1.6
17.	Transport	– 0.1	1.1	0.4	0.4

Source: Belgian National Planning Office

Table 4.14: The average growth rates of sectoral labour productivity per hour in Belgium

		1953–64	1964–74	1974–81	1953–81
1.	Agriculture	5.5	7.5	4.9	7.0
2.	Mining – coal	3.4	2.5	– 2.9	1.6
3.	Mining – others	9.2	9.0	3.3	8.3
4.	Food	2.1	6.8	4.9	4.5
5.	Textiles	5.7	5.8	8.6	7.1
6.	Clothing	8.0	4.5	4.2	5.6
7.	Wood	8.4	8.4	7.5	8.5
8.	Paper	2.8	4.1	4.2	3.8
9.	Chemical industry	5.8	9.8	4.4	8.0
10.	Glass	3.2	6.3	6.1	5.7
11.	Iron, steel	3.2	5.9	6.8	6.4
12.	Metal construction	5.6	7.3	4.0	6.0
13.	Diverse	– 0.5	10.9	3.9	5.1
14.	Construction	1.8	3.3	1.7	2.9
15.	Energy	6.4	10.2	6.3	8.0
16.	Distribution	3.1	4.3	0.6	3.1
17.	Transport	5.4	3.4	2.5	4.3

Source: Belgian National Planning Office

factor standing for technological progress. Consequently, employment is positively influenced by the (sectoral) production level and the annual reduction in individual working time and it is negatively influenced by increased labour productivity.

Table 4.15: Employment forecasts for Belgium, 1982–99, assuming three different average annual growth rates

	Reference	'Normal' growth	'High' growth
1. Agriculture	– 5.8	– 5.1	– 4.1
2. Mining – coal	– 9.3	– 8.5	– 7.4
3. Mining – others	– 6.0	– 4.5	– 2.2
4. Food	– 2.0	– 2.0	– 1.9
5. Textiles	– 7.0	– 5.6	– 3.5
6. Clothing	– 6.0	– 5.0	– 3.5
7. Wood	– 4.4	– 3.7	– 2.6
8. Paper	– 1.4	– 0.9	– 0.3
9. Chemical industry	– 0.3	0.4	1.8
10. Glass	– 6.8	– 5.2	– 2.7
11. Iron, steel	– 6.0	– 4.7	– 2.5
12. Metal construction	– 2.2	– 1.4	– 0.1
13. Diverse	– 2.9	– 2.0	– 0.7
14. Construction	– 4.4	– 3.8	– 2.7
15. Energy	– 2.9	– 1.9	– 0.4
16. Distribution	– 0.2	0.4	1.4
17. Transport	– 0.3	0.5	1.9

Source: Belgian National Planning Office.

Sectoral output for 17 sectors is deduced by an elasticity coefficient with respect to GNP. The reduction in annual working time is deduced from the latest Maribel forecast for the period 1982–87 and is assumed to be the same in all sectors. The evolution of capital intensity per hour has been assumed to be continuous with past evolution (with some adjustments for certain sectors, however, after discussion with the sectoral specialists at the Planning Office).

Three different growth scenarios have been simulated: first, a 'reference' GNP growth of 1.3 per cent during the period 1982–87 with an acceleration up to 2 per cent for the last three years; second, a 'normal' growth rate of 3 per cent from 1984–90; and third, a 'high' growth rate for the same period.

The average employment growth rates per sector for the period 1982–90 obtained in the three simulations are given in Table 4.15; the annual growth rates of total employment, in Table 4.16. Only the simulation using a high GNP growth rate results in positive annual employment growth rates after 1986, and even in this simulation the employment level of 1981 is only reached in 1989.

The sectoral average growth rates under any growth assumption indicate that all industrial sectors will continue their decline; if new employment is to be provided it will be in the tertiary sectors, transport/communications and distribution/services. The latter, representing 35 per cent of enterprise employment in 1981, is in particular responsible for an overall positive effect on total employment growth. Unfortunately a distinction between subsectors is not available in Belgium. Crucial for the distribution/services sector is the relatively

Table 4.16: The annual growth rates of total employment in Belgium, assuming three different average annual growth rates

	Reference	'Normal' growth	'High' growth
1984	– 2.3	– 2.3	– 1.8
1985	– 2.9	– 1.9	– 0.6
1986	– 1.3	– 0.0	1.5
1987	– 1.3	– 0.1	1.8
1988	– 1.6	– 0.2	1.4
1989	– 1.2	– 0.1	1.5
1990	– 1.1	– 0.1	1.6

low rate of increase of labour productivity: if productivity should increase through a massive introduction of robotics, the need for additional employment, when growth is accelerating, would be much less. In this case the results presented here will be far too optimistic.

In these simulations, employment in the government sector is held constant at its 1981 level. However, a high rate of growth would increase fiscal revenue so that additional employment might then be created.

An important restriction on a high rate of economic growth is the trade balance: input/output matrices show that for every 1 per cent of GNP growth, imports have to increase by 0.4 per cent so that in order to preserve the trade balance, an export growth of 0.4 per cent is also required. This, however, requires an international context which is much more expansive than it has been in recent years.

As long as the conditions for accelerated growth are not met in Belgium, other solutions to unemployment have to be sought, such as a reduction in individual working time.

The sectoral employment model is too mechanical to simulate such a policy. This requires a more extended model; however, as is explained earlier in more detail, it is not the model in itself but rather the economic scenario chosen that will determine the results of such a policy.

BIBLIOGRAPHY

The SERENA model

Pollefliet, E. and Floridor, J. *Prices and monetary effects with SERENA*, Paper presented at the Ninth International Conference of Applied Econometrics, Budapest, April (1982).

d'Alcantara, G. *Regional Investment*, Paper presented at the 21st European Congress Regional Science Association, August (1981)

The Maribel model

de Biolley, T. and Bogaert, H. *Maribel: A medium-term model for the Belgian economy*, to be published by the Belgian Planning Office.

The Sectoral Employment Model (SEM)

Pollefliet, E. and Vanden Boer, M. *Sectoral Employment Forecasts for Belgium, 1982–1990* (internal document), Brussels, Belgian Planning Office AD/3032, December (1982).

Chapter Five

FREIA and employment policies in the Netherlands

B.H. Hasselman, J.H.M. Kok and V.R. Okker, Central Planning Bureau, the Hague, the Netherlands

5.1 INTRODUCTION

In 1983 the Central Planning Bureau (*CPB*) of Holland introduced a new operational medium-term model (*FREIA*) with which the financial and the real sectors of the economy could be analysed in a comprehensive manner. This model describes these two sectors and the interactions between them. The main difference from its predecessor (*VINTAF*) is that it incorporates the monetary sector and, in consequence, the role which endogenous monetary variables (eg interest rates) play in equations for expenditure.

Sharply rising government budget deficits, imbalances in the current account of the balance of payments and extremely volatile interest rates and exchange rates have led to an increasing interest in monetary phenomena and in the interactions between these and the real sector of the economy. Some years ago, therefore, the *CPB* started research into the possibilities of building a financial submodel and incorporating it in a real model. This research resulted in *FREIA*.

This chapter contains a brief description of the *FREIA* model in section 5.3 and some simulations with possible employment policies in section 5.5. Certain relevant parts of the model are explained in some detail in section 5.4 in so far as this is necessary for understanding these simulations. Section 5.2 provides an overview of the main problems facing the Netherlands' economy today, such as unemployment, underutilisation of capacity production and government budget deficits. The final section of the paper considers what lessons can be drawn from the model simulations with respect to these economic problems.

5.2 THE CURRENT ECONOMIC SITUATION IN THE NETHERLANDS

In this section we describe some of the main features of the present-day Netherlands' economy. The most serious depression of the world economy since the 1930s, which started in 1980, faced the open economy of the Netherlands with:

1. a slow-down in the growth rate of world imports, especially oil
    refinery products;
2. a high real interest rate; and
3. a decline in the demand for natural gas and a corresponding drop
    in prices.

These factors had a considerable influence on the Netherlands'
economy. Some statistics are presented in Table 5.1.

   In spite of foreign market gains induced by relative labour cost reductions, the growth in exports has not compensated for the decrease in
domestic expenditure. The main reason for this is the lack of adequate
export opportunities due to diminished world trade growth but the
situation is made worse by an export structure which is dominated by
oil refinery products, chemical products and natural gas (standard international trade classification SITC-3). High real interest rates, low

Table 5.1: Some economic indicators in the early 1980s

	Growth in percentage			
	1980	1981	1982	1983[e]
Production of enterprises (vol)	1	− 1	− 2	0
Investments of enterprises: excl. dwellings (vol)	− 7	− 12.5	− 1	3
Private consumption (vol)	0.25	− 2.5	− 1.5	− 2
Exports of goods excl. SITC-3: (vol)[a]	3	4	0	3.5
World trade of goods: excl. SITC-3 (vol)	4	− 0.5	0.5	1
Exports SITC-3 (vol)	− 6.25	− 11.5	− 3.25	1
Employment in enterprises	0.25	− 1.75	− 2.5	− 2
Government employment	1.5	1.75	0.5	− 0.25
Consumption prices	7	6.5	5.5	2.75

	Percentage of net national income			
	1980	1981	1982	1983[e]
Current balance	− 1.5	2.5	3	3
Government budget deficit[b]	7.25	8.25	9.5	10.5
Government interest payments	4	5	5.75	6.5
Natural gas revenue	4	5.75	6	5.5
Unemployment[c]	5.25	7.25	10.75	13.5
Utilisation rate of capacity: production (manufacturing)[d]	0.80	0.78	0.76	0.78

a. Reweighted by the geographical composition as well as the production mix of
Netherlands exports.
b. Netherlands definition (ie including net loans to the private sector by the
Government).
c. Netherlands definition, percentage of labour supply, before 1983 revision.
d. Based on inquiries; 1980–82 yearly average, 1983 June figure.
e. Forecast (June 1983).
Source: Central Planning Bureau, the Netherlands.

profitability and a decrease in disposable income from wages, transfers and benefits have also contributed to the fall in domestic expenditure. Increasing unemployment, moderate wage claims and reductions in government-paid salaries, transfers and social security benefits have been the cause of this decline in disposable income. Hence production growth has stagnated and become negative and underutilisation of capacity production has increased. These developments, together with high interest rates and low levels of profitability, diminish the propensity to invest and thereby the creation of new jobs. Large surpluses on the current balance, upward pressure on exchange rates and low inflation rates are important consequences of these trends in domestic and foreign markets.

Employment figures running parallel with production figures show a downward trend. This rise in unemployment is even sharper because of the increasing labour supply. In comparison with other countries, this growth in the labour supply is very high and will remain so in the near future, as can be seen from Table 5.2. The main causes of this are the high birth rates until 1970 and the sharp increase in female participation rates, which start from a relatively low level in the Netherlands in the 1970s.

Table 5.2: Average annual growth of labour supply (in percentages)

Country	1981–86
United States	1.2
Canada	1.7
Japan	0.8
Belgium	0.3
France	0.3
West Germany	− 0.2
Italy	0.6
Sweden	0.9
United Kingdom	− 0.1
The Netherlands	1.5

Source: CPB forecast based on *Labour Force Statistics 1969–1980* (OECD, 1982), and *World Population Prospects as assessed in 1980* (United Nations, 1980).

Government budget deficits have risen sharply and continuously over the last few years. The reason for this is the growth of expenditure in the public sector. Due to the economic recession, both natural gas and tax revenues turned out to be lower than the initial projections.

Expenditure in connection with unemployment and interest payments increased considerably – the latter as a result of increased government indebtedness, as well as the higher interest rates which were themselves partly caused by the higher level of government borrowing.

This rise in the budget deficit has caused growing concern. A higher level of government borrowing leads to higher interest rates which in turn depress private investment, the so-called crowding-out phenomenon and, in the longer run, employment. Continuing high deficits and the accompanying increase in interest rates raise the burden of interest payments and subsequently the deficit, interest rates, and so on, creating an upward spiral. Before long society could be faced with a situation in which the government deficit has reached the limits at which it can be financed. For this reason a reduction in the government deficit is currently an important target of economic policy; this conflicts with other targets such as a reduction in unemployment and in the underutilisation of capacity production by means of an expansionary policy.

To sum up, the Netherlands' economy is characterised by under-utilisation of capital and labour, large surpluses on the current account and a low inflation rate, for all of which an expansionary policy would be an appropriate remedy. Unfortunately government budget deficits have risen to a dangerous level so that their reduction has become a primary goal; as a result an expansionary policy is hardly possible. On the other hand, though a reduction of the government deficit would have the effect of lowering interest rates, the impact of lower interest rates on investment is lessened by the high underutilisation of capital. In that situation, the propensity to invest and so to create new jobs is low.

5.3   THE *FREIA* MODEL IN A NUTSHELL

The model consists of two major submodels: the income-expenditure block and the financial block.

5.3.1   The income-expenditure submodel

The income-expenditure block can be divided into three parts: the market sector for goods and services, the labour market and the public sector.

5.3.1.1   *The market sector for goods and services*

The supply of goods and services is partly produced domestically and partly imported. Potential domestic supply, ie capacity production, is determined within a vintage model of production with fixed technical coefficients for capital and labour. Capacity production therefore depends on the size of investments, past and present, and on the economic and technical age of capital. The economic age of capital is determined by real labour costs. Actual domestic production is assumed to equal the demand for domestically produced goods. Imports depend on demand and the utilisation rate (equals production/capacity production) which in equilibrium equals a normal value (0.90).

Endogenous components of demand are private consumption, exports of goods excluding SITC-3, private investment in equipment and construction and inventory formation. Apart from prices, important explanatory variables are disposable income for private consumption, world trade and competing prices for exports, expected profitability and demand, together with the utilisation rate for investment in equipment and construction. Inventory formation is mainly determined by final sales. Monetary factors also play a part: interest rates in the equations for private consumption and investment in equipment and a monetary disequilibrium indicator in the inventory formation equation.

The prices of demand components are determined by cost and demand factors. The cost components are the unit cost of capital and labour and the prices of imported raw materials and semi-manufactures, intermediary services and energy. Demand factors are the prices offered by foreign competitors and the level of the utilisation rate. The influence the level of the utilisation rate has on prices implies that the price mechanism in the market sector can contribute to equilibrium, albeit in the (very) long run.

5.3.1.2   *The labour market*

The main assumption made about the labour market is that wages do not adjust quickly to changing demand and supply conditions in order to achieve continuous equilibrium. A state of excess demand for labour or excess supply is therefore a common occurrence. In the case of excess demand for labour, supply is the bottle-neck and therefore the main determinant of employment and vice versa. Employment is therefore calculated as a weighted average of supply and demand; the size of the weights depends on the labour market situation.

Labour supply is determined by demographic factors; excess supply on the labour market can produce the discouraged worker effect. Labour demand is linked to labour required when production is at capacity, and the utilisation rate. This implies that in times of underutilisation, enterprises hold on to a cyclical labour reserve. Wages follow labour productivity and the price of private consumption. The incidence of direct taxes and social security contributions also has an influence on wages. Finally, excess demand for labour – the so-called Phillips curve effect – influences wages, generating long-run equilibrating forces on the labour market.

5.3.1.3   *The public sector*

The public sector consists of the government and the social security system. For the government, the model includes equations for tax receipts and expenditure. These, together with non-tax receipts, determine the size of the government budget deficit, which is an important variable in the financial submodel.

Tax receipts have three components: the direct taxes on wage and income, direct taxes on non-wage income, and indirect taxes. In the equations for the direct tax receipts, the progressive nature of these taxes is taken into account, together with the inflation-indexed adjustment of the rates. Indirect taxes are linked to the components of final sales, each with their own specific exogenous tax rate.

Government expenditure consists of interest payments, consumption, wages and transfer payments. Interest payments depend on interest rates and the size and composition of government debt. The remaining expenditure categories have an exogenous quantity and an endogenous price component. The wage rate is a major influence on the latter, especially for transfer payments.

For the social security system both contributions and benefits are at least partly endogenous. On the benefits side, a distinction is made between unemployment insurance and the other social security insurance and pensions. The quantity components of benefits, with the exception of those for unemployment, are exogenous; the price components are endogenous and based on the current indexation schemes. Social security contributions are set in such a way that they cover benefits after adjustments for central government contributions. The incidence of pension fund contributions is exogenous.

5.3.2   The financial submodel

The framework of the financial submodel is given by a flow-of-funds account which supplies a review of additions to and withdrawals of financial assets from, and of the way these changes are financed through changes in liabilities, ie saving or borrowing.

The financial model consists of five different sectors: government, the central bank, the banking sector, the foreign sector and finally the (non-bank) private sector. The government consists of the central government and local authorities; the central bank is De Nederlandsche Bank (*DNB*). The banking sector comprises commercial banks and other money-creating institutions. The private sector is highly aggregated and includes households, firms and so-called institutional investors (savings banks, pension funds, life insurance companies and social insurance funds).

With the financial submodel the quantity traded and the interest rate of each financial instrument can be determined. In general there are three different ways of describing the operation of the financial markets of the model:

1. the interest rate follows from the assumption of equilibrium of supply and demand;
2. the interest rate is determined by a price-setting function for one side of the market and the quantity traded is determined by the other side of the market;
3. the interest rate is determined by a price-setting function and the quantity trade is determined as a minimum or weighted average of supply and demand.

In the first case, supply and demand equations are developed for each sector. Equality of supply and demand determines the interest rate and the quantity traded. In the second case, the interest rate is set on the supply side and the quantity traded determined on the demand side, given the interest rate. In the third case, a demand and a supply schedule can be formulated and simultaneously one of the market participants sets the interest rate. In this case the market will generally not be in equilibrium and a method of determining the quantity traded therefore needs to be specified.

All three market configurations are represented in the financial submodel. The equilibrium approach is applied to the markets for short-term government debt and domestic bonds and equities. The corresponding interest rates are the domestic short- and long-term interest rates. The assumption of continuous equilibrium in both these markets seems reasonable enough, as the interest rates react to daily changes in supply and demand.

The price-setting approach is applied, amongst others, to the markets for demand, time and savings deposits. As the impact of the Netherlands external capital flows on foreign interest rates is likely to be negligible, foreign interest rates are also assumed to be exogenous to the model.

The third approach, that of 'disequilibrium', is applied to the market for bank loans. Traditionally the bank loan rate is linked to the discount rate of the central bank. This implies that in general the bank loan rate is not an equilibrium price. However, it does not seem reasonable to assume that banks will meet all demand at all times at the current interest rate. Banks might set certain requirements concerning the creditworthiness of potential customers. Moreover, in the presence of a credit restriction regulation, banks will not honour all demand if, by doing so, they would exceed the credit ceiling. This implies that a state of disequilibrium exists in (parts of) the market for bank loans. This means that either suppliers or demanders will not be able to realise their plans. If actual transactions at a *micro* level are determined according to the 'minimum rule', then under certain conditions actual transactions at the *macro* level can be determined as a non-linear weighted average of macro supply and demand.

In the current version of the model exchange rates are assumed to be fixed. This means that the central bank absorbs any excess demand for, or excess supply of, foreign exchange.

Following this discussion of the operation of financial markets, a short outline will now be given of the specification of the financial submodel.

On the market for (short-term) bank loans, the quantity of outstanding bank loans is determined by the given supply of loans by banks and demand for loans by the private sector. The main factors behind demand are interest rates, the financial surplus of the private sector, and the difference between investment and non-wage income, as a measure of the extent to which private investment has to be financed externally. Apart from interest rates, time and savings deposits also play their part on the supply side as a possible credit ceiling.

The *private sector*, given the size of its financial surplus and the actual quantity of bank loans available, determines what to invest in the different financial assets. The distribution of available means depends, amongst other things, on domestic and foreign interest rates and the above-mentioned difference between investment and non-wage income, which is an important influence on net private supply on the capital market.

The available means of *banks* comes mainly from decisions of the private sector; the exception is the financial surplus of banks which depends on net interest income receipts: the difference between interest income received and interest income paid. Given the balance sheet total and the actual quantity of bank loans available, banks decide on the distribution of their means on the basis of interest rates and the share of savings deposits in the balance sheet total.

The *foreign sector* decides what to invest in Netherlands bonds and equities, given foreign and domestic interest rates.

The *central bank* determines the discount rate as a weighted average of the foreign and domestic short-term interest rates. Because of the assumption of fixed exchange rates, its net foreign assets are defined as the difference between the balance of payments surplus of the non-monetary sectors and the change in net foreign assets of banks and the government.

Finally, the *government* borrows on the domestic bond market to the extent to which its budget deficit is not covered by issuing short-term debt and changes in its balance with the central bank.

5.3.3   The interaction of the income-expenditure and financial submodels

From the preceding discussion of the two submodels, the main influence the financial side of the model has on the income-expenditure submodel appears to be through the long-term interest rate and, to a lesser extent, the short-term interest rate and the disequilibrium on the credit market. Interest rates can have both a direct and an indirect influence. They have a direct influence on several domestic expenditure components such as private consumption and investment in equipment and an indirect influence on capital costs, which affect prices and replacement and expansion investment. Interest payments made by the government also depend on interest rates.

There are several links between the income-expenditure submodel and the financial submodel. The most important are the financial surpluses of the private, public and foreign sectors, investment and non-wage income. Additional links are relative export prices, as a measure of exchange rate expectations, and the capacity utilisation rate as a business cycle indicator.

The financial surplus of a sector, defined as the difference between savings and investment, supplemented by net capital transfer payments received, determines the change in net financial wealth of that sector. It is an important factor in determining the financial behaviour of the different sectors.

An important determinant of the demand for long- and short-term loans by the private sector is the gap between investment and non-wage income: as investment increases and the level of non-wage income drops, the opportunities for internal financing become less; in consequence the demand for external financing will be greater. This will lead, all other things being equal, to a rise in interest rates which in its turn will have a moderating influence on investment, bearing in mind the previously mentioned effects of interest rates in the income-expenditure submodel.

5.4 EMPLOYMENT IN THE FREIA MODEL

This section deals with those parts of the model which contribute to the determination of employment patterns: the equations relating to capacity production and full capacity labour requirements, the labour market submodel, and finally the investment equation.

5.4.1 Capacity production and labour requirements

The production function as used in the FREIA model is an amendment of the standard vintage clay-clay production function with two factors of production, capital and labour. The main characteristic of a vintage model is disaggregation of existing capital into annual vintages of capital goods, each with a specific labour productivity. The capital-output ratio is assumed equal for all vintages. Labour productivity for each vintage is, by assumption, determined by both embodied and disembodied labour augmenting technical progress.

Capacity production in year t sustained by a vintage installed in year

τ and still in use in year t is calculated according to:

$$(1) \qquad yn_{t-\tau} = \frac{byn_t}{\varkappa} \, \Omega_{t-\tau} \, (ioa_\tau + ioa_{\tau-1})/2$$

where: $yn_{t-\tau}$ = capacity production in year t on a vintage installed in year τ,

byn_t = index of effective machine hours in year t,

ioa_τ = investment in equipment in year τ (excluding investment in the natural gas sector),

$\varkappa$ = capital output ratio, and

$\Omega_{t-\tau}$ = survival faction after $t-\tau$ years of operation of a vintage.

The size of vintage τ is assumed to be equal to the average of investment in year τ and τ-1, due to an assumed lag in starting to make use of new machinery. Labour requirements for vintage τ in year t are given by:

$$(2) \qquad an_{t,\tau} = \frac{yn_{t,\tau}}{ban_t \, \phi(1 + \epsilon)^t \, (1 + \mu)^\tau}$$

where: $an_{t,\tau}$ = labour requirements in year t for a vintage installed in year τ,

ban_t = index of effective labour time in year t,

ϕ = labour productivity for vintage 0 in year 0,

ϵ = rate of disembodied labour augmenting technical progress, and

μ = rate of embodied labour augmenting technical progress.

Total capacity production and total requirements in year t are obtained by adding (1) and (2) over all vintages still in use in year t. A vintage remains in operation as long as its quasi-rent is positive. The year of installation for the oldest vintage in use is thus determined from:[1]

$$(3) \qquad py_t \cdot yn_{t,obj_t} = lb_t \cdot an_{t,\,obj_t}$$

where: py_t = price per unit of output,

lb_t = (money) wage rate, and

obj_t = year of installation of the oldest vintage still in use in year t.

Substitution of (2) in (3) leads to the following equation for obj_t:

$$(4) \qquad obj_t = \frac{ln\left(\frac{lb}{py}\right)_t - ln\phi - tln(1 + \epsilon) - lnban_t}{ln(1 + \mu)}$$

In the model two restrictions are placed on obj_t: first, that the economic age[2] cannot be larger than the technical age of capital goods;[3] second, that capital goods scrapped in previous years cannot be put into operation in later years.[4]

The full set of equations relating to the capacity submodel can be found in Table 5.3. In the empirical application of the vintage model, some amendments have been made to the basic model. A constant has been added to the equation for capacity production (Table 5.3, equation 2) in order to take account of an (apparently) increasing capital output ratio in the period before 1960.[5] A distinction is thus made between average and marginal capital output ratio. The labour requirements equation has also been amended: the marginal capital output ratio has been replaced by the average capital output ratio (see Table 5.3, equation 3).

Table 5.3: The capacity submodel

Equations

1. $kou = \sum\limits_{\tau = obj}^{t} \Omega_{t-\tau} \; \frac{1}{2} (ioa_\tau + ioa_{\tau-1})$

2. $yn = yn_o + \dfrac{1}{x} \; byn \cdot kou$

3. $an = \dfrac{yn}{byn \cdot kou} \times \dfrac{byn}{\phi \cdot ban \cdot \prod\limits_{j=1}^{t} (1 + \epsilon_j)} \times$

   $\sum\limits_{\tau = obj}^{t} \Omega_{t-\tau} \dfrac{\frac{1}{2} (ioa_\tau + ioa_{\tau-1})}{\prod\limits_{j=1}^{\tau} (1 + \mu_j)}$

4. $obj = \max \left\{ obj_{-1}, \; \dfrac{\frac{1}{4} \sum\limits_{i=0}^{3} ln \left(\frac{lb}{\cdot 01py}\right)_{-i} - ln\phi - lnban - ln \prod\limits_{j=1}^{t} (1 + \epsilon_j)}{ln(1 + \mu)} \right.$

5. $sou = .5 \; ioa + .5 \; ioa_{-1} - kou + kou_{-1}$

6. $skk = 100 \; sou/kou_{-1}$

7. $qy = 100 \; y/yn$

8. $byn = hdn^{.72} \; hun^{.58}$

9. $ban = hdn^{.87} \; hun^{.70}$

Table 5.3: *Continued*

Coefficients in the equations have the following values:

yn_0 = 12.307
x = 1.228
ϕ = 9.478
μ = 0.0377 until 1975; decreasing annually by 0.001 until 1982; thereafter 0.03
ϵ = 0.0157 until 1975; decreasing annually by 0.0037 until 1978; thereafter 0.0

where: an = labour requirements at full capacity, in 000s of work years,
han = index-effective labour time (1970 = 1),
hdn = index of working days per year (1970 = 1),
hun = index of hours worked per day (1970 = 1),
hyn = index of effective machine time (1970 = 1),
ioa = investment in equipment, excluding natural gas sector,
kou = capital stock, equipment,
lb = wage rate, enterprises,
obj = year of installation of oldest vintage still in use,
sou = scrap of capital,
skk = scrap as a percentage of the lagged capital stock,
py = price production of enterprises, excluding natural gas (1970 = 100),
qy = capacity utilisation rate,
y = production of enterprises, excluding natural gas,
yn = capacity production,
μ = rate of embodied labour augmenting technical progress,
ϵ = rate of disembodied labour augmenting technical progress,
ϕ = labour productivity in 1948 of vintage 1948,
x = (marginal) capital output ratio,
t, ζ = time indices (0 in 1948).

Effective machine and labour time (see Table 5.3, equations 8 and 9) are linked to the indices of the number of days worked per year and the number of hours worked per day by means of elasticities. These have been derived with the aid of assumptions about the impact of a reduction in the number of days worked per year and the number of hours worked per day on machine operating time and labour productivity. Approximately 28 per cent of production involving approximately 15 per cent of all jobs occurs under conditions where machine operating time is fixed. Under these conditions a reduction in the number of days worked per year will have no impact on capacity production and will lead to a proportional increase in the number of jobs available. The elasticity of effective machine time with respect to the number of days worked per year therefore equals 1 – .28 = .72. The corresponding elasticity for the number of jobs is – .15; the elasticity for effective labour time[6] then equals .72 – (– .15) = .87.

A similar calculation can be made for the elasticities with respect to the number of hours worked per day. On the assumption that capacity production decreases by 0.8 per cent if the number of hours worked per day is reduced by 1 per cent, due to increased daily efficiencies, effective machine time decreases by 0.8 × 0.72 = 0.58 per cent.

Furthermore, on the assumption that labour productivity increased by 0.2 per cent if the length of the working day is decreased, the number of available jobs in the fixed machine operating time sectors will increase by 0.8 per cent. This implies that effective labour time decreases by $0.58 - 0.15 \times (-0.8) = 0.70$ per cent.

5.4.2 Labour market

The labour market submodel consists of behavioural equations for:

1. labour demand of enterprises;
2. labour supply;
3. employment in enterprises, and
4. wages rate in enterprises.

Government employment and the number of self-employed are assumed to be exogenous. The equations and a list of definitions are presented in Table 5.4.

Labour demand (equation 1) is determined by capacity labour requirements and the utilisation rate of capacity production. Fluctuations in the latter are only partly reflected in labour demand;[7] the assumption is that enterprises hold on to a cyclical labour reserve. The change in labour supply (equation 2) is linked to structural labour supply, which is determined on the basis of demographic factors and long-run trends in participation rates and the difference between total labour demand and structural labour supply. The latter influence provides an approximation to the so-called 'discouraged worker' effect.

As mentioned in the general section on the *FREIA* model, a state of disequilibrium is assumed to be normal for the labour market. Employment could therefore be determined as the minimum of demand and supply. However, on the macro-economic level this would imply a sharp change from excess demand to excess supply; moreover, where there is excess demand, unemployment would be zero, contrary to empirical evidence. An alternative approach, developed by Kooiman and Kloek (1979), has been applied in the model. Their basic idea is that the labour market consists of a large number of submarkets; in each of these, employment is determined as the minimum of supply and demand. Macro-demand and macro-supply are defined as the sum of demand and supply for all the submarkets. Assuming a lognormal distribution of demand and supply in the submarkets, it can be shown that employment is a non-linear weighted average of (macro) demand and supply.[8] The weights depends on relative excess demand in the labour market (see Table 5.4, equations 5, 6, 7, and 8); if demand is smaller than supply it gets the large weight and vice versa. Furthermore, the method of constructing the weights implies that employment is never larger than the minimum of demand and supply. From Table 5.4,

Table 5.4: The labour market

Equations

1. $abd = an(1 - .539(1 - .01qy))$

2. $\Delta as = \Delta ast + .1\Delta(abd + ag - ast)_{-\frac{1}{2}}$

3. $as = as_{-1} + \Delta as$

4. $asb = as - ag$

5. $aps = 200\,\dfrac{abd - asb}{abd + asb}$

6. $aud = 1 - \Phi\left[\dfrac{aps}{\sigma} + .005\sigma\right]$

7. $aus = \Phi\left[\dfrac{aps}{\sigma} - .005\sigma\right]$

8. $ab = aud \times abd + aus \times asb$

9. $aw = as - ab - ag$

10. $\overset{0}{lb} = \overset{0}{p}_{cps_{-\frac{1}{2}}} + \overset{0}{hys} + apl + afw$

11. $apl = \max\left\{-2.5, .3\,aps_{532}, .75aps_{532}\right\}$

where:		
ab	=	employment, enterprises,
abd	=	labour demand,
afw	=	shifting variable (wage equation),
ag	=	employment, government,
an	=	labour requirements at full capacity,
apl	=	Phillips curve influence on wage rate,
aps	=	excess demand on labour market as a percentage of the average of supply and demand,
as	=	labour supply,
asb	=	labour supply available to enterprises,
ast	=	structural labour supply,
aud	=	demand weight in employment equation (8),
aus	=	supply weight in employment equation (8),
aw	=	unemployment,
hys	=	structural labour productivity,
lb	=	(money) wage rate, enterprises,
p_{cps}	=	cost of private consumption, excluding indirect taxes, and cost of medical services,
qy	=	utilisation rate of capacity production (%),
$\phi(x)$	=	$1/\sqrt{2}\,\pi \int_{-\infty} \exp(-\frac{1}{2}t^2)dt$

equations 5, 6, 7 and 8, it can be seen that the process of determining employment involves the parameter σ, for which no easy prior numerical evaluation is possible. However, frictional unemployment, defined as equilibrium unemployment, can be approximated by:

(5) $$\overline{w} = \sigma/\sqrt{2\pi}$$

where: $\overline{w}$ = frictional unemployment as a percentage of labour supply (asb).

This relationship can be used as a check on the plausibility of numerical values for σ. Until 1964, σ is 4.51, implying a frictional unemployment rate of 1.8 per cent; from 1964 until 1980, σ increases by 0.14 annually, leading to a frictional unemployment rate of 2.7 per cent in 1980 and later years. These results roughly agree with those obtained by Kuipers and Buddenberg (1978).

Finally we turn our attention to the wage rate equation (Table 5.4, equation 10). Wages are currently inflation indexed, inflation being measured by the cost of private consumption, excluding indirect taxes, and the cost of medical services. The wage rate is therefore linked to this cost, with a lag of half a year, and a coefficient of 1. Additional influences on the wage rate are structural labour productivity, the Phillips curve and partial shifting of the incidence of direct taxes and social security contributions. The Phillips curve is assumed to be piecewise linear. With relative excess demand lower than -8.33 per cent, the influence on the wage rate is a constant -2.5 per cent. In other situations the impact of excess demand ($aps > 0$) wages is approximately twice as great as the impact of excess supply ($aps < 0$).

The last relevant variable (afw) is the shifting of the incidence of taxes and social security contributions but in order to keep the size of this paper down to manageable proportions, any detailed discussion of this will be omitted. The variable is based on the transition from gross wages to disposable wage income. It depends on social security premiums paid by employers and employees, direct taxes on wage income, wage-replacing payments and child benefits.

5.4.3   Investment in equipment

The equation explaining investment in equipment[9] may be found in Table 5.5. The basic idea underlying this equation is that a distinction can be made between investment for expansion and replacement. The latter, represented by the first term in the investment equation (skk), is equal to the scrap of capital with a distributed lag. Investment for expansion occurs supposedly for two reasons: increased profitability and demand expectations.

Profit-based investment is represented by the second term in the investment equation, in which the after-tax rate of return on new investment, adjusted for the average rate of capacity utilisation (90 per cent), is compared with the after-tax long-term interest rate. The constant (8 per cent) is based on a rate of technical decay (3 per cent) and a risk premium (5 per cent). The coefficient of the profit differential is assumed to depend on the rate of capacity utilisation: lower utilisation rates lead to a smaller coefficient. The reason for this is that a high potential rate of return cannot be realised with low utilisation rates.

The rate of return on new investment is equal to the revenue per unit of output expressed as a percentage of capital invested per unit of

Table 5.5: Investment in equipment

Equations

1. $iok = skk_{1111} + .35f(qy) \cdot (.9rnj - (1 - u) rl - 8)_{-1\frac{1}{2}} + .52\dfrac{y_{4321}}{\bar{x}_{-1}}$

$+ .16 \dfrac{(qy - 90)_{-1}}{\bar{x}_{-1}} + 2.71$

where: $f(qy) = \min\{1, \max\{1 + .05(qy - 90)_{-1}, 0\}\}$

2. $rnj = 100 \cdot \dfrac{byn}{1.228} \cdot \left\{ \dfrac{py - 1.448 \dfrac{100\, lb}{9.478ban \; \prod\limits_{j=1}^{t} (1 + \epsilon_j)(1 + \mu_j)}}{XOU \cdot p_{iou} + .17XGB \cdot p_{igb}} \right\}$

3. $K = \dfrac{byn \cdot kou}{yn}$

4. $XOU = \dfrac{1 - .01b_{ou} - .01\, u\, ZOU}{1 - u}$

5. $XGB = \dfrac{1 - .01b_{gb} - .01\, u\, ZGB}{1 - u}$

6. $ZOU = 10 \dfrac{1 - (1 + .01d)^{-10}}{1 - (1 + .01d)^{-1}}$

7. $ZGB = \dfrac{100}{3} \dfrac{1 - (1 + .01d)^{-10}}{1 - (1 + .01d)^{-1}}$

8. $d = \{(1 - u)rl\}_{111} + 5$

where:
b_{ou}	= investment credit rate (%), equipment,
b_{gb}	= investment credit rate (%), structures,
d	= discounting rate,
ban	= index-effective labour time,
byn	= index-effective machine time,
iok	= investment in equipment, excluding natural gas, as a percentage of the capital stock, lagged one year,
kou	= capital stock, equipment,
lb	= wage rate, enterprises,
p_{igb}	= price investment in structures,
p_{iou}	= price investment in equipment,
py	= price production of enterprises, excluding natural gas (1970 = 100),
qy	= utilisation rate of capacity production (%),
skk	= scrap of capital as a percentage of capital stock, lagged one year,
rl	= long-term interest rate,
rnj	= rate of return on newest vintage (%),
u	= profit tax rate,
XOU	= capital cost multiplier, equipment,

Table 5.5: *Continued*

XGB	=	capital cost multiplier, structures,
y	=	production of enterprises, excluding natural gas,
yn	=	capacity production,
ZOU	=	present value of tax-deductible depreciation allowances, equipment,
ZGB	=	present value of tax-deductible depreciation allowances, structures.

output (see Table 5.5, equation 2). In the numerator of this expression the factor 1.448 is intended to take account of future increases in real labour costs.[10] The multipliers XOU and XGB in the denominator take into account tax-deductible depreciation allowances[11] and investment credits.

Expansion investment based on demand expectations is represented by the last three terms in the investment equation. It is based on an accelerator model with desired capacity determined by expected demand growth and lagged capacity utilisation.

5.5 SOME SIMULATIONS ON EMPLOYMENT POLICY

5.5.1 Introduction

In this section we present some simulation experiments on employment policy. They are presented as deviations from the base run,[12] thus giving some insight into the effectiveness of the policy measures concerned.

Three kinds of employment policy are simulated with FREIA:

1. expansionary policies;
2. policies involving a reduction in wage rates, and
3. policies involving a reduction in working time.

As mentioned above, an expansionary policy conflicts with the target of reducing the government budget deficit; this is currently an important issue in Netherlands macro-economic policy.

In 5.5.2 we investigate the effects of policies aimed at stimulating consumption and investment and the crowding-out issue. First, we simulate an increase in public expenditure by 0.5 per cent of national income, equally distributed between government consumption of goods and services and income transfers to households. Second, we calculate the effects of increasing investment subsidies to such an extent that 0.5 per cent of national income is required in 1983. In each alternative, moreover, we distinguish two different methods of financing the expenditure: borrowing on the capital market and sales of short-term debt to the central bank. The last method of financing is equivalent to pure money creation, since the level of the base money increases.

In 5.5.3 we calculate the effects of a reduction in wage rates. Two alternatives are simulated: a once-and-for-all 2 per cent reduction in 1983 and a 2.5 per cent reduction over a four-year period combined with a reduction of tax incidence on wage income (0.5 per cent of national income) in order to lessen the decline in consumption as far as is permitted by budget deficit constraints.

In 5.5.4 we describe the effects of a 10 per cent reduction in working time (days per year), spread out over four years.

Since a number of non-linearities occur in the model, the policy simulations are fairly sensitive to the results of the base projection; the impact of underutilisation of capacity on prices, the impact of unemployment on wages and the impact of underutilisation on the coefficient of the rate of return on investment, play an especially important role. The base run itself is not presented explicitly. Its projection for the next decade can be characterised as a sequel to developments in the recent past. In spite of planned reductions in government expenditure, the budget deficit will remain high. Underutilisation of capacity, unemployment and the surplus on the current account will also remain sizeable. The non-linearities just mentioned, which are all relevant in the current deep depression, slow down the equilibrating process. An assumed small growth in world trade (3–3.25 per cent per annum) and small increases in international prices (including energy and natural gas prices) are further important elements in this projection.

5.5.2 Expansionary policies

Financed by borrowing on the capital market

Table 5.6 presents the results of an increase in public expenditure by 0.5 per cent of national income equally distributed between government consumption of goods and services and income transfers to households. They can be explained as follows.

The direct effects of the increase in public expenditure are a rise in domestic expenditure and growing imports. The higher level of borrowing on the capital market and the deterioration of the current account lead to a gradual increase in interest rates, especially the long-term interest rate. Prices rise because of the higher capacity utilisation rate and the increase in the cost of capital. This, in turn, results in a gradual fall in exports. Investment outlays initially rise due to the accelerator. After two years, however, the higher long-term interest rate makes itself felt and investment begins to decline. In the long run investment drops below the level of the base run. This is the so-called crowding-out phenomenon, which manifests itself only after a couple of years.

Table 5.6: An increase in (government consumption) expenditure by 0.5 percent NNP (long-term financing) (cumulated changes from base run)

		Year First	Second	Third	Fourth	L[e]
Wage rate, enterprises	(%)[a]	.0	.1	.1	.2	.2
Price of private consumption	(%)	.0	.1	.1	.1	.2
Price of commodity exports	(%)	.0	.1	.1	.1	.1
Real labour costs	(%)	.0	.0	.0	.1	-.1
Rate of return on private investment	(% pnt)[b]	.0	.0	.0	-.1	.0
Volume of private consumption	(%)	.3	.4	.4	.4	.3
Volume of commodity exports	(%)	.0	-.1	-.1	-.1	-.1
Volume of private non-residential investment	(%)	1.0	1.7	1.3	.4	-.6
Volume of commodity imports	(%)	.4	.6	.4	.3	.1
Volume of production of enterprises	(%)	.4	.4	.4	.3	.1
Capacity utilisation	(% pnt)	.3	.2	.1	.1	.0
Labour requirements (full capacity)	(1000MY)[c]	1.0	3.0	6.0	7.0	4.0
Employment, enterprises	(1000MY)	7.0	9.0	8.0	7.0	4.0
Unemployment	(1000MY)	-7.0	-8.0	-7.0	-6.0	-4.0
Financial surplus, government	(% NNP)[d]	-.3	-.3	-.3	-.4	-.7
Tax revenues	(% NNP)	.0	.1	.1	.1	.1
Current account of balance of payments	(% NNP)	-.3	-.4	-.4	-.3	-.3
Capital account of balance of payments	(% NNP)	.2	.3	.3	.2	.2
Long-term interest rate	(% pnt)	.1	.1	.2	.2	.4

a. percentage of base run.
b. percentage points.
c. MY = man-years.
d. NNP = net national product.
e. L = ninth-year impact.

Employment moves in line with labour requirements and capacity utilisation rates. Therefore unemployment falls initially but begins to rise again after a few years. In the long run, however (ie after nine years), unemployment still lies somewhat below the level in the base run. The government deficit gradually rises, largely because of increasing interest payments. The higher long-term interest rate attracts foreign capital flows and results in a surplus on the capital account, partially offsetting the deficit on the current account.

A policy of stimulating private investment can be simulated by an increase of the investment credit rates (described in 5.4) to such an extent that in 1983 additional investment premiums would amount to 0.5 per cent of national income. It should be noted that the size of the government expenditure at issue depends on the amount of private investment and is therefore less manageable from the government's point of view than a policy of increasing public consumption and transfer payments. The results are presented in Table 5.7. The increase

Table 5.7: An increase in investment credit rates by 0.5 per cent *NNP* (long-term financing) (cumulated changes from base run)

		Year First	Second	Third	Fourth	L[e]
Wage rate, enterprises	(%)[a]	-.1	-.2	-.2	-.2	-.1
Price of private consumption	(%)	-.1	-.3	-.4	-.6	-.6
Price of commodity exports	(%)	-.1	-.1	-.2	-.3	-.4
Real labour costs	(%)	.2	.3	.5	.8	1.0
Rate of return on private investment	(% pnt)[b]	1.4	1.3	1.2	1.1	1.1
Volume of private consumption	(%)	.1	.2	.2	.3	.3
Volume of commodity exports	(%)	.0	.1	.2	.3	.7
Volume of private non-residential investment	(%)	.3	3.0	5.8	6.2	1.7
Volume of commodity imports	(%)	.1	.4	.8	.9	.5
Volume of production of enterprises	(%)	.1	.3	.6	.8	.7
Capacity utilisation	(% pnt)	.1	.2	.3	.1	-.4
Labour requirements (full capacity)	(1000MY)[c]	-1.0	0.0	4.0	11.0	34.0
Employment, enterprises	(1000MY)	1.0	5.0	11.0	14.0	20.0
Unemployment	(1000MY)	-1.0	-5.0	-10.0	-13.0	-18.0
Financial surplus, government	(% NNP)[d]	.0	-.2	-.4	-.5	-1.2
Tax revenues	(% NNP)	.0	.0	.0	.1	.1
Current account of balance of payments	(% NNP)	-.1	-.3	-.6	-.6	-.4
Capital account of balance of payments	(% NNP)	.0	.2	.4	.4	.3
Long-term interest rate	(% pnt)	.0	.1	.2	.2	.5

a. percentage of base run.
b. percentage points.
c. MY = man-years.
d. NNP = net national product.
e. L = ninth-year impact.

of investment credit rates initially leads to an increase of the rate of return on private investment and a decrease of capital costs. Because of lags, this gradually results in an increase in private investment, a decrease in prices and a higher level of real labour costs.

As a result, economic scrapping increases; the resulting loss of jobs is more than offset by the increase in jobs created by investment. Labour requirements therefore slowly increase, leading to a steady rise in employment. These influences are absent in the previous simulation and therefore the decrease in unemployment is larger in the present simulation. The decrease of prices also leads to a sizeable increase of exports of commodities due to the improved competitive situation.

The government budget deficit shows a substantial increase caused by the higher credit rates, the increase in private investment outlays and increasing interest payments. Increased government borrowing on the capital market and the deficit on the current account of the balance of payments gradually lead to a higher long-term interest rate.

Table 5.8: An increase in (government consumption) expenditure by 0.5 per cent NNP (base money financing) (cumulated changes from base run)

		Year First	Second	Third	Fourth	L[e]
Wage rate, enterprises	(%)[a]	.0	.1	.1	.1	.1
Price of private consumption	(%)	.0	.1	.1	.1	.0
Price of commodity exports	(%)	.0	.1	.1	.0	.0
Real labour costs	(%)	.0	.0	.1	.1	.2
Rate of return on private investment	(% pnt)[b]	.0	.0	.0	.0	− .1
Volume of private consumption	(%)	.3	.5	.5	.6	.7
Volume of exports of commodities	(%)	.0	− .1	− .1	− .1	.0
Volume of private non-residential investment	(%)	1.1	2.0	1.9	1.3	.9
Volume of imports of commodities	(%)	.4	.6	.5	.4	.4
Volume of production of enterprises	(%)	.4	.5	.4	.4	.5
Capacity utilisation	(% pnt)	.3	.3	.2	.1	.0
Labour requirements (full capacity)	(1000MY)[c]	1.0	4.0	6.0	8.0	13.0
Employment, enterprises	(1000MY)	7.0	10.0	10.0	10.0	13.0
Unemployment	(1000MY)	− 7.0	− 9.0	− 9.0	− 9.0	− 12.0
Financial surplus, government	(% NNP)[d]	− .3	− .2	− .2	− .3	− .1
Tax revenues	(% NNP)	.0	.1	.1	.1	.0
Current account of balance of payments	(% NNP)	− .3	− .4	− .4	− .3	− .3
Capital account of balance of payments	(% NNP)	− .2	− .1	− .1	− .1	− .1
Long-term interest rate	(% pnt)	− .1	− .1	− .1	− .1	− .2

a. percentage of base run.
b. percentage points.
c. MY = man-years.
d. NNP = net national product.
e. L = ninth-year impact.

As in the previous simulation, this leads to some crowding out of private investment. After the fourth year this results in a slowing down of the decrease in unemployment and a decrease in private investment.

A comparison of this simulation with the previous one shows that the policy of increasing investment credit rates is more effective in stimulating investment and exports at the cost of a larger government budget deficit.

Financed by sales of short-term debt to the central bank

In Tables 5.8 and 5.9 it is shown that base money financing of public expenditure results in a slight fall in interest rates. Consequently, increased public expenditure does not lead to a crowding out of private expenditure. The impact on domestic expenditure therefore remains positive even in the longer run and unemployment shows a continuous

Table 5.9: An increase in investment credit rates by 0.5 per cent NNP (base money financing) (cumulated changes from base run)

		Year First	Second	Third	Fourth	L[e]
Wage rate, enterprises	(%)[a]	-.1	-.2	-.2	-.3	-.2
Price of private consumption	(%)	-.1	-.3	-.5	-.7	-.9
Price of exports of commodities	(%)	-.1	-.1	-.2	-.3	-.5
Real labour costs	(%)	.2	.3	.6	.8	1.3
Rate of return on private investment	(% pnt)[b]	1.4	1.3	1.2	1.1	1.1
Volume of private consumption	(%)	.1	.2	.4	.5	.7
Volume of exports of commodities	(%)	.0	.1	.2	.4	.9
Volume of private non-residential investment	(%)	.4	3.3	6.4	7.1	3.2
Volume of imports of commodities	(%)	.1	.5	.9	1.0	.9
Volume of production of enterprises	(%)	.1	.4	.7	.9	1.1
Capacity utilisation	(% pnt)	.1	.3	.3	.3	-.4
Labour requirements (full capacity)	(1000MY)[c]	-1.0	0.0	5.0	12.0	43.0
Employment, enterprises	(1000MY)	1.0	6.0	13.0	17.0	29.0
Unemployment	(1000MY)	-1.0	-6.0	-12.0	-15.0	-26.0
Financial surplus, government	(% NNP)[d]	-.1	-.2	-.3	-.3	-.6
Tax revenues	(% NNP)	.0	.0	.0	.0	.0
Current account of balance of payments	(% NNP)	-.1	-.3	-.6	-.7	-.4
Capital account of balance of payments	(% NNP)	-.3	-.1	.0	.1	.0
Long-term interest rate	(% pnt)	-.1	-.1	-.1	-.1	-.1

a. percentage of base run.
b. percentage points.
c. MY = man-years.
d. NNP = net national product.
e. L = ninth-year impact.

fall. The main differences between the two alternative policies nevertheless remain, such as the initial impact, price developments and composition of the growth of private expenditure.

In both alternatives the current account, and the sum of the capital and current account, show a continuous deficit (with respect to the base projection). This raises some doubts as to whether the central bank would be able to maintain the exchange rate of the guilder, especially in the longer run.

5.5.3   Wage reduction

This simulation concerns the impact of a once-and-for-all 2 per cent reduction in the wages paid by enterprises in 1983. Some results are given in Table 5.10. Wage reduction has a diversified impact in the model:

Table 5.10: A 2 per cent once-and-for-all wage reduction (cumulated changes from base run)

		Year First	Second	Third	Fourth	L[e]
Wage rate, enterprises	(%)[a]	− 2.4	− 3.0	− 3.3	− 3.4	− 3.3
Price of private consumption	(%)	− .8	− 1.0	− 1.1	− 1.1	− 1.5
Price of exports of commodities	(%)	− .3	− .4	− .5	− .5	− .5
Real labour costs	(%)	− 1.4	− 1.7	− 1.7	− 1.8	− 1.5
Rate of return on private investment	(% pnt)[b]	.5	.6	.6	.6	.5
Volume of private consumption	(%)	− .6	− 1.3	− 1.4	− 1.4	− 1.1
Volume of exports of commodities	(%)	.2	.5	.7	.8	.9
Volume of private non-residential investment	(%)	− .8	− 1.6	− 1.8	− 1.8	2.9
Volume of imports of commodities	(%)	− .4	− .7	− .7	− .5	.3
Volume of production of enterprises	(%)	− .1	− .2	− .2	− .1	.4
Capacity utilisation	(% pnt)	− .2	− .3	− .3	− .3	− .1
Labour requirements (full capacity)	(1000MY)[c]	9.0	17.0	24.0	29.0	31.0
Employment, enterprises	(1000MY)	4.0	7.0	14.0	20.0	26.0
Unemployment	(1000MY)	− 4.0	− 7.0	− 13.0	− 18.0	− 24.0
Financial surplus, government	(% NNP)[d]	.0	.1	.1	.2	.7
Tax revenues	(% NNP)	.0	− .1	− .1	− .1	− .1
Current account of balance of payments	(% NNP)	.2	.5	.6	.7	.3
Capital account of balance of payments	(% NNP)	− .1	− .3	− .4	− .4	− .1
Long-term interest rate	(% pnt)	.0	− .1	− .2	− .3	− .5

a. percentage of base run.
b. percentage points.
c. MY = man-years.
d. NNP = net national product.
e. L = ninth-year impact.

1. private consumption decreases as a result of the fall in wage income;
2. exports increase as the prices of exports fall relative to those offered by foreign competitors;
3. lower real labour costs lead to less scrapping of capital and a higher rate of return on new investment;
4. after some years the government budget deficit starts to decline as a result of the decrease in wage-sensitive expenditure.

In the first two years these developments lead to a decrease in production and the utilisation rate; in consequence, private investment also falls. After the fourth year, however, the positive impact of the rate of return exceeds the negative impact of the accelerator, leading to a gradual recovery of private investment.

Because the impact of less economic scrapping exceeds the impact of a lower utilisation rate on employment, unemployment shows a small decline even in the first year. This decline continues in later years under

Table 5.11: Wage reduction (2.5 per cent) combined with lower taxes on wage income (0.5 per cent NNP) (four years) (cumulated changes from base run)

		Year First	Second	Third	Fourth	L^e
Wage rate, enterprises	(%)^a	-3.2	-7.1	-11.0	-14.8	-15.9
Price of private consumption	(%)	-1.0	-2.2	-3.4	-4.6	-5.0
Price of exports of commodity	(%)	-.4	-.9	-1.4	-1.9	-2.0
Real labour costs	(%)	-1.8	-4.0	-6.3	-8.5	-8.6
Rate of return on private investment	(% pnt)^b	.6	1.4	2.1	2.7	2.4
Volume of private consumption	(%)	-.3	-1.2	-2.3	-3.5	-3.5
Volume of exports of commodities	(%)	.3	.9	1.7	2.7	3.9
Volume of private non-residential investment	(%)	-.2	-.9	-1.7	-2.5	8.4
Volume of imports of commodities	(%)	-.1	-.5	-.9	-1.1	1.1
Volume of production of enterprises	(%)	.1	.1	.2	.4	2.1
Capacity utilisation	(% pnt)	.0	-.3	-.4	-.5	-.1
Labour requirements (full capacity)	(1000MY)^c	13.0	37.0	65.0	92.0	148.0
Employment, enterprises	(1000MY)	10.0	27.0	47.0	69.0	131.0
Unemployment	(1000MY)	-10.0	-25.0	-43.0	-63.0	-118.0
Financial surplus, government	(% NNP)^d	-.4	-.7	-.9	-1.1	.1
Tax revenues	(% NNP)	-.5	-1.0	-1.5	-2.1	-2.0
Current account of balance of payments	(% NNP)	-.1	.2	.6	1.1	.7
Capital account of balance of payments	(% NNP)	.1	-.1	-.2	-.4	-.3
Long-term interest rate	(% pnt)	.0	.0	.0	-.1	-.6

a. percentage of base run.
b. percentage points.
c. MY = man-years.
d. NNP = net national product.
e. L = ninth-year impact.

the influence of a gradual increase in production and investment. In the long run unemployment will have decreased by approximately 20,000 work-years. The larger surplus on the current account of the balance of payments and the lower government budget deficit lead to a gradual fall in the long-term interest rate, providing an additional positive impact on private investment. However, private consumption remains about 1 per cent lower than in the base run. These results must be interpreted with caution, however. A larger wage reduction might not have a proportionally larger impact on, for example, unemployment if and when economic scrapping reaches its limit.[13] A policy of moderate wage reductions spread over several years would probably give better results in such a situation. It should be noted, too, that the apparent effectiveness of wage reduction hinges to some extent on whether or not the Phillips curve mechanism is operative. If it does operate, then the fall in unemployment will lead to subsequent wage increases, partially offsetting the initial reduction.[14] One disadvantage of a policy of wage reduction is the decline in private consumption. A policy of combining wage reduction with tax reduction might be more advisable in the current economic situation as it would minimise the decline in private consumption. The policy mix that we have simulated involves an *annual* wage reduction of 2.5 per cent combined with an *annual* reduction of taxes on wage income of 0.5 per cent NNP[15] for a *period of four years*. The results are given in Table 5.11. The combination has been chosen in such a way that the government budget deficit will not increase in the long run. In the short run, however, the deficit increases as the impact of wage reduction takes some time to emerge, whereas the tax reduction has an immediate impact on the deficit. Private consumption still decreases but to a lesser extent than would have been the case with no tax reduction. The outcome of this type of policy needs no further elaboration, bearing in mind the discussion of the impact of a once-and-for-all wage reduction.

5.5.4 Shorter working year

This simulation is intended to illustrate the impact of a 10 per cent reduction in the number of days worked per year spread out equally over a period of four years. This ultimately leads to reductions in effective machine and labour time of 7.3 per cent and 8.8 per cent respectively; this implies that approximately 28 per cent of total capacity remains constant.[16] Capacity production will also decrease, at least initially, and capacity utilisation will increase. In the current economic situation, with low utilisation rates, it seems unrealistic to expect this increase in capacity utilisation to lead to higher investment. An (autonomous) correction has therefore been introduced in the equation for investment in equipment.[17] The smaller number of working days is also assumed to apply to government employees and the government is assumed to increase its employment proportionally. The results of the simulation can be found in Table 5.12.

Initially the shorter working year leads to lower-capacity production but not to higher-(capacity) labour requirements. The reason is the lagged influence of real labour costs on scrapping, in contrast to the immediate impact of effective labour time.[18] Employment does increase initially, however, because of the higher-capacity utilisation rate. Labour productivity decreases; this leads to a lower wage rate which ultimately, through its impact on economic scrapping, almost compensates for the decrease in effective labour time. Employment steadily increases to a level which is approximately 4 per cent higher than in the base run; this leads to a decrease in government unemployment expenditure. Prices go up because the cost of capital per unit of output increases. Private consumption declines because of lower wage incomes and rising prices. Exports of commodities also fall as the price of exports increase.

Table 5.12: A 10 per cent reduction in the number of days worked per year (cumulated changes from base run)

		Year First	Second	Third	Fourth	L[e]
Wage rate, enterprises	(%)[a]	– 1.7	– 3.2	– 4.9	– 6.7	– 8.1
Price of private consumption	(%)	.3	.8	1.3	1.7	1.6
Price of exports of commodities	(%)	.1	.4	.6	.8	.9
Real labour costs	(%)	– 2.0	– 4.3	– 6.6	– 9.0	– 10.4
Rate of return on private investment	(% pnt)[b]	– .4	– .6	– .8	– 1.0	– .4
Volume of private consumption	(%)	– .8	– 1.9	– 2.9	– 4.0	– 4.4
Volume of exports of commodities	(%)	– .1	– .4	– .7	– 1.1	– 1.5
Volume of private non-residential investment	(%)	1.0	2.4	2.2	.3	.4
Volume of imports of commodities	(%)	– .1	– .4	– .9	– 1.5	– 1.3
Volume of production of enterprises	(%)	– .4	– 1.1	– 1.8	– 2.6	– 2.8
Capacity utilisation	(% pnt)	1.6	2.8	3.6	4.1	4.5
Labour requirements (full capacity)	(1000MY)[c]	– 27.0	– 31.0	– 12.0	22.0	67.0
Employment, enterprises	(1000MY)	13.0	37.0	73.0	117.0	169.0
Unemployment	(1000MY)	– 31.0	– 71.0	– 122.0	– 180.0	– 223.0
Financial surplus, government	(% NNP)[d]	– .1	.0	.1	.2	1.2
Tax revenues	(% NNP)	– .1	– .2	– .2	– .3	– .7
Current account of balance of payments	(% NNP)	.1	.4	.7	1.1	1.4
Capital account of balance of payments	(% NNP)	– .2	– .5	– .7	– 1.0	– 1.0
Long-term interest rate	(% pnt)	.0	.0	– .1	– .2	– 1.2

a. percentage of base run.
b. percentage points.
c. MY = man-years.
d. NNP = net national product.
e. L = ninth-year impact.

Private investment increases in the first years due to the increase in scrapping. Thereafter the negative production impact dominates and investment falls back to the level of the base run.

On balance, domestic expenditure declines and so do both domestic production and imports of commodities. Utilisation of capacity production, however, increases permanently as capacity production declines more than production and investment does not react fully to the increased utilisation.[19]

The government budget deficit declines because of the lower level of unemployment and decrease in interest payments. In combination with the larger surplus on the current account, this leads to lower long-term interest rates. The capital account is therefore in deficit.

In terms of employment, the reduction in the number of working days has a 40 per cent effectiveness. This estimate must be regarded with some caution, however. If wages less than fully compensate for the decline in productivity, the effects on employment will be less favourable.[20] Furthermore, a decrease in the number of working days per year could easily lead to an increase in the labour supply because of the greater opportunities for part-time work. Finally, our knowledge of the effects of a shorter working year at the micro-economic level is not sufficient to warrant hard-and-fast answers to questions about the possible consequences.

5.6   FINAL REMARKS

Given the current economic situation in the Netherlands, the simulations with the model just described give rise to the following remarks.

1. The crowding-out phenomenon, ie the displacement of private expenditure by government expenditure through high interest rates, is a relevant issue in the long run but its importance is fairly minimal nowadays, with underutilisation of capacity production and a surplus on the current account. After nine years, the crowding-out consequences of an expansionary policy would still not have cancelled out the initial positive effects on employment. As far as financing an expansionary policy by borrowing on the capital market is concerned, we conclude:
    a. the short-run positive effects of an expansionary policy on employment will be reversed in the long run;
    b. expenditure cuts by the government lead to a deterioration in the employment situation in the short- and medium-term; only in the very long run does the fall in interest rates lead to a rise in investment and employment, which can compensate for the initial decrease.
    Short-term targets must therefore be weighted up against long-term targets.
2. Base money financing of government expenditure prevents a rise in the long-term interest rate and the subsequent decrease in investment. In the longer run, however, this method of financing presents problems concerning the external position of the guilder and the inflation rate. It is clear that the level of international reserves, in consequence of the current account development in the base run, as well as the underutilisation rate of capacity production, determine the extent to which this method of financing can be applied. For a small and open economy the opportunities are rather limited. Internationally concerted action in this field would reduce the negative impact on the external position and, additionally, increase world trade growth. Such a scenario, however, is beyond the scope of FREIA, in which world trade is an exogenous variable; it is also

beyond the scope of the national government of a small country like the Netherlands.

3. The recent sharp fall in consumption mentioned in 5.2 would primarily recommend a policy aimed at stimulating consumption. As was shown in section 5.5.2, this is indeed more effective in the short run. In the long run, however, a rise in investment credit rates results in a higher level of employment.

    It would seem paradoxical to stimulate investment in times when overcapacity is large. However, as mentioned briefly in Section 5.2, the Netherlands' production structure is largely oriented to a few sectors, especially SITC-3 and low-graded chemical products. Upgrading and diversification should be carried out so as to enable the Netherlands to face structural changes and developments in the world economy.

4. Moderate wage reductions, spread out over several years, have a positive impact on employment. This is because of a slowing down of the scrapping process (ie the substitution of capital for labour), an increase in exports and a decrease in private consumption and imports. In order to prevent too sharp a fall in private consumption, wage reductions could be combined with tax reductions to an extent permitted by a controlled budget deficit development in the long run. This does mean a 'beggar my neighbour' policy which, if applied all over the world, would further depress the world economy. Nevertheless, for small countries with an open economy and a relatively high labour supply growth rate, such a policy may well be inevitable for in such countries a slowing down in the process of substitution of capital for labour is greatly needed.

5. Unemployment figures will soon surpass the 1 million mark (ie 19 per cent of the labour supply). None of the policies considered so far seem able to make any sizeable impression on unemployment so one must consider a reduction in working time. This cannot of course solve the unemployment problem itself but it does distribute the misery more fairly. However, since the reduction in working time would enable enterprises to reduce overcapacity and labour reserves in a rapid and elegant manner, the results for employment are not particularly impressive.

6. If the model adequately describes the economy of the Netherlands, as it should do, the conclusions to be drawn with respect to the results of possible employment policies are rather pessimistic. Most of the policies simulated have little success; they are mere drops in the ocean. The fact that any policies that will increase the budget deficit are now out of order, the reduction of this deficit having become a primary target, must make any conclusions even more negative. Only a very strong 'beggar my neighbour' policy, without reaction from the neighbours, and an internationally co-ordinated expansionary policy, mostly financed by base money creation,

could possibly solve the unemployment problem within a reasonable period.

NOTES

1. Provided, naturally, that both the first year quasi-rent and μ are positive.
2. $t\text{-}obj_t$
3. 45 years.
4. $obj_t \geqslant obj_{t-1}$.
5. This, admittedly *ad hoc*, amendment originated with Den Hartog and Tjan (1979).
6. See Table 5.3, equation 3.
7. The coefficient of qy is smaller than 1.
8. For the derivations see Kooiman and Kloek (1979:28). Average is not the proper term, since the weights do not add up to 1.
9. Excluding investment in the natural gas sector.
10. If 1.448 is replaced by 1., then rnj would equal the rate of return in the first year of operation.
11. Depreciation for tax purposes is assumed to be linear.
12. The figures in the accompanying tables, when designated by (%), are cumulated percentage deviations from the corresponding level in the base run. The other figures are simply absolute differences from the level in the base run. The first year of the simulations, designated as year 1, is 1983.
13. See note 4.
14. See Knoester (1982) for some experiments.
15. NNP = net national product.
16. See Section 5.4, 260-261, and Table 5.3, equations 8 and 9.
17. The correction is 0.0, -0.2, -0.4, -0.6 in the first four years and -0.8 thereafter; see Table 5.5, equation 1. Autonomous corrections have also been introduced in the price equations in order to compensate for the effects of productivity coefficients differing from 1.
18. See Table 5.3, equation 4.
19. See page 281 and Footnote 17 above.
20. See subsection 3 on the wage reduction simulation.

BIBLIOGRAPHY

Den Hartog, H., and Tjan, H.S. *A Clay-Clay vintage model approach for sectors of industry in the Netherlands*, Occasional Paper, 17, The Hague, Central Planning Bureau (1979).

Knoester, A. *Economic policy and employment*, Discussion Paper 8201, The Hague, Ministry of Economic Affairs (1982).

Kooiman, P. and Kloek, T. *Aggregation of micro markets in disequilibrium, theory and application to the Dutch labour market, 1948–1975*, Working Paper, Rotterdam, Econometric Institute, Erasmus University (1979).

Kuipers, S.K. and Buddenberg, F.H. 'Unemployment on account of market imperfection in the Netherlands since the Second World War', in *De Economist*, Leiden, 126, (1978).

Chapter Six

Labour market simulations for six OECD countries using INTERLINK with a three-factor putty-clay supply block: Results and their limitations

Peter H. Sturm*, Growth Studies Division, Organisation for Economic Co-operation and Development, Paris, France

6.1 INTRODUCTION

This chapter reports on labour market simulations with an experimental version of the OECD INTERLINK model. The supply blocks on which this paper is based have so far been constructed for six OECD member countries: the United States, Japan, the Federal Republic of Germany, France, the United Kingdom and Canada. They are part of the ongoing development work for the OECD INTERLINK system.[1] The core of the INTERLINK system is a multi-area model of the world economy developed by the OECD secretariat as a tool to assist in economic forecasting and policy analysis. The structure of this model broadly reflects the organisation of the OECD secretariat's regular forecasting exercise, the results of which are reported semi-annually in the OECD *Economic Outlook*. A major function of the INTERLINK system is to assure consistency (by enforcing both domestic and international accounting identities) throughout the multi-country forecasting round which involves thousands of data series and in which all divisions of the OECD Economics and Statistics Department participate. At present the INTERLINK system is used in combination with 'traditional' forecasting procedures (as described, for example, in OECD 1965) to generate the baseline forecasts periodically published by the OECD. Once this baseline forecast has been constructed, the INTERLINK system is used to generate alternative projections based on different assumptions for economic policy and other exogenous (to the system) variables.[2] The supply blocks discussed in this paper are to be integrated into the standard operating version of the INTERLINK system after review and

* This paper draws on joint work being done in the Economics and Statistics Department in which a number of colleagues have been involved (see references). The views expressed in this paper are those of the author and do not necessarily represent those of his colleagues nor of the OECD.

discussion by modelling experts from OECD member countries that met in Paris in September 1983.

The chapter consists of five sections: Section 6.2 gives a summary description of the INTERLINK model structure, with special attention to the supply block. Section 6.3 explains the various labour market simulations run and summarises their results. Some shortcomings and limitations of the model are discussed in Section 6.4, while the final Section 6.5 indicates model improvements, either planned or already under way.

6.2 MODEL STRUCTURE

This section gives an overview of the country models with which the labour market simulations reported in Section 6.3 below were carried out. First, the supply blocks are presented in some detail. Thereafter, a brief overview of the remaining model blocks and their interaction with the supply block is given.

6.2.1 The supply block[3]

Underlying the supply block specification is an incremental putty-clay production function with three factor inputs: labour (L), capital (K) and energy (E). The corresponding (marginal) output concept (Q) is change in gross value-added plus change in intermediate energy inputs (at constant prices). The incremental output measure also allows for output lost due to scrapping of obsolete capacity:

$$(1) \qquad\qquad Q = X - X_{-1}(1 - d)$$

where: X = gross output, including value of intermediate energy
            inputs,
      d = scrapping rate.

The scrapping rate has been endogenised. Assuming that equipment is scrapped whenever the variable production cost associated with it exceeds the market value of its output, the following approximation to the correct expression for the scrapping rate can be derived:[4]

$$(2) \qquad\qquad d = d_0 + d_1/(1 - v) + d_2\, \dot{v}$$

where: v = variable cost as per cent of market value,
      d_1 = estimated parameters,
      Z = percentage change in variable Z.

The following estimation results were obtained for the parameters d_1

with *t*-values indicated in parentheses behind each coefficient:

Country	d_0	d_1	d_2
United States	0.083 (1.5)	0.017 (1.1)	–
Japan	0.059 (9.8)	–	0.19 (4.5)
Germany, Fed. Rep. of	0.060 (0.1)	0.006 (1.6)	–
France	0.090 (0.9)	–	0.17 (1.8)
United Kingdom	0.100 (0.7)	–	0.06 (0.9)
Canada	0.030 (1.2)	0.015 (5.4)	–

The functional form chosen for the (marginal) production function is a nested CES function, with capital (K) and energy (E) forming the inner input bundle, which is combined with aggregate labour in the outer bundle, eg:

$$(3) \qquad Q = f\left(g\left(K,\ E\right),\ L\right) A(t)$$

where: $f(\cdot)$ and $g(\cdot)$ represent CES functions with constant returns to scale.[5]

Technical progress $A(t)$ is assumed to be embodied in new capital vintages, so that the capital-labour and capital-output ratios of old vintages remain unchanged after capacity has been installed. Combining this production function with the assumption that firms minimise their expected cost of production allows calculation of optimal (marginal) input-output ratios for the three production factors. This is done by minimising the aggregate cost function subject to the technological constraint.[6] The resulting optimal input-output ratios are (rather complicated) functions of time, factor prices and substitution elasticities between factors:

(4) $RKO^* = h\ (t,\ r;\ s,\ s_1;\ e,\ u,\ w)$; optimal capital-output ratio

(5) $REO^* = j\ (t,\ r;\ s,\ s_1;\ e,\ u,\ w)$; optimal labour-output ratio

(6) $RENO^* = k\ (t,\ r;\ s,\ s_1;\ e,\ u,\ w)$; optimal energy-output ratio

where: t = time index,
r = technical progress coefficient,
S = elasticity of substitution between capital and energy,
S_1 = elasticity of substitution between labour and the capital-energy bundle,
$e,\ w,\ u$ = prices of energy and labour, and user cost of capital respectively.

The key substitution elasticities s and s_1 were estimated from an annual logarithmic investment equation derived from equation 4, assuming adaptive expectations for the formulation of output and price expectations. The estimation results are as follows:

Country	Incremental production function	Elasticity of substitution between	
		Capital and energy (s)	Capital-energy and labour (s_1)
United States	CES-CD	0.25	1.00
Japan	CES-CES	0.97	0.70
Germany, Fed. Rep. of	CES-CES	0.40	0.60
France	CES-CD	0.16	1.00
United Kingdom	CES-CES	0.20	0.25
Canada	CES-CD	0.37	1.00

Using these (estimated) substitution elasticities and (observed) input prices, the optimal input-output ratios can be calculated. The final semi-annual investment equation was estimated as:

$$(7) \quad \ln K = a_0 + \sum_i a_{1i} \ln Q_{-1} + \sum_j a_{2j} \ln RKO_{-j} + a_3 t$$
$$\text{with} \quad \sum_i a_{1i} = \sum_j a_{2j} = 1$$

In this equation RKO differs from RKO* defined in equation 4 by exclusion of the time trend: the technical progress coefficient is estimated separately in equation 7.

Given the synthetic input-output ratios calculated above and gross investment, the optimal levels of labour ($ETOPT$) and energy ($ENTOPT$) inputs at full capacity utilisation can be computed from the following recursive formulae:

$$(8) \quad ETOPT = ETOPT_{-1}(1 - d) + K_{-1} \cdot REO^*_{-1}/RKO^*_{-1}$$

$$(9) \quad ENOPT = ENOPT_{-1}(1 - d) + K_{-1} \cdot RENO^*_{-1}/RKO^*_{-1}$$

Similarly potential output (POTB) can be calculated as:[7]

$$(10) \quad POTB = POTB_{-1}(1 - d) + K_{-1}/RKO^*$$

and the corresponding measure of capacity utilisation (GAP) is defined as:

$$(11) \quad GAP = X/POTB.$$

Given the synthetic series for optimal energy and labour inputs, actual demand for these factors is modelled as a lagged adjustment of actual to desired input levels based on either a partial stock adjustment or an error correction adjustment process[8] – typically including *GAP* as an additional explanatory variable. In some countries these employment adjustment equations include a variable related to hours worked. The treatment of hours worked in the context of labour demand merits a detailed description, given the political importance which the discussion of shortening work time has acquired: in the model, hours worked deviate from exogenous trend hours worked[9] whenever the capacity utilisation rate or the output growth rate deviate from their mean values. The effect of these deviations is asymmetrical, depending on whether they are positive or negative. Employment-level adjustment cost effects were captured by including the share of non-wage labour cost in total compensation as an explanatory variable. The complete equation for hours worked is thus:[10]

$$(12) \quad HW = HTREND + [a^+ (GAP - \overline{GAP})^- + a^- (GAP - \overline{GAP})^+ + b^+$$
$$(\dot{X} - \overline{\dot{X}})^+ + b^- (\dot{X} - \overline{\dot{X}})^-] * (c + d\,PAR)$$

where:
HW	= average hours worked per semester,
$HTREND$	= (quadratic) time trend of hours worked,
$(GAP - \overline{GAP})^{-(+)}$	= negative (positive) deviation from normal capacity utilisation,
$(\dot{X} - \overline{\dot{X}})^{-(+)}$	= negative (positive) deviation from average output growth rate,
PAR	= share of non-wage labour cost in compensation of employees in the business sector.

Estimation results for this equation are summarised in Table 6.1. In all retained equations the coefficients *c* and *d* were set equal to either 0 or 1, cf the explanation of column headings in Table 6.1. This specification allows us to distinguish between trend average hours worked and cyclical deviations from it. It is the former variable which entered the employment adjustment equation, the results of which are presented in Table 6.2. The non-cyclical component of hours worked (*HWNC*) was computed as the difference between actual hours worked and cyclical deviations. For all countries (except Canada), changes in capacity utilisation as well as the non-cyclical component of hours worked attenuated changes in employment.

Apart from private sector employment and hours worked discussed in detail above, the supply blocks include the following labour market equations and variables:

Table 6.1: Estimation of the hours worked equation

Annual data (1964–78)	Constant	T (time)	T²	I	II	III	IV	V	VI	R²	DW	SEE
United States	1876 (162.0)	−6.07 (3.3)	−0.21 (3.0)	436.7 (6.4)	253.7 (6.6)					0.998	3.15	0.18
Germany, Fed. Rep. of	1918 (40.8)	−12.14 (1.8)	0	266.3 (1.6)	244.2 (3.7)			286.1 (1.3)	124.8 (0.6)	0.998	2.67	0.23
France	2041 (69.5)	−17.67 (4.1)	0.10 (0.7)	827.0 (4.6)	133.1 (1.1)	829.4 (4.6)	133.5 (1.1)	169.4 (3.0)	185.6 (2.6)	0.999	2.80	0.18
United Kingdom	2226 (156.4)	−0.76 (0.3)	−0.80 (7.0)	310.7 (1.0)	479.0 (2.6)					0.997	2.26	0.33
Japan	2069 (84.0)	−17.70 (4.2)	0.19 (1.1)	1068.2 (2.9)	828.8 (3.1)					0.984	1.89	0.55
Canada	2539 (43.2)	−34.87 (4.5)	0.75 (3.0)	133.9 (1.7)	1405.0 (7.3)			227.5 (2.9)	296.6 (1.1)	0.999	3.24	0.11
	2137 (28.1)	−32.43 (2.8)	0.76 (1.8)			826.2 (2.0)	186.0 (0.9)			0.962	2.02	0.56

I = $(GAP - \overline{GAP})^+$; II = $(GAP-\overline{GAP})^-$; III = $(\dot{X}-\dot{\overline{X}})^+$; IV = $(\dot{X}-\dot{\overline{X}})^-$; V = $(GAP-\overline{GAP})^+ \cdot PAR$; VI = $(GAP-\overline{GAP})^- \cdot PAR$.

Source: Artus (1983).

Table 6.2: Growth in private sector employment (estimated equations)
(Dependent variable X = ln(ETB/ETB(− 1))

United States
$$X = 0.42 LN((ETOPT/ETOPT(-1))^*GAP/GAP(-1)) - 8.82 LN(HWNC/HWNC(-1)) +$$
$$0.043\ LN(ETOPT(-1)^*GAP(-1)/ETB(-1))$$

Japan
$$X = 0.015 + 0.11\ LN(ETOPT^*GAP/(ETB(-1)HWNC))$$

Germany, Federal Republic of
$$X = 0.97 + 0.34\ LN(ETOPT^*GAP/(ETOPT(-1)^*GAP(-1)))$$
$$- 0.77\ LN(HWNC/HWNC(-1)) + 0.20$$
$$LN((ETOPT(-1)^*GAP(-1)/(HWNC(-1)^{**}0.77^*ETB(-1))))$$

France
$$X = 0.73\ LN(ETOPT(-1)) - 2.32\ LN(HWNC/HWNC(-1))$$
$$+ 0.08\ LN(ETOPT(-1)/ETB(-1))$$

United Kingdom
$$X = 0.026 + 0.41\ LN(ETOPT^*GAP^{**}0.66/(ETB(-1)^*HWNC^{**}1.21))$$

Canada
$$X = -33.97 + 0.19\ LN(ETOPT^*GAP^{**}1.59\ EXP(0.013^*TIME)/ETB(-1))$$

(a) *exogenous variables*
LF	labour force
EG	government employees

(b) *behavioural equations*
$ES = ES_{-1} \times ETB/ETB_{-1}$ — self employed

(c) *identities*
$ET = ETB + EG$	total employment
$EEP = ETB - ES$	private sector employees
$EET = ETB + EG$	employees, total
$UN = LF - ET$	unemployment
$UNR = UN/LF$	unemployment rate

6.2.2   Remaining country model blocks

Besides the supply block, the experimental INTERLINK country models include the following blocks:

Wage-price block

In this block the rates of change of implicit price deflators for the various final expenditure components are determined by use of a modified cost mark-up model.

The estimated wage equation is of the general form:

(13) $WR = CO + C1 \times 1/UNR + C2 \times UNR + C3$
$\times PE + C4 \times PROD + C5 \times MIW$

where: *WR*   = percentage increase in average wage rates,
   UNR = unemployment rate; per cent,
   PE   = expected price increase (computed as average of lagged price increases); per cent,
   PROD = expected increase in productivity (computed as average of lagged productivity increases); per cent,
   MIW = percentage increase in minimum wage rate.

Estimation results are presented in Table 6.3 below. Not all the explanatory variables in equation 13 were significant in all countries.

Expenditure block

In this block final expenditure components (with the exception of business fixed investment, exports and imports) are determined. In the model version used for the present paper, changes in inventories are exogenous.

External block

In this block total import volumes (disaggregated into five components) are determined on the basis of appropriate demand and relative price indicators. Export volumes are determined on the basis of exogenous (to the country) world demand and relative export prices.

Fiscal block

This block determines endogenous tax revenues and government expenditure components on the basis of exogenous policy parameters (eg tax and benefit rates). The major exogenous policy instruments on the expenditure side are: government employment, government non-wage consumption expenditure and government investment.

Income distribution block

The major function of this block is to determine business profits and household disposable income (nominal and real): both these variables are an aggregate of wage income, transfers and residual income (profits and self-employed income), but this distinction in the expenditure block plays no role.

Table 6.3: Wage equations

	Estimated coefficients (t-statistics)						Estimation statistics			
	Constant	$1/UNR$	UNR	PCP	$PROD$	NIW	R^2	DW	SE	Fit period[a]
United States	-0.67 (2.4)	7.67 (7.0)	-	0.92 (3.2)	-	0.02 (2.6)	0.95	1.53	0.25	1959:2 -1982:2
Japan	-4.04 (4.9)	10.81 (9.0)	-	0.87 (9.0)	-	-	0.88	1.62	1.16	1967:1 -1982:2
Germany, Fed. Rep. of	-	0.91 (3.0)	-	0.89 (7.2)	0.64 (3.6)	-	0.67	2.09	1.01	1967:1 -1981:1
France	3.70 (8.9)	-	-0.42 (4.6)	0.98 (7.6)	-	0.06 (2.0)	0.92	2.07	0.61	1964:1 -1981:2
United Kingdom	2.34 (6.0)	-	-0.14 (1.8)	1.00	-	-	0.70	1.63	1.49	1961:2 -1981:2
Canada	-1.01 (1.2)	10.16 (2.9)	-	1.00 (9.7)	-	-	0.73	2.27	1.18	1965:2 -1982:1

a. Year and a quarter.

Financial block

This block determines interest rates (short- and long-term) and various monetary aggregates. Monetary policy can be simulated either to follow a target for the short-term interest rate or the money supply.

The major linkages between the supply block and the remainder of the model are business investment, feeding directly into total demand, and business employment and hours worked which co-determine household income and thus private consumption expenditure. Besides these links, the capacity utilisation rate computed in the supply block enters the price determination process and, in some cases the determination of export and import volumes.

Conceptually the model allows the distinction between two types of unemployment: cyclical unemployment, ie unemployment caused by deviation from full capacity utilisation, and structural unemployment, ie unemployment which remains even when installed productive capacity is fully utilised. Given that older capital vintages have, on average, lower capital-labour ratios and thus are associated with higher variable cost of production, a decline in capacity utilisation should lead to a more than proportional decline in unemployment if the latter were to adjust instantaneously. Lagged adjustment of actual to desired employment modifies this relationship in most countries: only in the Canadian employment equation does the elasticity of employment with respect to capacity utilisation exceed unity (cf Table 6.2).

The putty-clay technology underlying the supply block implies fixed coefficients *ex post*, so that maximum employment in the private sector in each period is determined by the available capital stock and the (fixed) capital-labour ratios of its various vintages. The difference between the labour force and the maximum employment thus determined (both net of government employment) constitutes 'structural' or 'capital shortage' unemployment which can only be eliminated through either reductions in the labour force or additions to the capital stock which more than compensate for the loss of jobs from the scrapping of obsolete capacity. Wage moderation tends to reduce structural unemployment both by reducing the capital-labour ratio of new investment and delaying the scrapping of old (labour-intensive) vintages. On the other hand, wage moderation may lead to an increase in cyclical unemployment if it entails a reduction in effective demand and thus in capacity utilisation. In fact, this latter effect – through the multiplier/accelerator mechanism – may lead to a reduction in investment. This tends to augment structural unemployment, attenuating the positive impact on labour demand from the substitution effect of wage moderation.

6.3 MODEL SIMULATIONS

This part of the paper reports selected simulation results from six country models of the experimental version of the OECD INTERLINK system described in the previous part. All simulations are run in unlinked and fixed exchange rate mode. A time-span of 11 model-periods (ie five and a half years) has been simulated, using the period 1980:1 to 1985:1 as the simulation baseline. Actual values of key variables of the baseline forecast are presented in Table 6.4.[11] The simulations were designed to show the effects of various input price and economic policy shocks on labour demand implied by the model. Since the main interest of the simulations is focused on the labour market the following variables are reported:

ET   = total employment
ETB   = total employment in the private sector
ETOPT = optimal employment in the private sector (for specific factor price combinations and assuming full-capacity utilisation).

For their general interest the following demand and price variables are also reported:

GDPV = gross domestic product at constant prices
PCP   = implicit private consumption deflator
IBV   = business fixed investment, volume

All variables in the simulation reports are given as per cent deviations from baseline values.

6.3.1   Simulations

To facilitate the analysis of causal relationships in the model, two sets of simulations were carried out. The first set consists of 'diagnostic' simulations in which some of the variable interactions in the model are suppressed to isolate pure substitution and pure scale (or output) effects respectively. Consequently, in the simulations in which the three input prices are shocked, output is held constant. Thus changes in employment in response to these input price shocks are due solely to inter-factor substitution. Alternatively, in a simulation where output is shocked, input prices are held constant. Resulting changes in employment and business investment are thus due solely to an increased scale of production. In summary, the following diagnostic simulations were run:

A.1 A sustained 4 per cent increase in the wage rate above the baseline level, output held constant.

A.2 A sustained 20 per cent increase in the price of intermediate energy inputs above the baseline level, output held constant.

A.3 A sustained 6 per cent increase in the user cost of capital above the baseline level, output held constant.

A.4 A sustained 1 per cent increase in aggregate output (GDPV) above the baseline level, input prices held constant.

In the second set of simulations all variable interactions in the respective country models are allowed to operate. For the purpose of comparison with the diagnostic simulations the input price and demand shocks experimented within simulations A.1 to A.4 are repeated in the fully interactive mode (simulations B.1 to B.4). Thereafter, a number of policy simulations are carried out. Their purpose is to show how various policy instruments can influence employment in the framework of the given model. The following simulations were run:

C.1 A sustained increase in government non-wage expenditure by 1 per cent of baseline GDP/GNP:
   a. with accommodating monetary policy (short-term interest rates kept at baseline values);
   b. with non-accommodating monetary policy (money stock held at baseline values).

C.2 A sustained decrease in the personal income tax by 1 per cent of baseline GDP/GNP. (Given the structure of the model this is identical to an equal size increase in transfer payments to households.)

C.3 A sustained decrease in the long-term interest rate by 10 per cent below baseline values.

C.4 A sustained increase in government employment by 4 per cent above baseline values.

C.5 A sustained 5 per cent investment tax credit.

C.6 A sustained decrease in personal income taxes by 1 per cent of baseline GDP/GNP combined with a (roughly) equivalent reduction in wage claims, accompanied by accommodating monetary policy (consensus scenario).

6.3.2 Simulation results

The results of simulation C.6 are presented in Table 6.5 below; detailed numerical results of the other simulations are available from the author on demand. Some of the major transmission mechanisms from the variables, shocked in the simulations to optimal and actual employment, will be briefly discussed in qualitative terms.

Table 6.4: Baseline values for simulation runs

Country	Variable	Units	80:1	80:2	81:1	81:2	82:1	82:2	83:1	83:2	84:1	84:2	85:1
Canada	ET	10**6	10.6	10.8	11.0	11.0	10.7	10.5	10.5	10.5	10.7	10.8	10.9
	EEP	10**6	7.6	7.7	7.8	7.8	7.5	7.3	7.4	7.5	7.6	7.6	7.6
	ETOPT	10**6	8.7	8.9	9.1	9.3	9.4	9.6	9.6	9.5	9.4	9.4	9.3
	GDPV	10**9CU	129.8	131.0	135.0	134.0	129.5	126.5	128.7	132.1	135.2	138.0	141.1
	PCP	Index	1.9	2.1	2.2	2.3	2.4	2.5	2.6	2.7	2.7	2.8	2.9
	IBV	10**9CU	20.8	21.1	22.3	22.1	20.8	18.5	18.1	18.2	18.5	19.0	19.4
France	ET	10**6	21.7	21.7	21.6	21.5	21.4	21.4	21.3	21.2	21.1	21.0	21.0
	EEP	10**6	14.3	14.2	14.2	14.0	14.0	13.9	13.9	13.9	13.8	13.8	13.8
	ETOPT	10**6	17.2	17.1	17.0	16.9	16.9	16.8	16.8	16.8	16.7	16.6	16.6
	GDPV	10**10CU	111.9	111.4	111.3	112.8	113.8	114.2	113.8	113.4	114.1	114.8	115.5
	PCP	Index	2.3	2.5	2.6	2.8	3.0	3.1	3.2	3.4	3.5	3.6	3.8
	IBV	10**10CU	15.0	15.1	15.0	14.8	15.2	15.1	15.0	14.8	14.8	15.0	15.1
Germany, Fed. Rep. of	ET	10**6	25.7	25.7	25.6	25.5	25.2	25.0	24.8	24.7	24.7	24.6	24.6
	EEP	10**6	18.5	18.6	18.5	18.4	18.2	17.9	17.8	17.8	17.8	17.7	17.7
	ETOPT	10**6	19.1	19.3	19.4	19.6	19.8	19.8	19.8	19.8	19.8	19.9	20.0
	GDPV	10**10CU	127.1	125.7	125.8	126.5	125.4	124.3	125.1	126.4	127.4	128.4	129.4
	PCP	Index	1.1	1.1	1.2	1.2	1.2	1.3	1.3	1.3	1.3	1.3	1.4
	IBV	10**10CU	16.0	16.0	15.7	15.4	14.8	14.5	14.6	14.9	15.2	15.5	15.8
Japan	ET	10**6	55.1	55.5	55.7	55.8	56.2	56.4	57.1	57.4	57.7	58.1	58.4
	EEP	10**6	34.5	35.1	35.4	35.4	36.0	36.0	36.7	37.1	37.4	37.7	38.1
	ETOPT	10**6	55.8	56.2	56.5	57.6	59.4	61.2	62.1	63.7	64.9	65.8	66.8
	GDPV	10**12CU	187.6	191.8	195.7	198.3	200.7	205.0	207.6	211.1	214.7	218.8	222.7
	PCP	Index	1.3	1.3	1.4	1.4	1.4	1.4	1.4	1.4	1.4	1.5	1.5
	IBV	10**12CU	31.6	32.6	33.7	34.0	34.4	34.7	34.4	35.0	35.6	36.3	37.0

United Kingdom	ET	$10^{**}6$	25.2	24.7	24.2	23.8	23.6	23.2	23.0	22.9	22.9	22.9	22.9
	EEP	$10^{**}6$	17.5	17.0	16.4	16.1	15.8	15.5	15.3	15.2	15.2	15.2	15.2
	ETOPT	$10^{**}6$	23.4	23.7	23.9	24.1	24.3	24.5	24.8	25.1	25.4	25.6	25.9
	GDPV	$10^{**}9$CU	115.1	112.5	111.5	111.4	112.0	113.5	114.4	115.4	116.7	118.4	119.8
	PCP	Index	1.8	1.9	2.0	2.1	2.2	2.3	2.3	2.4	2.5	2.6	2.6
	IBV	$10^{**}9$CU	12.3	12.2	11.4	12.3	12.4	12.7	12.6	12.7	12.8	13.0	13.2
United States	ET	$10^{**}6$	99.4	99.2	100.4	100.3	99.6	99.3	99.5	100.3	101.5	102.8	104.1
	EEP	$10^{**}6$	75.9	75.6	77.0	76.8	76.2	75.9	76.1	76.9	77.8	78.9	80.0
	ETOPT	$10^{**}6$	64.5	66.0	67.4	69.1	71.0	72.6	73.7	74.6	75.3	76.1	77.1
	GDPV	$10^{**}10$CU	147.6	147.1	150.4	150.0	147.4	147.9	149.8	154.0	156.9	159.9	163.0
	PCP	Index	1.7	1.8	1.9	1.9	2.0	2.0	2.1	2.1	2.2	2.2	2.3
	IBV	$10^{**}10$CU	16.7	16.5	16.9	17.4	16.9	16.2	16.1	16.1	16.6	17.1	17.6

ET = Total employment
EEP = Private sector employment
ETOPT = Optimal employment at full-capacity utilisation (and baseline factor prices)
GDPV = Gross domestic product, volume P
PCP = Private consumption, deflator P
IBV = Business fixed investment, volume.

Table 6.5: Consensus scenario (Simulation: C.6; Deviation from baseline %)

Country	Variable	80:1	80:2	81:1	81:2	82:1	82:2	83:1	83:2	84:1	84:2	85:1
Canada	*ET*	0.08	0.26	0.44	0.64	0.85	1.04	1.20	1.34	1.45	1.54	1.61
	EEP	0.10	0.31	0.54	0.79	1.06	1.31	1.49	1.66	1.79	1.93	2.04
	ETOPT	0	0.03	0.30	0.67	1.07	1.51	1.91	2.30	2.62	2.89	3.13
	GDPV	0.32	0.74	0.95	1.16	1.37	1.54	1.63	1.69	1.74	1.78	1.80
	PCP	-0.61	-1.35	-1.62	-1.91	-2.10	-2.25	-2.47	-2.63	-2.70	-2.69	-2.59
	IBV	0.22	0.65	0.93	1.01	1.28	1.75	1.94	1.93	1.81	1.70	1.61
France	*ET*	0.02	0.11	0.27	0.42	0.57	0.70	0.84	0.95	1.05	1.11	1.14
	EEP	0.02	0.14	0.33	0.52	0.70	0.87	1.03	1.17	1.28	1.36	1.39
	ETOPT	0	0.09	0.22	0.37	0.52	0.66	0.81	0.90	0.96	0.97	0.92
	GDPV	0.09	0.44	0.64	0.77	0.93	1.10	1.24	1.37	1.45	1.52	1.56
	PCP	-0.15	-0.27	-0.37	-0.52	-0.65	-0.76	-0.61	-0.34	0.01	0.43	0.95
	IBV	0.14	1.08	1.48	1.58	1.72	1.95	2.21	2.53	2.67	2.82	2.97
Germany, Fed. Rep. of	*ET*	0.08	0.20	0.33	0.46	0.58	0.70	0.83	0.94	1.04	1.14	1.23
	EEP	0.09	0.24	0.39	0.54	0.68	0.83	0.98	1.11	1.23	1.34	1.44
	ETOPT	0	0.07	0.24	0.46	0.70	0.91	1.13	1.32	1.49	1.64	1.77
	GDPV	0.23	0.48	0.68	0.82	0.94	1.07	1.20	1.29	1.35	1.40	1.46
	PCP	-0.24	-0.47	-0.73	-1.06	-1.18	-1.30	-1.40	-1.44	-1.46	-1.47	-1.47
	IBV	-0.23	0.10	0.48	0.57	0.62	0.63	0.81	0.89	0.85	0.78	0.70
Japan	*ET*	0.04	0.12	0.24	0.38	0.54	0.69	0.83	0.95	1.04	1.12	1.17
	EEP	0.04	0.13	0.26	0.42	0.58	0.75	0.89	1.02	1.13	1.20	1.25
	ETOPT	0	0.47	0.47	0.62	0.75	0.92	1.06	1.23	1.31	1.38	1.43
	GDPV	0.33	0.75	1.04	1.30	1.50	1.64	1.77	1.93	2.07	2.14	2.20
	PCP	-0.69	-1.61	-1.98	-2.07	-1.94	-1.59	-1.14	-0.75	-0.42	-0.17	0.01
	IBV	-0.03	0.28	0.73	1.35	2.06	2.75	3.26	3.60	3.76	3.55	3.43

United Kingdom	ET	0.10	0.35	0.68	1.05	1.42	1.84	2.25	2.65	3.00	3.28	3.49
	EEP	0.13	0.45	0.90	1.38	1.88	2.44	3.00	3.53	3.99	4.36	4.63
	ETOPT	0.03	0.12	0.33	0.67	1.14	1.72	2.35	2.98	3.57	4.07	4.42
	GDPV	0.32	0.92	1.43	1.80	2.08	2.32	2.50	2.63	2.64	2.55	2.41
	PCP	-0.44	-0.86	-1.31	-1.82	-1.91	-2.02	-2.05	-1.95	-1.70	-1.30	-0.77
	IBV	0.91	2.81	5.53	7.43	9.61	10.95	12.12	12.33	11.54	9.96	8.20
United States	ET	0.22	0.51	0.75	1.01	1.30	1.53	1.73	1.87	1.98	2.08	2.12
	EEP	0.26	0.62	0.89	1.21	1.55	1.83	2.06	2.22	2.36	2.47	2.51
	ETOPT	0.00	0.13	0.40	0.77	1.24	1.78	2.31	2.82	3.29	3.74	4.13
	GDPV	0.53	1.18	1.59	2.01	2.40	2.61	2.72	2.75	2.77	2.75	2.63
	PCP	-0.13	-0.35	-0.64	-0.97	-1.14	-1.16	-1.09	-0.93	-0.73	-0.52	-0.32
	IBV	0.97	2.45	3.69	4.95	6.46	7.79	8.63	9.36	9.72	9.60	8.60

ET = Total employment

EEP = Private sector employment

ETOPT = Optimal employment at full-capacity utilisation (and baseline factor prices)

GDPV = Gross domestic product, volume P

PCP = Private consumption deflator P

IBV = Business fixed investment, volume.

6.3.2.1   *Diagnostic simulations (A)*

A.1. Increase in labour costs, output and capacity utilisation held constant.

The increase in labour cost leads to input substitution of capital and energy for labour *at the margin*. The (marginal) optimal capital-output and energy-output ratios will go up while the (marginal) optimal labour-output ratio will decline. The result is a decline in desired employment followed by a fall in actual employment. There will also be an increase in business investment and energy inputs, but given that output is fixed in this simulation the employment repercussions of this change in demand are not allowed to work through the model (cf simulations B below for the consequences of relaxing this assumption).

A.2. Increase in the price of intermediate energy inputs, output held constant.

This will increase the relative cost of energy and thus lead to input substitution of labour for the capital-energy bundle at the margin. Within the capital-energy bundle, capital will be substituted for energy. Thus the optimal labour (energy) output ratio will unambiguously increase (decrease), leading to a rise in desired employment which is followed by an increase in actual employment. The change in the optimal capital-output ratio is indeterminate, depending on the relative size of the two elasticities of substitutions S and $S1$. Thus, business investment may in principle either increase or decrease in response to a rise in energy prices.

A.3. Increase in the user cost of capital, output held constant.

This case is symmetric to the previous case. Thus there will be an unambiguous increase in desired and actual employment and a decline in investment, while the *a priori* effect on energy inputs is ambiguous.

A.4. Increase in output, input prices held constant.

The increase in demand leads via the accelerator to an increase in business investment, while all desired input-output ratios remain constant by assumption. This increases optimal employment, followed with a lag by a rise in actual employment. Due to multiplier-accelerator interaction the transition from the low to the higher demand-level growth path can be very different between countries. But, given the constraint of constant returns to scale imposed on the supply blocks and the fact that input prices are fixed in this simulation, the final increase in business employment – after all adjustments have worked their way through – will be proportional to the increase in demand levels which, of course, are different between countries and depend on the size of the multiplier/accelerator.

6.3.2.2   *Factor price and output shocks under general equilibrium conditions (B)*

The four partial equilibrium simulations discussed above are repeated here, allowing for simultaneous changes in factor prices and output, which in some cases involve significant changes in the employment results. In particular, an increase in labour costs – unambiguously lowering employment on account of substitution effects – has an initial positive effect on employment through increased income and demand. But in all countries the negative effect regains the upper hand around the middle of the simulation period, lowering employment by the end of the period by more than is accounted for by the substitution effects alone, since by then business investment has also fallen below the baseline value.

6.3.2.3   *Policy simulations[12] (C)*

C.1. Increase in government non-wage expenditure.

   a.   Accommodating monetary policy.
      The increase in demand leads – via the accelerator process – to an increase in investment which, in turn, raises desired and actual employment. The price level also rises (by very different amounts in different countries), inducing an increase in labour costs which dampens the expansionary effect on employment.
   b.   Non-accommodating monetary policy.
      In this case the demand expansion is less, and it is accompanied by an increase in interest rates and thus the user cost of capital. Consequently, optimal and actual employment increase less. In fact, given the price-induced wage increase, optimal employment falls below its baseline value at the end of the simulation period in some countries (eg France).

C.2. Cut in personal income tax.
Except for first-round saving leakages, this case is identical to shock C.1 (increase in non-wage expenditure). Consequently, effects on output, prices and employment (both optimal and actual) are in the same direction but weaker.

C.3. A decline in (long-term) interest rates.
This shock (brought about by an increase in the money supply) entails a decline in the user cost of capital. This in turn entails a negative substitution effect (ie capital-energy for labour) but a positive output effect on labour. In most countries the net effect of these opposing influences is an initial decline in optimal employment, followed by an increase when the positive output effect outweighs the negative

substitution effect; the net effect on actual employment remains positive throughout (except in the case of France).

C.4. Increase in government employment.

The significant difference between this simulation and the increase in government non-wage consumption expenditure is that the first round output effect occurs in the public rather than in the private sector. Thus, despite a comparable overall change in GDP and employment, business investment is much less stimulated in the present case, entailing little change in private employment (either optimal or actual).

C.5. A sustained investment tax credit.

Given the neo-classical user cost of capital formula used in the model this shock is similar to a cut in profit taxes or a liberalisation of depreciation allowances.[13] It lowers the user cost of capital, though this effect is attenuated by upward pressure on the interest rate induced by the increasing budget deficit. As a result, the desired capital-output ratio increases, leading to higher investment. Thus, there is a contractionary substitution effect on employment and an expansionary output effect. The latter will, however, only be transitory unless the measure leads to a permanently higher output path.

C.6. Combination of income tax cut, wage restraint and accommodating monetary policy (Table 6.5).

Given the dominant policy preoccupation with inflation and the resulting reluctance to use expansionary demand management in the face of high unemployment, a 'consensus scenario simulation' was run, combining an income tax reduction with (nominal) wage restraint and accommodating monetary policy. Simulation results correspond to the optimistic prejudice of the standard neo-Keynesian paradigm: employment increases, fostered by both a positive substitution and demand effect. Substitution and demand effects are in opposite directions as far as investment is concerned, but in most countries the demand effect dominates, thus inducing an increase in business investment as well. Inflation declines due to a reduction in wage cost pressure. There is an initial increase in the government deficit, though subsequent output expansion and induced wage restraint among government employees reduce the deficit rapidly.

6.4 MODEL LIMITATIONS

The experimental INTERLINK model discussed above has been designed as a general purpose macro-model to assist in forecasting and policy simulations. Consequently, its capability to carry out in-depth analysis on specific aspects of the economy (eg the labour market) are limited.

Many questions which are of great importance for a comprehensive appraisal of medium-term labour market aspects cannot be analysed with the model as it presently stands because structural details of the labour market and/or labour market specific policy instruments are missing from the model. Besides these shortcomings specific to labour market analysis, there are some more general problems with the model in its present form which also impinge on labour market projections. It is thus useful to distinguish three types of problems which limit the model's effectiveness for medium-term labour market projections:

a.   missing labour market details;
b.   missing labour market policy instruments;
c.   general model problems.

6.4.1 Missing labour market details

Probably the most obvious omission with respect to labour market analysis is the lack of an endogenous labour supply. Presently the labour force is an exogenous variable in the model. This is unsatisfactory, given the overwhelming evidence showing the cyclical sensitivity of participating rates. Therefore labour supply should be endogenised, determined as the product of exogenous population variables times endogenous (ie behaviourally determined) participation rates. Among the key variables determining participation rates are real wage rates (both male and female), unemployment rates, and certain types of non-wage (transfer) incomes. Ideally, various sex and age-group specific participation rate equations should be estimated.

The question of the trade-off between average hours worked and employment has been gaining steadily in importance in the economic policy debate. It would therefore be desirable to integrate average hours worked formally into the supply block framework.[14] There are numerous conceptual as well as practical difficulties to carrying out such an improvement, the most basic of which, on the practical side, is the lack of reliable comprehensive data on average hours worked. On the theoretical side, major difficulties arise because a given reduction in average hours worked (per semester and person) may have quite different effects on employment, depending on the actual format the reduction in working time takes (eg fewer daily hours versus longer holidays).

Since both output and labour inputs are treated as single aggregates in the model, there is no room conceptually for unemployment caused by labour market mismatches, either 'normal' (ie frictional unemployment) or more permanent (structural) professional mismatches. Similarly, regional labour market mismatches cannot conceptually be captured by the model.

6.4.2 Missing policy instruments

With rapidly rising unemployment figures virtually everywhere in the OECD area, specific policy instruments aimed at the labour market have gained increasing importance. Among these instruments are the following:

 a. employment subsidies;
 b. government training schemes;
 c. changes in unemployment eligibility criteria and benefits;
 d. early retirement schemes.

This list is not meant to be comprehensive. None of these instruments has been built into the INTERLINK model, though in several countries their application is known to have an important impact on labour market performance and/or statistics. Similarly, other specialised policy instruments which are not aimed directly at the labour market but are known to have important repercussions on employment (eg migration legislation, legal school-leaving age) are not represented in the model.

No distinction is presently made between foreign workers and indigenous members of the labour force, though in many European countries the former constitute a significant percentage of the labour force. Changes in their number will thus have a noticeable impact on labour supply. While international migration is in principle a demographic variable (and treated in official statistics as such), there is no doubt that in practice it is largely controlled by policy decisions. In the model the number of foreign workers – if introduced as a separate variable – should therefore realistically be treated as a policy instrument.

6.4.3 General model problems

A more fundamental question than the problems arising from missing details concerns the appropriateness of the basic structure of the model; notwithstanding the full specification of the supply side, the model is essentially demand driven. Potential output will always adjust to total demand (net of import leakages). Import leakages from total demand are variable according to relative price performance and relative demand pressure, but the model does not allow for demand remaining unsatisfied due to lack of profitability. In fact (except for Canada), profitability of real capital does not enter any of the behavioural equations in the model directly or indirectly. Given the key role expected profits play in real world investment decisions, this is disconcerting.[15] The 'real world' most probably consists of a combination of alternative disequilibrium regimes where output may be demand, supply or factor-supply constraint in different production units. The relative importance of these various disequilibrium regimes supposedly changes both over time and during the cycle, but such a scheme is very difficult to model.

A particularly worrying problem concerns the ability of the supply block to track actual developments outside the 'estimation period. Evidence on this becomes only gradually available, since all existing observations were used at the time of estimation (1981–82) in order to maximise the degrees of freedom. For some countries the prediction error for most recent periods is large (eg 20 per cent for the key variable business investment) and seems to be increasing. It is likely that this problem is largely due to the pronounced non-linearities in the key supply block equations and to the sensitivity of these equations to the values of the factor substitution elasticities. The latter cannot be reliably determined on the basis of observed data, ie standard errors of the estimates are large relative to the size of parameter changes and this is sufficient to change simulation results significantly.[16]

In the present model scrapping is assumed to be an identical proportion of all capital vintages in each period, though it may differ between periods according to cost/price relationships. This is not quite consistent with the assumption of putty-clay technology. For the latter, scrapping should be concentrated on older vintages for which variable cost exceeds the market price of output produced. Similarly, the assumption that *all* technical progress is embodied in fixed investment does not necessarily correspond to reality. Both assumptions were necessary to reduce the complexity of the model, but it is not clear what biases result from these 'assumptions of convenience'.

Several important stock-flow relationships are missing from the model: there are no wealth effects in any of the final expenditure functions, and the level of inventories has no effect on output decisions in the model. The absence of wealth effects in particular (eg in the household consumption function) is likely to reduce significantly the forecasting performance in times of rapidly changing inflation rates.

Wherever expectations play a role in the model they are based on an 'adaptive', rather than 'rational', expectation formation mechanism. This exposes the model to the standard criticism of the rational expectations school. To the extent that this criticism is justified, the effects of economic policy measures produced by the models can be misleading.

6.5 PLANS FOR IMPROVEMENT

As noted above, the INTERLINK system is a general purpose forecasting and simulation model. It is thus not desirable to build into it detailed sectoral and/or institutional aspects tailor-made to analyse specific problems. Thus, most development work presently under way is not specifically aimed at improving labour market forecasts, though the latter would necessarily benefit from any general model improvement. Given the growing importance of labour market problems in economic policy debate, such improvement is highly desirable. The areas in which work is presently under way and which are likely to affect the labour market projections significantly are the following:

6.5.1 Labour supply

Behavioural equations for aggregate male and female participation rates are presently estimated. Explanatory variables in these equations are: real wage rates (male and female), age structure, real non-wage income, degree of labour market slack (ie the unemployment rate).

6.5.2 Output supply constraints

Efforts are made to introduce (expected) profitability into the factor demand functions and the investment function in particular. While this is still a far cry from embodying the recent insights of the disequilibrium theory with alternative rationing regimes in the model, it is thought to be a step in the right direction, ie recognising the possibility of supply constraints and structural unemployment originating from lack of business profitability. Complementary experiments to estimate an aggregate supply function are also under way. The explanatory variables are total demand (minus imports), profitability, and the stock level. If successful, this approach would lead to determination of changes in inventories as the difference between domestic supply plus imports minus final demand.

6.5.3 Monetary policy modelling

The financial blocks in the presently operating INTERLINK model are rather rudimentary, with monetary policy being simulated by changes in the (exogenous) domestic credit expansion variable. Work on more fully specified central bank policy instruments is at present under way.

NOTES

1. Another important development area within the INTERLINK system is FINLINK, a model of international capital flows and exchange rate determination, on which work is carried out parallel to the supply block development.
2. A detailed description of the INTERLINK system, including both its structure and functions, can be found in OECD (1982) and – of an early version of the system – in OECD (1979). Also see OECD (1980) for a demonstration

of the application of the model in a specific simulation exercise.

3. A detailed description of the development work leading to the present supply block specification can be found in Artus (1983). The presentation in this section draws on this material and other sources mentioned therein.

4. For a detailed discussion of the derivation of this formula and the non-linear estimation of its parameters (jointly with the investment function), see Artus (1983: 14–19) and Annex 2.

5. Where empirically the substitution elasticity between labour and the capital-energy bundle turned out to be close to unity, a Cobb-Douglas function instead of a CES function was chosen for $f(.)$; this was the case for the United States, France and Canada; cf table on page 307.

6. See Footnote 3 above.

7. Appropriate benchmark values for *ETOPT, ENOPT* and *POTB* were determined with the help of the OECD's resident country experts.

8. The theory and application of error correction models are discussed in some detail in Salmon (1982).

9. Trend hours worked are modelled as a second degree polynominal in time which reproduces satisfactorily the slower decrease in average hours worked in the late 1970s.

10. Individual country equations do not make use of all the explanatory variables included in equation 12 which represents the most general specification.

11. Except for marginal changes, this baseline corresponds to the forecast published in *Economic Outlook*, 33 (1983), where more details and a comprehensive discussion of the underlying assumptions can be found. Due to non-linearities in the model, especially in the supply and wage-price blocks, the simulation results are partly baseline dependent.

12. In principle, each fiscal policy simulation can be carried out alternately under a regime of accommodating and non-accommodating monetary policy, as done for simulation C.1 above. To avoid an excessive number of simulations, all subsequent fiscal policy simulations were run with an intermediate stance of monetary policy in which expansionary fiscal measures lead to both an increase in interest rates *and* the money supply.

13. All these measures lead to a fall in the user cost of capital and a decline in government revenues, though there is no precise quantitative equivalence in both these areas.

14. To treat the average hours worked, employment trade-off properly requires integrating at least the two major alternatives of cutting average working time, ie fewer daily hours and an increased number of holidays, into the model.

15. The explanation of this discrepancy lies probably in the fact that neo-classical theory, on which most investment functions are based, has until recently been predominantly equilibrium theory assuming perfect competition. Within such a theoretical framework, profits will be zero by definition.

16. For example, a change in $S1$ (elasticity of substitution between labour and the capital-energy bundle) from 0.8 to 0.7 reverses the direction of change of investment in response to a wage shock by reversing the size ordering of the resulting substitution and output effects on business investment.

BIBLIOGRAPHY

Artus, P. *Capital, energy and labour substitution: The supply block in OECD medium-term models*, Working Paper 2, Paris, OECD (1983).

OECD 'Structure and operation', in *OECD INTERLINK System*, Paris, 1 (1982).

OECD 'Fiscal policy simulations with the OECD International Linkage Model', in *Economic Outlook*, Occasional Studies 4–32, July (1980).

OECD *'The OECD International Linkage Model'*, in *Economic Outlook*, Occasional Studies, 3–33, January (1979).

OECD *Techniques of economic forecasting* OECD Paris, (1965).

Salmon, Mark 'Error correction mechanisms', in *Economic Journal*, Cambridge, 92, pp. 615–29, September (1982).

Chapter Seven

Unemployment prospects for the OECD area: Alternative scenarios with the Project LINK system

*Peter Pauly, University of Pennsylvania, United States**

7.1 INTRODUCTION

For the Organisation for Economic Co-operation and Development (OECD) area as a whole and most individual countries in the industrialised world, persistent and high unemployment rates have emerged as the major cause of concern for economic policy. Ever since 1973 – roughly coinciding with the first oil shock – unemployment rates have been rising during recessions but, except for the United States and Canada, have failed to come down during the recovery. Rather, the growth rates achieved in the second half of the 1970s were barely enough to stabilise unemployment rates at the plateau achieved during the respective down-swings.

The present situation and the consensus forecast for the short- and medium-term are essentially characterised by a similar pattern. While a modest recovery is expected over the next two years, with inflation picking up again only slightly – helped in particular by stable real food and energy prices – no improvement on the labour markets is seen. This is certainly true for the European economies while in the United States and Canada unemployment rates should decrease, though it is generally held that the natural rate for both economies has increased substantially over the past five years.

It is the purpose of this chapter to examine a number of policy options aimed at reducing unemployment rates in the short- and medium-term on a broad scale. The econometric world model of Project LINK is used to simulate alternative 'recovery' scenarios for the period 1983–88. Policy options include traditional demand management policies, industrial policies, development aid and selective structural policies.[1] While some of these policies include measures focusing on the developing world, the analysis in this paper will concentrate on the OECD area. The primary reason is that at present the developing country models in Project LINK do not support a consistent labour market analysis, even

* The simulations reported in this paper have been performed by C.A. Bollino and C.E. Petersen.

though some of the models include a certain amount of labour market detail. The GNP and trade balance reaction can give an idea about some of the expected labour market effects for these countries and areas.

This chapter is organised as follows. In Section 7.2 we shall give a brief overview of the present status of the LINK system. Section 7.3 contains a summary of the most recent LINK forecast for the period 1983–88, which is used as a baseline solution for subsequent scenarios. In Sections 7.4 and 7.5 are presented the results of our alternative scenarios, concentrating first on demand management and industrial strategies and finally on selective structural policies in a number of industrialised countries. The concluding Section 7.6 contains a brief summary of the results and an attempt to evaluate critically the capabilities of present generation large-scale macro-economic models with regard to the analysis of labour market phenomena.

7.2 THE LINK MODEL

The purpose of Project LINK is to tie together major macro-econometric models being used in each of the main countries or regions of the world and generate a *consistent* model system for studying the world economy. The LINK approach is to accept models from each country or area as they are designed by resident model builders for their *own* use, based on the assumption that each model builder knows his own country or area best. The technical linkage, explained below, imposes only a minor degree of homogeneity across the models. The LINK system includes a broad range of different models containing from 30 to more than 1,000 equations per country. The major industrial countries account for the larger models. There are significant differences in the amount of detail implemented in these models with regard to the level of disaggregation, the representation of channels for transmitting economic policy, the simultaneous determination (endo-genisation) of certain variables, and many more characteristics. At present there are 37 countries or areas in the LINK system (see Table 7.1). The system includes 24 models for OECD countries, eight models for centrally planned economies and four regional models for developing countries. The system is completed by a residual category for 'the rest of the world'.

By far the most important mechanism linking different economies is the international flow of merchandise exports and imports. The centre-piece of linkage and the technique by which consistency is maintained is the *world trade matrix*, an accounting design that lays out the inter-country and inter-regional trade flows on a bilateral basis. Consistency is achieved by requiring that the exports of each country or region be estimated as a weighted sum of the imports of trading partners. Essentially what the procedure amounts to for the individual country or

Table 7.1: LINK participants

	Models for OECD countries
Australia	University of Melbourne
Austria	Institut für Hoehere Studien, Vienna
Belgium	Université libre de Bruxelles
Canada	University of Toronto
Denmark	Danmarks Statistík, Copenhagen
Finland	Bank of Finland, Helsinkí
France	INSEE, Paris
Germany, Federal Republic of	Universität Hamburg
Greece	KEPE, Athens
Iceland	LINK Central, Philadelphia
Ireland	Central Bank of Ireland
Italy	Università di Bologna
Japan	Kyoto University
Netherlands	Central Planning Bureau, The Hague
New Zealand	Reserve Bank of New Zealand
Norway	LINK Central, Philadelphia
Portugal	LINK Central, Philadelphia
Spain	Universidad Autónoma de Madrid
Sweden	Stockholm School of Economics
Switzerland	Université de Lausanne
Turkey	LINK Central, Philadelphia
United Kingdom	London Business School
United States	University of Pennsylvania/WEFA, Philadelphia
Yugoslavia	LINK Central, Philadelphia

	Models for centrally planned economies
Bulgaria	
Czechoslovakia	United Nations
German Democratic Republic	
Hungary	University of Lodz
Poland	Market Research Institute, Budapest
Romania	Wharton EFA, Philadelphia
USSR	
China	Stanford University

	Regional models for developing countries
Africa	
Asia	
Latin America	United Nations
Middle East	
Pacific Far East	

area model is that the model is required to generate *import* and *export prices*, while the linkage procedure generates a consistent set of *export* and *import prices* to be passed back into the model.

Both these transformations can be done on a commodity or subgroup basis as well as for total trade. The common agreement within LINK is to disaggregate foreign trade into four standard international trade classification (SITC) subgroups: SITC-0, SITC-1 (food, beverages and tobacco), SITC-2, SITC-4 (industrial materials), SITC-3 (mineral fuels) and SITC-5 to SITC-9 (manufactures and other). For LINK purposes, the trade and price relations in these variables are estimated in United States dollars, the *numéraire* of the system.

No comparable linkage mechanism is available for service flows. While individual country models generally provide a fair amount of detail for service flows *vis-à-vis* the rest of the world, the lack of bilateral data makes it impossible to provide a direct linkage, as well as to enforce consistency; the latter problem is particularly troublesome since, in the available data sets, consistency is not enforced.

Similar problems make it, for the majority of the countries, impossible to model capital flows on a bilateral basis. Again, most of the models contain a certain amount of information with regard to capital flows but this cannot be used to establish bilateral linkages. This however does not mean that there are no monetary linkages. Rather, they assume the form of direct linkages via interest rates and exchange rates. The exchange rate submodel is designed to provide a consistent set of exchange rate equations for the big ten industrial countries. In addition, countries with some sort of pegging scheme are represented in the system with that particular set of basket weights to the extent these weights are available.

The treatment of the labour market differs substantially across models in the system. As a general characterisation of the labour market sub-sectors in the models for the major industrial countries, however, the following structure is representative: employment is explained – usually on a sectoral level – as a function of output and relative factor prices with appropriate time lags. The production technology varies across sectors; in some models (France and the Federal Republic of Germany, for example) the production technology for the industrial sector is putty-clay. Labour supply – often disaggregated by age and sex groups – is determined by exogenous population trends, expected real wages and wealth. Unemployment is generally determined residually. A similar structure, though usually on an aggregate level, is implemented in most of the OECD models (see Chapter 6). For both the centrally planned economies and the developing countries, (and Newly Industrialised Countries), severe data problems make it in most cases impossible to obtain unemployment forecasts. Quite often employment and labour force data are indices; for a number of countries such data is simply non-existent. A consistent labour market analysis for these areas in the system is therefore at present not feasible.

7.3 THE LINK BASELINE FORECAST

In this section we shall discuss briefly the present forecast for the world economy as generated with the LINK system, dated September 1983.

While the primary purpose of this is to illustrate the baseline solution from which the policy scenarios presented below were run, it is also of some interest to look at these projections, which are quite in line with those presented by other organisations. In Tables 7.2, 7.3 and 7.4 some of the characteristics of the forecast with regard to GDP, inflation and unemployment are summarised for the major areas. Note that in Table 7.4 the unemployment figures for Denmark and France are in thousands and millions respectively, rather than percentages; the figures for Switzerland give employment in thousands.

The GDP growth rate forecast for 1983 is in the 2–2.5 per cent range while for 1984 a growth rate of around 4 per cent is expected stimulated by the anticipated strong performance in the United States (Table 7.2). Growth will slow down again in subsequent years but an average rate of around 2–2.5 per cent will be maintained.

Significant changes have occurred for the developing area. As a result of weak performances in Africa, Latin America and the Middle East, the growth rate for the entire area is seen to be close to zero in 1983. Following the world recovery, coupled with a stabilisation of real oil prices, the situation will however improve in 1984 and subsequent years. The exception to the rule will be Africa; it is now projected that the average growth rate for the continent (excluding South Africa and the oil-producing countries) will hardly exceed 1 per cent for the entire forecast period. This makes Africa a prime target for improved development aid and subsistence programmes. The centrally planned economies are expected to continue to grow at a rate of around 3 per cent on average; the Polish economy, though still stagnant in 1983, is expected to recover in later years.

Even with a modest recovery under way, it appears as if the previous improvements in inflation can be defended. The present forecast incorporates a slight increase in OECD inflation in 1984 and 1985, but the general tendency is one of stability.

Unemployment continues to be the major problem for the Western European economies. While for the United States and Canada it seems likely that unemployment rates will fall by about 2 per cent (or more) over the next couple of years, no sign of relief is apparent for Europe. The major countries (France, Federal Republic of Germany and United Kingdom), as well as Belgium and Spain, among others, continue to be faced with stagnant high unemployment rates well in the double-digit range. There is every indication that this problem is likely to continue until at least the middle of the decade. Policy scenarios with the LINK system also suggest that there is little hope for improvement, based on traditional demand management policies. Proponents of the classical real wage argument also have to acknowledge that two (or even three) years of falling real wages have not brought about any significant improvement. It remains to be seen whether medium-term structural policies, such as reducing the average working week, could contribute

Table 7.2: Forecasted GDP growth rates

	1983	1984	1985	1986	1987	1988	1983–88
22 LINK OECD countries	2.3	4.0	2.6	2.3	1.7	2.5	2.6
North America	3.3	5.3	2.5	1.6	1.3	2.2	2.7
Developed Eastern countries	2.0	3.2	3.2	3.7	2.5	3.0	2.9
Nine LINK EEC countries	0.7	1.9	2.5	2.9	1.9	3.0	2.7
Rest of OECD Europe	1.5	2.7	3.2	3.1	2.3	2.8	2.6
Developing countries – total	0.2	2.6	4.1	3.8	3.1	3.1	2.8
Developing countries – non-oil producing	0.5	2.6	4.2	3.9	3.0	2.9	2.9
Africa	-0.7	0.6	0.8	0.6	1.4	1.8	0.7
Asia	3.9	4.2	5.4	5.3	4.0	4.6	4.6
Latin America	-2.6	1.4	3.9	3.2	2.3	1.2	1.5
Middle East	-1.9	2.6	3.4	3.5	4.0	4.6	2.7
Centrally planned countries	3.1	3.1	3.1	3.1	3.3	3.4	3.2
World	2.3	3.7	3.0	2.7	2.3	2.9	2.8
World level, nominal	8,765.9	9,585.5	10,820.1	12,035.5	13,030.0	13,962.6	11,366.6
World level, real	4,740.0	4,914.1	5,059.6	5,196.5	5,315.3	5,466.9	5,115.4

Source: World summary of economic activity (annual percentage change), Project LINK, University of Pennsylvania.

Table 7.3: Private consumption deflator growth rates

	1983	1984	1985	1986	1987	1988	1983–88
22 LINK OECD countries	8.3	8.5	9.1	9.0	8.5	8.0	8.6
North America	4.1	5.1	6.5	6.7	5.5	4.8	5.5
Developed Eastern countries	3.4	3.9	3.9	4.3	3.5	2.1	3.5
Nine LINK EEC countries	11.1	10.7	10.4	10.4	9.9	10.6	
Rest of OECD Europe	22.5	19.5	17.4	16.8	16.3	15.3	18.0

Source: World summary of economic activity (annual percentage change), Project LINK, University of Pennsylvania.

to a revitalisation of the labour markets in Europe. Some policy experiments with trade liberalisation and capital transfer to developing countries indicate the possibility of slight additional gains in employment (see below). The trade balances follow essentially the same trend that has been incorporated in the previous forecast. The United States will experience major trade deficits for several years to come, while the EEC countries and Japan will continue to accumulate surpluses. For the oil-producing countries the moderate increase in the nominal price of oil will be sufficient only to preserve the present status while the trade balance for non-oil-exporting countries will continue to deteriorate.

On balance, the present forecast gives rise to cautious optimism, even though serious trouble spots remain. Also, in the background the debt problems for a number of countries still have to be resolved. Any disturbance could initiate a re-emergence of the debt issue with increased severity; for the present forecast this is, however, not considered to be the preferred assumption. It should also be pointed out again that this projection, though optimistic on average, incorporates large imbalances with regard to regional development.

Clearly, while the present forecast is being characterised as cautiously optimistic, this does not apply to the labour market outlook for Europe. The medium-term forecast shows an extraordinary persistence of today's double-digit unemployment rates. It is this lack of light at the end of the tunnel that is the major cause for concern. In a number of countries the persistence is due to medium-term labour force trends that show that new cohorts cannot be absorbed. Also, there is some indication that most of the investment having taken place over the past two or three years has been replacement investment, which translates into further tightness on the labour markets. The following scenarios are designed to examine some policy options for the troubled OECD labour markets.

Table 7.4: Unemployment (in percentages)

	1982:1	1983:1	% chg	1984:1	% chg	1985:1	% chg	1986:1	% chg	1987:1	% chg	1988:1	% chg
LINK, non-European OECD countries													
Australia	7.1	10.2	43.4	9.8	-4.2	9.4	-3.7	9.4	-0.7	9.1	-2.5	9.3	1.3
Canada	11.0	12.4	12.6	11.9	-4.1	11.0	-7.8	9.9	-9.5	9.8	-1.3	9.7	-0.5
Japan	2.5	2.2	-10.6	2.1	-5.0	2.0	-2.6	2.1	1.3	1.5	-25.5	1.2	-22.4
United States	9.7	9.8	1.7	8.8	-10.6	8.0	-9.3	7.5	-5.3	7.4	-1.4	7.0	-6.1
LINK, EEC countries													
Belgium	13.0	14.2	9.1	16.3	14.5	16.2	-0.2	16.3	0.3	15.6	-3.9	15.7	0.6
Denmark[1]	264.0	277.6	5.2	292.2	5.3	284.3	-2.7	269.7	-5.1	258.6	-4.1	255.2	-1.3
France[2]	2.1	2.3	9.4	2.4	6.6	2.6	5.8	2.6	2.0	2.7	1.9	2.7	-0.4
Germany, Fed. Rep. of	8.0	10.7	34.0	11.4	6.6	11.1	-2.5	10.7	-3.8	10.6	-1.2	10.4	-1.9
Italy	9.0	9.9	10.5	10.1	1.7	9.8	-2.8	9.4	-4.3	9.5	0.9	9.3	-1.9
United Kingdom	11.6	11.3	-2.8	11.6	2.7	10.8	-7.3	10.4	-3.4	10.2	-2.0	9.5	-6.6
LINK rest of OECD Europe													
Austria	3.6	4.6	27.4	5.1	10.8	5.4	4.6	5.5	2.2	5.2	-4.8	5.0	-3.5
Finland	5.9	6.3	7.0	6.3	-0.1	6.2	-1.4	5.8	-7.0	5.5	-5.3	5.6	1.6
Iceland	0.7	1.1	57.1	0.9	-18.2	0.9	0.0	1.1	22.2	1.2	9.1	1.3	8.3
Norway	3.0	4.6	55.2	3.1	-32.5	2.9	-6.2	1.7	-41.0	1.85	5.7	1.8	-0.7
Portugal	8.6	9.4	9.7	9.4	-0.1	8.9	-5.1	8.4	-5.2	8.1	-4.2	7.2	-10.7
Spain	16.8	17.2	2.0	17.0	-0.7	16.6	-2.6	15.8	-4.9	14.6	-7.3	13.2	-9.7
Sweden	3.3	3.2	-4.6	2.9	-8.6	2.2	-22.4	1.8	-17.2	1.8	3.8	1.5	-11.9
Switzerland[3]	2,955.1	2,912.8	-1.4	2,911.9	-0.0	2,931.2	0.7	2,960.7	1.0	2,965.3	0.2	2,957.8	-0.3
Turkey	18.2	18.1	-0.2	17.4	-4.0	17.4	0.3	17.7	1.5	18.1	2.0	18.8	4.0
Yugoslavia	11.1	10.8	-2.9	10.4	-3.1	10.1	-2.9	9.9	-2.3	9.7	-2.0	9.5	-2.0

[1] Figures given in thousands.
[2] Figures given in millions.
[3] Actual figures.
Source: World summary of economic activity (annual percentage change), Project LINK, University of Pennsylvania.

7.4 DOMESTIC POLICIES FOR INDUSTRIALISED COUNTRIES

In this section we report the results for alternative policy scenarios focusing on traditional domestic monetary and fiscal policy instruments in the major industrialised countries. The presentation will concentrate on summary results only; detailed country results are available upon request. All subsequent tables report deviations from the baseline as presented above.

7.4.1 Traditional demand management

In 1983 a number of politicians, economists, and international institutions called for a co-ordinated policy action to spur world recovery.[2] It is worth looking at the labour market implications of these proposals. It should be noted that some of the measures called for have in the meantime been taken not as the result of a concerted action but rather in the leader-follower framework between the United States and Europe. The centrepiece of the following analysis is the policy proposal put forward by the Institute for International Economics, the 'Bergsten proposal'.

In the set of scenarios described here we try to evaluate various aspects of the Bergsten proposal, as we interpret its major intentions. One of its basic ingredients seems to be the notion that among the big seven countries there is room for expansionary fiscal policy only in those countries with tolerable budget deficit prospects. In contrast, it is most likely that a co-ordinated interest rate reduction, if actually performed that way, will be feasible for all participants.

To implement a statistical calculation of the effects of the recommended policies on the world economy, in its various parts, we have quantified the different fiscal and monetary measures as inputs for the LINK system as follows.

For three of the seven summit nations (the United States, the United Kingdom and Canada) we changed appropriate monetary instruments to bring down short-term interest rates by two percentage points; for the other four the reduction was by only one percentage point. We further changed the inputs for the base case by increasing government expenditure in real terms by 2.4 per cent above the baseline path in Japan, the Federal Republic of Germany and the United Kingdom. For the United Kingdom, this amounts to a nominal rise of £3 thousand million. In order to restrain the United Kingdom deficit, a part of the fiscal policy package was to increase personal income taxes by 5 per cent in 1984 and by 10 per cent in 1985.

This stimulative package raises the OECD yearly growth rate by about 0.4 percentage points (1983–86). In the United States, Canada, the Federal Republic of Germany and Japan, the new path of GDP runs about 1.0 to 2.0 per cent or more above the base path, while for many other countries it is up by about 0.5 to 1.0 per cent.

The gain in the OECD growth rate reflects back on the developing countries through better export performance and raises their growth rate by about 0.1 percentage points. This ratio of gain (4:1) is a fairly standard result in calculations like these. There are only marginal gains for the centrally planned economies. The volume of world trade responds somewhat better than GDP to this growth stimulus and provides the source of improvement for the developing world.

The net external position of the OECD countries is slightly worsened, as far as merchandise trade is concerned, because the higher level of activity induces an import expansion in excess of their export expansion. Oil-exporting countries are estimated to be the main beneficiaries and this is surely part of the OPEC strategy in waiting for better times when the upturn takes hold.

In the present world environment this is not an inflationary policy. In the first place, lower interest rates feed directly into lower-cost values for figuring price indices. Second, there are some cyclical productivity gains to be realised and these hold down inflation. Fuel and food prices remain soft in this recovery scenario, which is not all that strong, and this contributes to continuing success in the working off of inflationary pressures. But most of all, the recovery leaves a residual of unemployment over the time-span of this projection and labour market conditions make for continuing wage moderation.

Unemployment rates are projected to fall as output growth recovers, but the improvement in unemployment does not restore labour markets to any accepted version of full employment by 1986. For the United States, the improvement amounts to 1.6 percentage points; for the United Kingdom, 1.2 points (but this soon comes to an end); for the Federal Republic of Germany, 0.4 points and for France only 0.1 point. This is an indication of the large structural component in European unemployment.

In addition to this basic package (MON.FISC) we tried to evaluate the implications of three alternative packages:

1. in view of large budget deficits, we cancel the fiscal stimuli but retain the monetary package (MON.POL);
2. here we extend the reduction in interest rates to the entire OECD area (M.F.OECD);
3. in addition to 2, we generate an additional 10 per cent depreciation of the effective United States dollar exchange rate (M.F.OECD).

The results of all four packages with regard to unemployment are summarised in Figures 7.1–7.4.

In deviations of real GDP from the baseline solution, the ranking across scenarios differs, reflecting again the differential impact of these

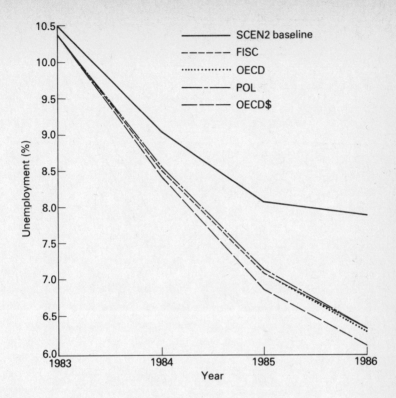

Figure 7.1: Unemployment rates, United States and Canada

policies on various regions. The absolute gain in world GDP by 1986 varies between US $65 and US $85 thousand million (in 1970 prices and exchange rates); of this improvement, between US $40 and US $60 thousand million are attributable to the United States and Canada. Moderate but significant improvements are noticeable for every other region in the world. This is true for any of the four scenarios examined here. In terms of real GNP, the level of world activity could, according to these results, be increased by at least 1–1.5 per cent.

At the same time, none of these packages is inflationary. The comparison of inflation rates projected under either scenario with the baseline forecast shows only minor deviations never exceeding the range 1–1.5 per cent. The average rate of inflation for the period 1983–86 remains almost unaffected; the scenario, including a dollar depreciation, even implies a 0.2–0.3 per cent reduction in the average rate.

With respect to the unemployment prospects, it is clear that the present results are far from satisfactory. While for North America any of these policies would lead to a substantial further reduction in the unemployment rate (which is expected to come down to around 8 per

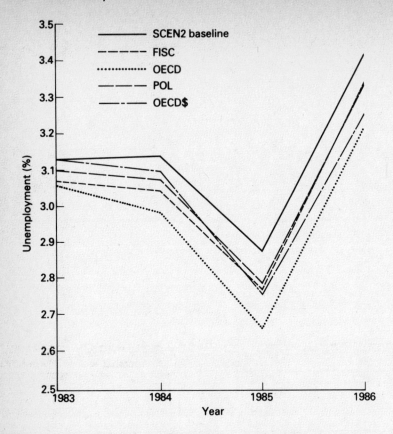

Figure 7.2: Unemployment rates, Japan and Australia

cent) in the baseline forecast already, a comparable result for the European countries does not materialise. Neither surplus nor deficit countries can expect to achieve significant improvements in the labour markets; the unemployment rates will not be reduced by more than 0.5 per cent. It is thus clear and, given the experience of previous years, not surprising that traditional demand management is likely to contribute little, if anything, to fighting high structural unemployment.

Finally, an attempt is made to analyse the effects of a 10 per cent investment tax credit in the seven summit countries. Table 7.5b summarises the effects of such a policy aimed at stimulating private non-residential investment outlays. It can be seen that even though the unemployment effects are mostly favourable, they are not as strong as for the original Bergsten package as summarised in Table 7.5a.

A combination of both demand-oriented fiscal and monetary stimulus and a supply-side stimulus, as the investment tax credit can be regarded, generates an appreciable stimulus for world economic activity. As can be seen in Table 7.6, world GDP can be expected to increase by about 2 per cent after about three years. The weighted unemployment rate

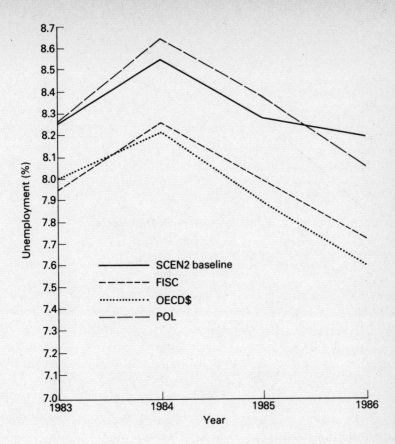

Figure 7.3: Unemployment rates, European OECD countries in surplus

difference is about 1 per cent in the medium term. This is by no means sufficient, but a reasonable gain, given that the policy stimulus is still rather modest.

7.4.2   How relevant are international conditions?

In this section the focus is on the assessment of labour market consequences of alternative international conditions. In this context we shall examine three possible factors that could – via improving domestic economic activity – have a positive impact on the labour market:

1. The price of basic materials has an important impact on labour demand and thus on unemployment. Depending on the degree of substitutability between labour, capital and imported materials, changes in relative prices affect employment. In addition, changes in import prices feed into domestic real activity. To assess the importance of this channel, we simulate the effects of a further

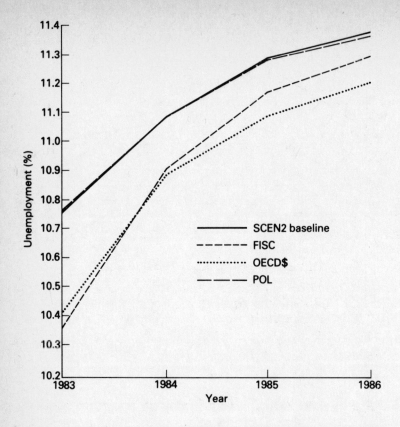

Figure 7.4: Unemployment rates, European OECD countries in deficit

drastic reduction in crude oil prices (US $5 in 1983 and US $10 in 1984–88).

2. Movements in exchange rates affect the economy via similar channels. In addition, though, they have a significant impact on capital flows and thus on wealth distribution. As an exercise to trace through the effect of a limited currency realignment we have simulated the effect of a 10 per cent depreciation of the Deutschmark and the Yen *vis-à-vis* the United States dollar (and hence *vis-à-vis* all other currencies).

3. The greater openness of most economies over the past several years has generally reduced traditional multipliers by increasing leakages. This has generated an increasing willingness to apply protectionist tariff schemes. By distorting relative prices, this will – in the long run – generate welfare losses. In order to evaluate the short-term effects of these policies, we examine in scenario 3 the effects of a worldwide reduction of tariff rates on manufactured goods by 5 per cent.

Table 7.5a: Unemployment effects of Bergsten package (in percentages)

	1982:1	1983:1	% chg	1984:1	% chg	1985:1	% chg	1986:1	% chg	1987:1	% chg	1988:1	% chg
LINK, non-European OECD countries													
Australia	0	0	0	-0.01	-0.1	-0.3	-0.3	-0.04	-0.4	-0.05	-0.5	-0.56	-0.5
Canada	0	-0.03	-0.3	-0.16	-1.3	-0.29	-2.5	-0.37	-3.2	-0.39	-3.4	-0.38	-3.4
Japan	0	-0.01	-0.5	-0.02	-1.2	-0.04	-1.9	-0.03	-1.5	-0.01	-0.9	0	0.3
United States	0	-0.10	-1.1	-0.07	-4.4	-0.57	-7.6	-0.71	-9.6	-0.69	-10.0	-0.46	-7.5
LINK, EEC countries													
Belgium	0	-0.12	-1.0	-0.41	-2.9	-0.65	-4.5	-0.84	-5.4	-0.84	-5.4	-0.75	-4.7
Denmark	0	-1.14	-0.4	-9.90	-1.3	-6.72	-2.3	-9.20	-3.2	-9.70	-3.3	-0.34	-2.6
France	0	0	-0.1	0	0	0.01	0.7	0.03	1.5	0.05	2.2	0.07	2.8
Germany, Fed. Rep. of	0	-0.03	-0.4	-0.02	-0.2	-0.02	-0.03	-0.16	-1.7	-0.29	-3.1	-0.39	-4.2
Italy	0	-0.02	-0.3	0	-0.9	-0.15	-1.7	-0.19	-2.4	-0.20	-2.6	-0.10	-2.5
United Kingdom	0	0	-0.2	-0.05	-0.5	-0.04	-0.4	-0.01	0.2	0.09	0.9	0.12	1.4
LINK rest of OECD Europe													
Austria	0	-0.04	-0.9	-0.16	-3.5	-0.02	-7.1	-0.51	-11.3	-0.67	-14.6	-0.74	-17.5
Finland	0	0	-0.1	-0.03	-0.5	-0.07	-1.1	-0.08	-1.6	-0.10	-1.6	0	1.3
Norway	0	0	0	0	0	0	0	0	0	0	0	0	0
Spain	0	0	0	0	0	0	0	0	0	0	0.1	0.01	0.1
Sweden	0	-0.02	-0.8	-0.07	-8.8	-0.07	-3.6	-0.07	-3.6	-0.04	-2.7	-0.01	-0.5
Switzerland	0	1.22	0.0	3.24	0.1	4.42	0.2	6.21	0.2	6.17	0.2	5.30	0.2

Table 7.5b: Unemployment: effects of a 10 per cent investment tax credit (in percentages)

	1982:1	1983:1	% chg	1984:1	% chg	1985:1	% chg	1986:1	% chg
LINK, non-European OECD countries									
Australia	0	0	-0.1	-0.01	-0.3	-0.05	-0.5	-0.08	-0.8
Canada	0	-0.10	-0.3	-0.50	-4.3	-0.82	-7.2	-0.96	-8.8
Japan	0	-0.06	-2.9	-0.10	-4.9	-0.11	-6.1	-0.07	-3.1
United States	0	-0.12	-1.3	-0.48	-5.6	-0.95	-12.5	-1.62	-21.7
LINK, EEC countries									
Belgium	0	-0.10	-1.5	-0.60	-4.3	-0.94	-6.5	-1.21	-7.7
Denmark	0	-2.17	-0.8	-6.72	-2.0	-11.22	-3.3	-15.19	-4.5
France	0	0	-0.3	-0.02	-1.10	-0.02	-1.0	-0.02	-0.9
Germany, Fed. Rep. of	0	-0.43	-4.4	-0.34	-3.4	-0.29	-3.0	-0.55	-5.7
Italy	0	-0.02	-0.2	-0.09	-0.9	-0.16	-1.8	-0.23	-2.8
United Kingdom	0	-1.18	-10.5	-0.37	-3.2	-0.13	-1.2	0.03	0.3
LINK, rest of OECD Europe									
Austria	0	-0.06	-1.4	-0.23	-5.0	-0.48	-10.0	-0.77	-15.7
Finland	0	-0.01	-0.2	-0.06	-1.0	-0.13	-2.0	-0.17	-2.7
Norway	0	0	0	0	0	0	0	0	0
Spain	0	0	0	0	0	0	0	0	-0.1
Sweden	0	-0.05	-1.6	-0.13	-5.0	-0.12	-6.0	-0.12	-6.2
Switzerland	0	1.99	0.1	5.05	0.2	7.44	0.3	9.97	0.3

Source: OECD *Economic Outlook* and LINK projection

Table 7.6: Scenario: monetary and fiscal stimulus, and investment tax credit

Country aggregate	Variable	1984	1985	1986	1987	1988
OECD	GDP % development	0.6	1.8	3.0	3.8	3.4
	PCDEF abs. dif.	0.4	− 0.6	− 0.1	0.2	0.6
	Tbal. abs. dif.	3.4	0.8	− 2.1	− 5.0	− 7.2
	Unempl. rate dif.	− 0.2	− 0.5	10.9	− 1.3	− 1.3
Australia/ Japan	GDP % development	0.5	1.5	1.8	3.3	4.4
	PCDEF abs. dif.	0	0.2	0.3	− 1.1	0.1
	Tbal. abs. dif.	2.4	5.0	7.9	10.9	10.2
	Unempl. rate dif.	0	− 0.1	− 0.2	− 0.3	− 0.3
Canada/ United States	GDP % development	0.5	2.1	3.9	5.0	4.0
	PCDEF abs. dif	− 0.7	− 1.3	− 0.3	0.6	1.3
	Tbal. abs. dif.	1.3	− 3.1	− 14.0	− 24.1	− 26.7
	Unempl. rate dif.	− 0.1	− 0.8	− 2.0	− 3.0	− 3.0
EEC (nine)	GDP % development	1.1	1.7	1.7	1.9	2.0
	PCDEF abs. dif.	− 0.1	0.2	0.2	0.1	0
	Tbal. abs. dif	− 0.8	− 1.4	3.5	7.7	9.0
	Unempl. rate dif.	− 0.5	− 0.3	− 0.2	− 0.1	− 0.1
Developing countries (all)	GDP % development	0.3	0.6	0.8	1.1	1.4
	PCDEF abs. dif.					
	Tbal. abs. dif.	− 5.3	− 4.5	− 2.7	− 0.7	0.3
	Unempl. rate dif.					
Developing countries (non-oil producing)	GDP % development	0.4	0.6	0.9	1.2	1.5
	PCDEF abs. dif.					
	Tbal. abs. dif.	− 5.9	− 7.1	− 8.5	− 10.0	− 11.5
	Unempl. rate dif.					
Developing countries (oil producing)	GDP % development	0.1	0.2	0.3	0.4	0.5
	PCDEF abs. dif.					
	Tbal. abs. dif.	0.6	2.6	5.7	9.3	11.8
	Unempl. rate dif.					
Planned economies	GDP % development	0	0	0.1	0.1	0.2
	PCDEF abs. dif.					
	Tbal. abs. dif.	1.3	2.2	2.6	3.1	3.3
	Unempl. rate dif.					
World	GDP % development	0.4	1.3	2.0	2.6	2.4

GDP percentage deviations: (scenario – baseline)/baseline
Private consumption deflator: differences in growth rates from baseline
Trade balance: absolute differences from baseline in thousand millions of United States dollars
Unemployment: rate of deviation from baseline

The results[3] for these three types of disturbances show that the unemployment effects of minor exchange rate adjustments seem to be small in either direction. This is in accord with previous studies showing that while exchange rate movements contribute substantially to fluctuations in activity, they are not instrumental in determining long-run labour market conditions. This is not surprising, given that exchange rates tend to follow some weak form of purchasing power relationship in the long run, thus being non-distortionary.

Quite surprisingly we find that a further reduction of oil prices would also not contribute to a reduction in unemployment. There are several reasons for this result: domestically, there seems to be a high degree of complementarity in a number of countries; more importantly, OPEC imports from OECD countries are reduced substantially, which has a major impact on GNP in these countries. The European countries and Japan are further faced with an appreciation of their currencies *vis-à-vis* the United States dollar, caused by the reduction of OPEC foreign assets denominated in dollars and an asymmetry in the price reaction across countries. On balance though, the GNP effects, and in particular the unemployment effects, of this adjustment are not significant.

On the contrary, however, a redirection in worldwide tariffs appears to have a major potential effect on world GNP by stimulating world trade in all areas. The unemployment effect is not overwhelming but recognisable. A slight appreciation of the dollar reduces the gain for the United States via a terms-of-trade effect.

It is worth noting that there is a potential problem with this policy in that it tends to worsen the trade deficit for the developing countries. This, however, is a direct consequence of our limiting the tariff reduction to manufacturing goods only; an extension to food and basic materials will not be likely to alter this result favourably.

Comparing these findings with those of the previous section, it is apparent that while there is a noticeable effect of international conditions on unemployment, the order of magnitude of this effect does not measure up to those generated in the previous set of scenarios.

7.5 WORLDWIDE DEVELOPMENT STRATEGIES

The policies analysed in the previous section have been conceived and implemented primarily in the developed world. Any effect upon the developing countries is therefore bound to be of a secondary order of magnitude. In this section we shall therefore concentrate on a number of strategies aimed at directly improving prospects for the Third World; to the extent that these countries maintain their re-spending patterns, these policies can also be expected to contribute positively to a reduction of unemployment rates in the developed countries.

In an alternative approach, we considered the problem of alleviating the export-earning shortfalls from the viewpoint of direct market intervention aimed at stabilising prices. In particular, we computed the necessary increase in the export deflator of developing countries for SITC subgroups 0 + 1 and 2 + 4, in order to provide these countries with an amount of resources to be used to finance import requirements equivalent to the full amount of the compensatory facility.

In yet another alternative, we explored the possibility of a more ambitious plan in the global context of North–South dialogue, namely the fulfilment of the targets for official development aid (ODA) as a percentage of GDP of developed countries at the end of the decade. On the basis of current discussion, we envisaged a worldwide reduction in defence expenditure in order to contribute to the financing of the ODA programme.

While the previous scenarios were specifically aimed at the developing countries, in the final set of simulations we have addressed the issue of trade liberalisation at the world level. We have interpreted this issue as a reduction in tariff rates for broad commodity groups, excluding energy.

The results for each of the scenarios discussed above have been treated in detail in the LINK studies previously mentioned. Perhaps the most important observation that can be made is that no one strategy by itself seems to be sufficient to impart a long-lasting improvement of respectable size on the world economy. In fact, the percentage deviation of world real activity from the baseline hardly exceeds a full percentage point. Moreover, the impact upon developing country activity is in most cases of secondary order of magnitude.

As far as long-run policies are concerned, we have analysed the impact of a compensatory financing facility (CFF) designed to assist developing countries with liquidity for shortfalls in commodity export earnings, according to the background elaborations and proposals of the UNCTAD secretariat since the Manila Resolution of 1979. Under this scheme, drawings from the facility would be used to finance commodity-related activities intended to stabilise the commodity sector and eradicate the root causes of instability such as short-term income support in individual commodity sectors and structural adjustment in cases of chronic over-supply or under-supply. Access to the facility is seen as conditional on the elaboration of commodity development programmes in which the intended uses of the resources would be specified and mutually agreed upon between the applicant country and the facility.

In order to implement the simulation exercises, we investigated the options available in the developed countries in order to contribute to the compensatory facility and the different impacts upon the economy. Briefly, the public authorities in these countries could: inject more liquidity into the international financial system; issue public notes; raise domestic taxation; and divert resources from domestic programmes to

Table 7.7a: Scenario: official development aid financed by defence expenditure reduction

Country aggregate	Variable	1983	1984	1985	1986	1987	1988
OECD	GDP % development	0.2	0.2	0.2	0.2	0.2	0.3
	PCDEF abs. dif.	0	0	0	0	0	0
	Tbal. abs. dif.	23.0	23.0	23.3	23.3	23.0	22.7
	Unempl. rate dif.	0	-0.1	-0.1	-0.1	-0.1	-0.1
Australia/Japan	GDP % development	0.6	0.7	0.6	0.6	0.6	0.6
	PCDEF abs. dif.	0.1	0.1	0.2	0.1	0.2	0
	Tbal. abs. dif.	6.0	6.0	5.8	5.9	6.1	6.2
	Unempl. rate dif.	0	-0.1	-0.1	-0.1	-0.1	-0.1
Canada/United States	GDP % development	0	0	0	0	0	0
	PCDEF abs. dif.	0	0	0	0	0	0
	Tbal. abs. dif.	7.9	8.4	8.3	8.3	8.7	9.2
	Unempl. rate dif.	0	0	0	0	0	0
EEC (nine)	GDP % development	0.6	0.6	0.4	0.4	0.5	0.6
	PCDEF abs. dif.	0	0	0	0	0	0
	Tbal. abs. dif	7.3	6.9	7.6	7.1	6.0	4.6
	Unempl. rate dif.	0	-0.1	-0.1	0	-0.1	-0.1
Developing countries (all)	GDP % development	1.5	1.7	1.8	2.0	2.2	2.3
	PCDEF abs. dif.						
	Tbal. abs. dif.	-25.9	-25.5	-25.1	-24.7	-24.3	-24.0
	Unempl. rate dif.						
Developing countries (non-oil producing)	GDP % development	1.7	1.9	2.1	2.2	2.4	2.6
	PCDEF abs. dif.						
	Tbal. abs. dif.	-26.3	-26.5	-26.6	-26.7	-26.8	-26.9
	Unempl. rate dif.						

Developing countries (oil producing)						
GDP % development	0	0	0	0	0	0
PCDEF abs. dif.	0.3	0.9	1.4	2.0	2.4	2.9
Tbal. abs. dif.						
Unempl. rate dif.						
Planned economies						
GDP % development	0	0.1	0.1	0.2	0.2	0.3
PCDEF abs. dif.	2.5	2.1	1.6	1.3	1.2	1.0
Tbal. abs. dif.						
Unempl. rate dif.						
World						
GDP % development	0.3	0.3	0.4	0.4	0.4	0.5

GDP percentage deviations: (scenario – baseline)/baseline
Private consumption deflator: differences in growth rates from baseline
Trade balance: absolute differences from baseline in thousand millions of United States dollars
Unemployment: rate of deviation from baseline

Table 7.7b: Official development aid financed by defence expenditure reduction (unemployment in percentages)

	1982:1	1983:1	% chg	1984:1	% chg	1985:1	% chg	1986:1	% chg	1987:1	% chg	1988:1	% chg
LINK, non-European OECD countries													
Australia	0	-0.06	-0.6	-0.13	-1.4	-0.15	-1.6	-0.15	-1.6	-0.14	-1.6	-0.13	-1.5
Canada	0	-0.01	-0.1	-0.01	-0.1	-0.01	-0.1	-0.02	-0.3	-0.02	-0.2	-0.01	-0.1
Japan	0	-0.04	-1.8	-0.04	-2.2	-0.04	-2.0	0	-0.03	0.01	1.1	0.01	1.5
United States	0	0	0.1	0.01	0.1	-0.02	-0.3	-0.05	-0.7	-0.06	-0.9	-0.06	-0.9
LINK, EEC countries													
Belgium	0	-0.49	-3.5	-0.89	-5.5	-0.92	-5.7	-0.92	-5.7	-0.93	-6.0	-0.97	-6.2
Denmark	0	-6.66	-2.4	-13.76	-4.7	-16.29	-5.7	-15.68	-5.8	-12.04	-4.7	-3.84	-1.5
France	0	-0.01	-0.8	-0.01	-0.7	0.01	0.4	0.01	0.6	0.01	0.4	0	0
Germany, Fed. Rep. of	0	-0.15	-0.8	-0.01	-0.7	0.01	0.4	0.01	0.6	0.01	0.4	0	0
Italy	0	-0.07	-0.8	-0.14	-1.4	-0.1	-1.6	-0.15	-1.6	-0.15	-1.6	-0.15	-1.7
United Kingdom	0	-0.18	1.6	0.08	0.7	-0.14	1.3	0.17	1.6	0.12	1.3	0.08	0.9
LINK, rest of OECD Europe													
Austria	0	-0.16	-3.6	-0.42	-8.1	-0.60	-11.1	-0.69	-12.6	-0.73	-14.0	-0.75	-14.9
Finland	0	-0.04	-0.8	-0.16	-2.5	-0.20	-3.2	-0.15	-2.7	-0.10	-1.9		-1.4
Iceland	0	0	0	0	0	0	0	0	0	0	0	0	0
Norway	0	0.01	0.3	0	0.3	0.01	0.5	0.01	0.8	0.01	0.9	0.01	0.3
Portugal	0	-0.02	-0.3	-0.07	-0.8	-0.08	-0.9	-0.06	-0.8	-0.03	-0.5	-0.01	-0.2
Spain	0	0	0	0.01	0.1	0.01	0.1	0.02	0.1	0.02	0.2	0.02	0.2
Sweden	0	-0.15	-4.7	-0.23	-8.1	-0.13	-5.8	-0.03	-1.9	0.02	1.6	0.06	3.9
Switzerland	0	7.35	0.3	10.00	0.3	9.46	0.3	8.34	0.3	7.58	0.3	7.13	0.2
Turkey	0	-0.04	-0.3	-0.09	-0.5	-0.11	-0.7	-0.15	-0.9	-0.19	-1.1	-0.24	-1.3
Yugoslavia	0	-0.03	-0.3	-0.10	-1.0	-0.14	-1.4	-0.16	-1.6	-0.16	-1.7	-0.17	-1.8

abroad. While the first option bears no apparent cost, this is only a superficial view. There is an inflationary feedback, largely manifested through higher interest rates, together with higher prices. The other options bring upward pressure on interest rates or perverse multiplier effects on real activity.

This point is illustrated in Tables 7.7a and 7.7b where we report the results for an increase in ODA towards the 0.7 per cent of GNP target, financed by a reduction in defence expenditures on a multilateral basis. There are minor, but by no means spectacular, gains in GNP for all areas – except, initially, for the United States – which translate into additional jobs and reduced unemployment rates by some minor order of magnitude.

The next step then is to try to combine several of these scenarios, which implies a co-ordination both across countries and of different policies. To achieve maximum effects we have simulated all these combinations on top of a first layer, which combines the preferred policy package from the preceding chapter. Figure 7.5 illustrates the different combinations looked at in this context. In running these scenarios we are obviously focusing primarily on trying to identify the 'degree of relative interdependence', which determines the feedback of these measures on OECD labour markets.

Scenario 1 has a non-negligible effect upon the world economy in the order of two or more percentage points deviation from the baseline in the long run. If we turn the attention to major areas, the percentage deviations for developed and developing countries are on average 3.5 per cent and 1.33 per cent respectively. This 3:1 ratio is a standard result in these types of simulations, where a policy is initiated in the developed countries. We may notice in the developed countries a sign-reversal pattern for inflation and trade balances.

The former occurs because of productivity gains, especially in the United States, which hold inflation in check at the beginning of the period. The latter phenomenon is due to healthy growth of imports generated by increased economic activity. It is through higher developed country imports that a positive effect is transmitted to developing countries. In turn, these latter expand their import requirements according to a standard two-gap hypothesis, generating a secondary stimulus outside their area. We interpret the degree of relative interdependence as the final outcome of the process described above.

Turning attention to scenario 2, we observe that adding tariff reduction improves the world activity by an additional half of a percentage point in the long run, while inflation is improved further. This can be contrasted with the result of the tariff reduction scenario above, where the deviation of world GDP from the baseline is in the order of a full percentage point. Scenario 2 shows, therefore, partial but not total offsetting of the individual policy proposals by which it is composed.

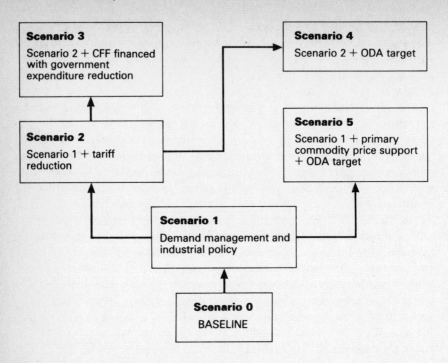

Figure 7.5: Alternative policy scenarios

The relative interdependence between developed and developing countries is in the order of 2.5 to 1. We can state therefore that for each desired percentage point of activity increase in developing countries, scenario 2 requires less increase in developed country GDP, with respect to scenario 1. This consideration seems important in evaluating the plausibility and the feasibility of expansionary policies initiated in the developed countries with the explicit objective of improving the outlook for developing countries.

The results of scenario 3 seem somewhat mixed. In fact, the world outlook changes only marginally. This is because the cost of financing the CFF in terms of reduced government expenditure partially offsets the original fiscal expansion set in motion according to scenario 1. This occurs especially in the United States at the beginning of the simulation period. It is important to notice, however, the reversal in sign occurring in the latter years and to contrast it with the results of the CFF scenario implemented by itself. In this latter case the impact upon the United States economy is negative throughout the entire period. This observation provides only one example of the importance of considering fully co-ordinated policies. In fact, from the viewpoint of the United States, the CFF strategy by itself may be unacceptable in terms of resource costs versus benefits, while it may be acceptable if in conjunction with other policy strategies.

As far as the developing countries are concerned, in scenario 3 they benefit, at the margin, by an additional amount between 0.75 per cent and a full percentage point. The relative interdependence ratio between developed and developing countries improves to values below 2 to 1 (1.6 and 1.7 to 1, depending on the years), showing therefore stronger spillover of the policies initiated by developed countries into the developing countries.

In scenario 4 we have added to scenario 2 an increase in official transfers financed by defence expenditure reduction. This scenario is therefore similar to the previous one with respect to the developed countries. It is different with respect to the centrally planned economies, which are assumed to reduce their defence expenditure and contribute to the transfer to the developing countries. Since activity in the planned economies responds less than developed country activity to defence expenditure reduction, their GDP actually improves marginally as a result of the induced world trade expansion.

Perhaps the most important conclusion that can be drawn from this scenario is that the measure of relative interdependence stabilises around values of 1:1 at the end of the period. In addition, the last scenario (5), which combines scenario 1 with official transfer financed by defence expenditure reduction and with primary commodity prices support policy, shows results similar to scenario 4 although the absolute size of the gain is somewhat smaller.

On the basis of the discussion of the preceding sections, we conclude that scenario 4 is the best case for at least three reasons. First, in comparison with other alternatives, it generates the highest increase in world activity with respect to the baseline projection (+ 3.5 per cent at the end of the period). Second, it consists of policies which are relatively feasible and desirable, although not necessarily easily implemented or politically popular among present governments. Third, on equity grounds, it seems to be a well-balanced policy strategy for the improvement, at the margin, of both developing and developed countries. The increments to production in each area are of equal size.

It is in this spirit that we interpret a world recovery as being potentially synonymous in the developing countries' recovery. It is also obvious, though, that even these massive packages cannot contribute to the much needed reduction in unemployment in European countries; however, the labour market effects for the United States and Canada are, as expected, quite favourable.

7.6   SUMMARY

The purpose of this chapter has been systematically to evaluate the effects of a variety of 'world recovery scenarios' on world economic activity and unemployment prospects in particular. The focus has been on both domestic and international policies. Several individual strategies have been combined to generate a maximum impact in the medium term.

A number of interesting conclusions emerge with respect to the types of policies examined in sections 7.4 and 7.5. From the international point of view, it is quite striking that – given the degree of inter-dependence of today's world economy – a substantial recovery in the OECD is indeed almost synonymous with a corresponding recovery in the developing countries; the converse is obviously not true. Also, the package of international instruments analysed in this paper can successfully be added to a suitably designed co-ordinated monetary and fiscal policy to improve GNP performance.

From the point of view of employment and unemployment, the prospects for the short- and medium-term given in this chapter are rather disappointing. There are positive effects to be expected from any combination of policies analysed here; none of these packages can, however, be expected to bring about spectacular reductions in unemployment rates. This is particularly true for the European economies. Reductions in the OECD unemployment rate in the order of magnitude of about 1.5 to 2 per cent by 1988 are not sufficient to consider any of these strategies unambiguously successful.

Are these results reliable? Clearly, macro-econometric models are known to have major problems in capturing some of the crucial features of the labour market. Regional and professional disaggregation, which is crucial given the lack of homogeneity in the market, are totally absent. Similarly, job qualifications are not taken into account properly in most cases. Econometric problems are notorious in attempts to obtain reliable estimates of such crucial parameters as the elasticity of substitution and household elasticities of labour supply with respect to real wages, etc. For the former set of arguments, one can safely assume that they contribute, if anything at all, to an underestimation of the adjustment problems. Any serious labour market analysis should therefore include an attempt to complement these macro-economic estimates with more specific micro evidence.

NOTES

1. The material presented in this paper draws extensively on a number of studies produced at LINK Central. See, eg, Bollino, C.A., Pauly, P. and Petersen, C.E. *Strategies for a worldwide recovery*, Philadelphia, University of Pennsylvania (April and June 1983) Parts I and II; Bollino, C.A., Pauly, P. and Petersen, C.E. *Tariffs and global development: Further results from Project LINK* Philadelphia, University of Pennsylvania, August (1983); Bollino, C.A. and Klein, L.R. *World recovery strategies in the 1980s: Is world recovery synonymous to LDC recovery?*, Philadelphia, University of Pennsylvania, September (1983).
2. Institute for International Economics *Promoting world recovery*, Washington, DC, December (1982): Schmidt, H. 'The world economy at

stake', in *The Economist*, 26 February (1983); United Nations Committee for Development Planning, *World economic recovery and international monetary and fiscal co-operation*, New York, (1982).
3.   Space limitation prevents full presentation of results.'

Chapter Eight

Employment and output in a semi-industrial economy: modelling alternative policy options in Mexico

Ajit Singh, Faculty of Economics, University of Cambridge

8.1 INTRODUCTION

This chapter reports on certain macro-econometric models which were developed to analyse major issues of economic policy in Mexico during 1976–82, the period of office of the last President, José Lopez Portillo. These models were of a rather different kind than those used elsewhere in the developing countries, for example in India. An assessment of this approach to modelling in relation to the actual evolution of the Mexican economy during the sexenium (the normal six-year period of a Mexican presidency) will not only throw some light on economic policy and the economic crises which came at the end of this period in Mexico, but will also be of wider relevance, particularly in relation to policy modelling in other semi-industrial mixed economies.

The chapter is organised as follows. Section 8.2 briefly reviews the salient features of the Mexican economy, its institutional framework and the nature of the employment problem the country faces. Section 8.3 outlines the main long-term policy options which Mexico faced when it became an 'oil economy' in the mid-1970s, as well as certain significant short- and medium-term policy issues. Section 8.4 comments on the methodological approach to macro-economic modelling of policy options which was used in the analyses reported here. Section 8.5 examines the application of this analysis to long-term policy issues, and section 8.6 to short- and medium-term issues of devaluation, import controls, and economic adjustment. Finally, Section 8.7 offers some concluding remarks on the strengths and limitations of these models.

8.2 MEXICO AS A SEMI-INDUSTRIAL ECONOMY

Mexico is a large semi-industrial economy, the absolute size of whose industrial sector is about three times that of South Korea's. Manufacturing industry accounts for about one-quarter of the country's total production and employs about 20 per cent of its labour force. Thus, compared with other major Third World oil producers such as Saudi

Arabia, the Islamic Republic of Iran, Venezuela, Indonesia and Nigeria, Mexico has a sophisticated economy with a relatively well-developed industrial structure. The level of Mexican industrial development may be compared with that of India, which is counted among the most advanced industrial economies of the Third World. Manufacturing in India accounts for less than 20 per cent of total output and employs about 10 per cent of its labour force. India, however, possesses a more developed capital goods industry than Mexico: the former produces and exports a wide range of advanced industrial products, eg railway locomotives, heavy electrical machinery and defence equipment. To put matters in further perspective, both India and Mexico today produce more steel and probably have a higher level of overall industrial development than Japan did in the early 1950s at the start of that country's spectacular post-war industrialisation drive.

As for the dimensions of the employment problem in Mexico, Mexico has a population of over 70 million, which grew at a rate of 3.3 per cent per annum during the 1960s and at a slightly lower rate in the 1970s. Despite some recent fall in the rate of population increase (3.0 per cent per annum during 1975–81, compared with 3.3 per cent earlier), the labour force is expected to expand at a rate of 3.5 per cent per annum because of previous population growth. The remunerated, economically active population comprises less than 25 per cent of the total (Brailovsky, 1981). In 1978, 33 per cent of Mexico's economically active population was engaged in agriculture, 1.5 per cent in mining and oil, 26 per cent in the secondary sector (including manufacturing) and the remaining 40 per cent in the tertiary sector. The overall long-term productivity growth rate of the economy as a whole between 1950 and 1973 was about 3.5 per cent per annum. Given the anticipated growth of labour supply, this suggests that GDP needs to grow at a rate of 7–8 per cent per annum simply to maintain the present degree of unemployment and underemployment. Just to provide employment for new entrants to the labour force is therefore a major objective and an enormous undertaking for all Mexican governments.

The relevant features of the institutional framework of the Mexican economy for purposes of policy analysis may be summarised as follows. First, it is a mixed, relatively open economy where imports of goods and non-factor services constituted about 15 per cent of GDP in 1980. Mexico had long operated a system of import controls based on quotas and licences. This system was greatly liberalised during the period 1977–80. Secondly, it was among the few Third World countries which until 1982 had maintained a more or less free convertibility of its currency. Mexican citizens were able to hold (subject to some restrictions) United States dollar deposits both in Mexican and in foreign banks. Thirdly, the country's political system had an important place for trade unions; the dominant political party, PRI, is officially a coalition of its three sections, the peasantry, the middle class and the working class. This means that, at least in the modern industrial sector, wage bargaining is done on a centralised basis.

8.3   OIL AND ALTERNATIVE ECONOMIC STRATEGIES

The presidency of José Lopez Portillo started in December 1976 in the midst of a major economic and currency crisis, financial instability and an IMF stabilisation programme. However, these negative aspects were very soon to be far outweighed by the international recognition of Mexico's enormous oil reserves. The availability of these reserves, among the world's largest, totally transformed the prospects of the economy. The central policy issue was how to translate this oil into economic development, to ensure that the oil added to total national wealth on a long-term basis rather than substituting for the existing sources of wealth, as had been the experience of many oil-producing countries, both rich and poor.[1]

For this purpose Mexico was essentially presented with two kinds of long-term strategies for the development of the economy. One, which was best articulated by the World Bank (1979), but which had many influential adherents in Mexico, consisted basically of seeking closer integration of the Mexican economy with the world economy and, *inter alia*, fast development of Mexico's oil resources. More specifically, some of the major features of this policy programme were: (a) fairly rapid dismantling of import controls and opening up of the economy so that the forces of world competition might compel Mexican industry to become more efficient; (b) reliance mainly on variations in the exchange rate for whatever level of protection Mexican industry might require in the interim; (c) lowering the growth of real wages and changing labour laws, as well as adopting other measures to induce employers not to substitute capital for labour, thus increasing employment; (d) encouragement of foreign investment. This set of policy measures clearly had a certain internal logic and coherence.

However, an alternative 'nationalist' long-term strategy for Mexico, which was pressed by a section of the party and the government (notably by the Ministry of Industry), contained the following main elements: (a) in the context of a world economy which was likely to grow much more slowly than it had in the past, retaining import controls and relying on fast growth of internal demand and domestic competition to induce productive efficiency; (b) relatively slower development of hydrocarbon resources (with a strict limit on their exports), and the use of oil revenues principally for investment in domestic agriculture and industry; (c) deepening the process of import substitution, particularly in relation to capital goods industries, and encouraging exports, both by means other than exchange rate variations; (d) increasing employment essentially by faster growth of manufacturing industry. The latter would not only increase employment directly but also lead indirectly to the creation of more jobs in other sectors; it would also bring about desirable long-term changes in the structure of the economy.[2]

The analyses underlying each of these two strategies are very different. From the standpoint of economic policy, the choice between them was clearly significant. A major aim of the macro-economic policy models considered below was to quantify the effects on production and employment of these alternative long-term perspectives. However, these models were also used to consider certain short- and medium-term policy issues which came up as the Mexican economy subsequently ran into a balance of payments constraint.

8.4 PLANNING AND POLICY ANALYSIS OF THE MEXICAN MODELS

The macro-economic models of the Mexican economy which were used to explore these alternative policy options and strategies were based on the two models of the United Kingdom economy currently in operation at the Department of Applied Economics at Cambridge, namely the Cambridge Growth Project (CGP) model under the direction of Richard Stone and Terry Barker,[3] and the Cambridge Economic Policy Group (CEPG) model directed by Wynne Godley and Francis Cripps. The Industrial Model of Mexico at the Secretaria de Patrimonio y Fomento Industrial, which provided the basis of the National Industrial Plan, was a dynamic multi-sectoral model disaggregated into 45 branches of activity, and was patterned on the CGP model; the macro-economic model constructed at Centro de Investigación y Docencia Económicas (CIDE) had a similar structure to that of the CEPG model.

The methodology underlying these models is somewhat different from that of either the planning models which have normally been used in development planning in Third World countries or that of the conventional forecasting models. It may be useful to comment briefly on these differences.

Planning models have principally been concerned with the growth and allocation of real resources over some planning period.[4] For example, the models used in Indian economic planning have been mainly consistency models which are designed to fit into a framework of specified overall targets.[5] Thus, given the perspective plan for the long run (say 25 years), the short-run *targets* of national income growth, requisite aggregate investment and other macro magnitudes are specified. Then the detailed plans have been used to work out consistent dynamic input-output models for these targets.

Forecasting models, on the other hand, provide forecasts of major real and financial aggregates (eg output, employment, trade, the balance of payments, inflation, the government's financial balance) conditional on external assumptions and government policy. The priority of the forecasting objective tends to determine the structure of the model. Such models often concentrate on the short-term outlook (12 months to 24 months) and use quarterly data. The models therefore require a considerable specification of short-run dynamics. Individual equations often contain complicated distributed lags to capture short-run properties of the time-series data, although the economic content of the equations is often by contrast very simple.

The Mexican models, while being close in structure to forecasting models (and which could be used as a forecasting tool), derive more from the tradition of macro-economic planning of resources. There are, however, a number of significant differences. The major purpose of these models is to evaluate alternative policy options. All projections are therefore strictly conditional in that the outcomes depend crucially upon the policy assumptions given to the model. Whilst a forecaster is trying to obtain the most accurate forecast of what is likely to happen in the economy (which includes forecasting what policies the authorities are likely to follow), the purpose of these models is to compare the effects of alternative policies. The model projections do not necessarily have the status of forecasts.

A second but related difference is that the Mexican models concentrated on the medium- and long-term-scale (three to five years or longer). Many of the quantitatively most important effects of government policy or external shocks have their main impact beyond the period of short-run forecasts. It is particularly important when evaluating alternative strategies to consider carefully these medium-term effects. Consequently, the models used annual data which reduced the degree of short-run dynamics which needed to be modelled. Whilst these models may not be as effective in capturing the short-run timing of economic changes, they are better able to deal with medium- and longer-term properties by analysing underlying trends in the structure of the economy. Statistical forecasting models may be quite successful in forecasting changes in the economy while normal external conditions and government policies prevail, but might require the complete respecification of equations and re-estimation of parameters should these circumstances change. Since the purpose of the Mexican models was to consider policy alternatives under possibly very different conditions, it was more important that these models give a good description of the macro-economic structure of the economy and its medium- and longer-term properties.

A macro-economic model is fundamentally a device which enables the user to work out the ultimate logical implications of the user's beliefs about how an economy functions, conditional on exogenous assumptions. It is, however, essential that the maintained beliefs about how the economy operates must be consistent with the evidence of observed historical data. An important step in the development work of the models was therefore testing the robustness of the behavioural equations against time-series of economic statistics.

The most important distinguishing characteristics of these models may be described as follows. First, these are essentially Keynesian models driven by demand; these models pay particular attention to the behaviour of the external sector and to the modelling of the balance of payments, as the latter is regarded as a crucial determinant of the level and the rate of growth of demand in an open mixed economy.[6] Second, on the supply side, they incorporated the Verdoorn relationship and, in particular, the view that the rate of growth of productivity in manufacturing industry is a function of the rate of growth of production (see, further, Section 8.5 below). Third, in the modelling of the labour market, wage changes are regarded as being determined by past price changes and an *ex ante* real wage target which the workers pursue; the latter is exogenous to the models but is assumed to be influenced by past changes in real wages, growth of productivity, and wages policies of the government. Fourth, in these models, the price level is essentially determined by international prices and domestic costs. The former are the main determinant, together with official price policies, of agricultural prices. Domestic normal costs (including imports, domestically produced raw materials and labour costs) determine industrial and service prices.[7]

8.5   OIL, INDUSTRIALISATION AND EMPLOYMENT: POLICY ANALYSIS OF LONG-TERM ISSUES[8]

The economic foundation of the nationalist strategy was based on the view that Mexico could achieve a fast long-term expansion of production and employment only through rapid industrialisation of the economy. This view is supported by a systematic body of economic analysis which not only explains why manufacturing industry should expand at a faster rate than the economy as a whole during the course of economic development, but which would also assign strategic causal significance to manufacturing in raising the overall rate of growth of productivity in the economy. Very briefly,[9] first, at the simplest level, as the income elasticity of demand for manufacturing is considerably greater than that for food and for agricultural products, manufacturing can be expected to grow relatively faster. Second, following the classic work of Allyn Young (and, of course, before that, of Adam Smith and other classical economists), the economists with a structural approach to economic growth argue that manufacturing is subject to increasing returns, both in the static and, more importantly, in the dynamic sense of Kaldor. Because of these favourable demand elasticities and the dynamic economies of scale, manufacturing industry not only grows more quickly than other sectors, but its growth is normally associated with increased employment. In agriculture, on the other hand, where there is usually considerable disguised unemployment, expansion of productivity and output is normally connected with a reduction in the labour force employed. The expansion of manufacturing industry thus helps to raise the rate of growth of productivity in agriculture in two ways: (a) by absorbing redundant labour; and (b) by providing modern industrial inputs, which incidentally raises both land and labour productivity. Third, it is argued that the expansion of manufacturing industry also increases the pace of technical change and helps raise productivity growth in sectors other than agriculture.

Tables 8.1 and 8.2 provide historical evidence on the growth of output, employment and productivity for the various sectors of economic activity in Mexico during the past 25 years. These data are in broad agreement with the structuralist theses concerning long-term economic growth outlined above. The following points are worth special attention. First, as Table 8.1 shows, by 1978 agriculture accounted for less than 10 per cent of Mexico's national production, although it still employed one-third of the country's economically active population. Second, during the 1960s, Mexico had achieved a long-run rate of growth of GDP of 7 per cent per annum. Thus, the government's objective in 1977 of creating 700,000 new jobs every year for the new entrants to the labour force, which would have required an economic growth rate of 8 per cent per annum, was by no means unfeasible, particularly in view of the country's new-found oil wealth.

Third, as implied by the structuralist thesis, the results of the regression analysis of the relationships between sectoral and overall growth reported in Table 8.2 show that the long-term growth elasticity of the industrial sectors (manufacturing, construction and electricity) with respect to GDP was well above unity, and also usually much greater than that observed for other sectors. Further, compared with other sectors, there was also a much closer relationship between manufacturing and overall growth.[10] This and other evidence for Mexico accorded with Kaldor's (1967) thesis that 'the faster the overall growth, the greater is the *excess* of the rate of growth of manufacturing production over the rate of growth of the economy as a whole'.

Fourth, the data in Table 8.1 indicate the highly significant role of manufacturing in generating employment and increasing productivity. Not surprisingly, there had been relatively little growth in employment in the primary sectors; more importantly, there was hardly any relationship between the growth of output and employment in these sectors. However, unlike the primary sectors, the tertiary sectors did register substantial employment growth. But again, as in the case of primary employment, increases in employment in the services were not directly related to increased output, but were relatively autonomous. The absorption of labour into this sector appears more a response to lack of employment opportunities elsewhere than to increased demand.

In the Mexican manufacturing industry, the Verdoorn relationships

Table 8.1: Mexico: growth and composition of output, employment and productivity in the long term, by sectors of activity, 1950–78[1] (percentages)

	Average annual growth rate[2]				Composition		
	1950–60	1960–68	1968–73	1973–78	1950	1968	1978
Output	5.52	7.12	6.21	3.96	100.0	100.0	100.0
Agriculture	4.52	3.58	1.44	2.58	17.82	12.39	9.21
Mining	1.70	2.20	4.16	2.69	1.70	1.23	1.09
Oil	9.45	8.50	5.32	11.97	1.67	2.66	3.70
Manufacturing	6.02	8.98	6.91	4.37	18.79	22.61	23.83
Construction	7.34	10.02	9.91	4.49	4.18	6.14	7.48
Electricity	12.79	13.04	9.57	7.76	0.22	0.67	0.93
Transport	5.52	6.49	6.78	6.63	2.15	2.05	2.39
Commerce[5]	6.16	7.60	6.43	3.02	27.05	29.78	28.76
Other services[5]	4.81	5.59	5.82	3.17	18.97	15.81	14.93
Government	4.37	8.92	8.32	5.01	6.46	6.61	7.68
Employment[3]	2.70	2.65	2.66	na	100.00	100.00	100.00
Agriculture	1.27	0.22	0.23	na	54.85	39.39	33.06
Mining	3.24	-1.46	-1.55	na	1.05	0.80	0.59
Oil	5.63	7.20	3.18	6.93	0.37	0.70	0.76
Manufacturing	4.71	5.18	3.34	2.79	12.82	18.90	19.60
Construction	6.12	3.94	4.56	2.99	3.01	4.61	5.39
Electricity	5.08	4.38	5.48	6.47	0.28	0.40	0.47
Transport	3.92	2.97	2.87	4.88	2.63	3.04	3.10
Commerce[5]	2.84	3.49	3.32	5.10	9.79	10.60	10.77
Other services[5]	4.47	4.71	4.76	4.43	10.92	15.20	17.11
Government	3.80	6.15	7.00	5.46	4.27	6.37	9.15

Table 8.1: Continued

	Average annual growth rate[2]				Composition		
	1950-60	1960-68	1968-73	1973-78	1950	1968	1978
Productivity[4]	2.75	4.35	3.46	n.a.	100.00	100.00	100.00
Agriculture	3.21	3.35	1.20	n.a.	32.30	31.46	27.58
Mining	-1.76	4.07	5.80	n.a.	256.78	160.60	191.70
Oil	3.62	1.21	2.07	4.71	445.03	379.31	374.62
Manufacturing	1.25	3.61	3.46	1.54	146.61	119.68	118.19
Construction	1.16	5.35	5.12	1.85	138.86	133.13	141.75
Electricity	7.33	8.30	3.87	1.21	79.78	166.19	171.88
Transport	1.53	3.42	3.80	1.67	81.55	67.41	72.12
Commerce[5]	3.22	3.97	3.02	-1.98	276.23	281.01	280.15
Other services[5]	0.33	0.83	1.01	-1.21	173.62	104.01	89.81
Government	0.55	2.27	1.23	-0.43	151.30	103.77	80.47

1. The years selected for the different periods correspond to peak points of the economic cycle.
2. Growth rates of output are calculated on 1975 prices.
3. Employment is defined as the remunerated economically active population.
4. The productivity index is calculated by dividing output per worker employed in each activity by the corresponding national average.
5. Commerce and services include workers in unclassified activities.
Source: Secretaría de Patrimonio y Fomento Industrial, Dirección General de Política e Inversiones Industriales: *Estadísticas Anuales de Producción por Rama da Actividad Económica, 1980*; and Secretaría de Programación y Presupuesto, Coordinación General del Sistema Nacional de Información: *Encuesta Continua de Mano de Obra*, several quarters.
(Reproduced from Brailovsky (1981))

Table 8.2: Behaviour of sectoral output, 1960–78: regression results

	c	$\bar{q}$	$(q-\bar{q})$	R^2	ser	DW
Output (q_i)						
Agriculture	0.0211	0.1311	0.7713	.32	.020	1.72
	(1.18)	(0.44)	(2.74)			
Mining	0.0175	0.1832	0.2337	.01	.043	2.46
	(0.46)	(0.29)	(0.40)			
Oil	0.1123	−0.5101	0.3632	.09	.038	2.18
	(3.37)	(0.91)	(0.70)			
Manufacturing	−0.0103	1.3530	1.1780	.81	.014	1.87
	(0.82)	(6.44)	(6.01)			
Construction	0.0147	1.7240	2.7857	.58	.047	2.20
	(0.35)	(2.47)	(4.28)			
Electricity	0.0105	1.5426	0.6936	.34	.038	1.99
	(0.31)	(2.72)	(1.31)			
Transport	0.0345	0.4797	0.7612	.29	.024	1.53
	(1.64)	(1.35)	(2.30)			
Commerce	−0.0219	1.4095	1.2197	.95	.007	1.98
	(3.62)	(13.85)	(12.85)			
Other services	0.0071	0.7331	0.1044	.56	.011	2.08
	(0.73)	(4.47)	(0.68)			

Notation: q_i = growth rate of output sector; c = constant; q = growth rate of total gross domestic product; $\bar{q}$ = long term growth rate of total gross domestic product; R = correlation coefficient; ser = standard error or the regression; DW = Durbin Watson statistic.

Notes: (1) The coefficients of $\bar{q}$ represent long-term elasticities of the different sectoral outputs in relation to total gross domestic product; the coefficients of $(q-\bar{q})$ short-term elasticities. (2) The growth rates are calculated as first differences of the natural logarithms of the variables. (3) Calculations of the trend values of gross domestic product are based on moving regressions over a 10-year period; $\bar{q}$ is the first difference of the natural logarithm of this variable. (4) The t statistics of the coefficients are in parentheses. (5) Gross domestic product excludes government.

Sources: As for Table 8.1.

(Reproduced from Brailovsky (1981))

between output, employment and productivity growth were seen to hold. On the basis of the annual data for the period 1960–75, Brailovskey (1981) estimated the following regression equations with respect to these variables:

$$e = .012 + .410\,q + 0.286\,(q - \bar{q})$$
$$(0.83)\quad(2.17)\quad\quad(1.64)$$

$$R^2 = 0.35;\ DW = 2.02$$

$$P = -.012 + .581\,q + 0.714\,(q - \bar{q})$$
$$(0.83)\quad(3.00)\quad\quad(4.09)$$

$$R^2 = 0.66;\ DW = 2.02$$

where: *e* is employment growth;
     q is output growth;
     p is productivity growth;
     $\bar{q}$ is the average growth of output.

(The parentheses give the *t* values of the coefficients.)

Thus, in Mexican manufacturing industry, a 1 per cent increase in production was associated in the long term with a 0.4 per cent increase in employment and a 0.6 per cent increase in productivity. These coefficients are broadly comparable with those for other semi-industrial countries. The United Nations Industrial Development Organisation (UNIDO) (1979) reported the following results from an inter-country *cross-section* analysis of the relationship between growth of manufacturing output, employment and productivity covering nine countries (Argentina, Brazil, Chile, Colombia, Ecuador, India, Mexico, the Republic of Korea and Venezuela) for the period 1968–74.

$$e = .91 + .48\, q$$
$$(4.77)$$

$$R^2 = 0.76$$

$$P = .66 + .47\, q$$
$$(4.86)$$

$$R^2 = 0.77$$

In addition to these long-run analyses of economic growth and economic structure, the proponents of the nationalist economic strategy at the Patrimonio (the Ministry of Industry) had a rather different interpretation than those of orthodox economists of the past experience of import substitution and of the 'efficiency' of the Mexican manufacturing industry. On the basis of a detailed disaggregated study of manufacturing over the last two decades, the Patrimonio economists believed that Mexican industry was characterised by a pattern of cumulative causation, in which the expansion of domestic demand leads to significant reductions in the import coefficient, and over time to a rise in exports. The growth of industrial output, productivity and even exports was regarded as being satisfactory by relevant comparative international standards. Thus, as Table 8.3 shows, in terms of volume, Mexican industrial exports expanded at a faster rate than the world trade in manufactures throughout the period 1965–78. Further, except between 1965 and 1969, the rate of growth of Mexican manufacturing exports was greater than that of manufactured imports into the United States, a country which accounts for nearly two-thirds of total Mexican exports. Equally significantly, Mexico's manufactured exports over this 15-year period increased at much the same rate as those of Japan or of

Table 8.3: Growth of GDP and of imports and exports of manufacturers, international comparisons, 1965–78 (average annual growth rates, in percentages, based on 1975 prices)

	1965–69	1969–73	1973–78
Gross national product			
World-wide[1]	5.3	4.9	3.1
Industrial economies	4.7	4.8	2.7
United States	4.0	3.5	2.8
Japan	11.9	9.7	4.4
Developing economies[2]	5.1	5.4	5.4
Mexico[3]	6.7	6.3	4.7[5]
Manufactured imports[4]			
World-wide	11.0	10.0	6.0
Industrial economies	12.2	10.4	4.1
United States	17.7	7.7	5.5
Japan	27.8	17.0	0
Developing economies[2]	8.7	8.1	6.4
Mexico	5.2	7.8	9.4[5]
Manufactured exports[4]			
World-wide	11.0	10.0	6.0
Industrial economies	11.0	9.8	5.8
United States	9.2	4.3	4.3
Japan	16.0	13.4	10.5
Developing economies[2]	17.5	15.2	8.6
Mexico:			
Excluding in-bond industries	16.9	10.9	8.6
Including in-bond industries	n.a.	19.8	7.9

1. Excluding centrally planned economies.
2. Excluding oil-exporting countries; includes exports of in-bond industries.
3. Gross domestic product.
4. Excluding trade in food, beverages and tobacco.
5. Period 1973–79.
Sources: Cambridge Economic Policy Review (University of Cambridge, Department of Applied Economics), Apr. 1979 (based on United Nations: *Yearbook of International Trade Statistics* and *Yearbook of National Accounts Statistics*); and Secretaría de Patrimonio y Fomento Industrial, Dirección General de Política e Inversiones Industriales; *Banco de datos del Modelo Industrial de México, 1980*; reproduced from Brailovsky (1981).

other developing countries. The Patrimonio economists, therefore, viewed the past industrial record as containing adequate promise that Mexican industry was in principle capable of carrying out the central task of the long-term structural transformation of the economy.

The foregoing conceptions and analyses of Mexico's historical experience provided the basis for a quantitative evaluation of the alternative long-run development strategies following the availability of oil resources. These exercises were carried out at the Ministry of Industry with the help of the dynamic multi-sector industrial model referred to earlier and a smaller, more abbreviated model developed specifically for this purpose.[11]

Two main long-term strategies whose chief elements are outlined in Section 8.3 were considered: (a) an 'oil strategy' based on fast development of Mexico's oil resources and a closer integration of the Mexican economy with the world economy; (b) a nationalist strategy based on protection, slow development of hydrocarbon resources and the use of oil revenues for investment in agriculture and industry, labelled as the 'agricultural and industrial strategy'. Simulations were done on the basis of common assumptions with respect to the growth of world trade, the growth of the United States economy and the world price of oil which at that time (ie in the aftermath of the massive 1979 price increase) was assumed to rise in real terms at an annual rate of between 5 and 7 per cent until the year 2000. In addition, a common target of 8 per cent growth of GDP (the government's objective to meet its employment goals), as well as a similar balance of payments target, were imposed on both strategies. The basic questions which were addressed were: How long will it take for the oil reserves to be 'exhausted', ie, reach a critical level of 15 times the annual rate of extraction?[12] What will be the structural characteristics of the economy and its potential for future growth at that time?

The answers to these questions are contained in Table 8.4. Assuming the Mexican oil reserves[13] to be 50 or 75 thousand million barrels, the table shows that, under the oil strategy, the reserves will be 'exhausted' by 1986 or 1987, whilst under the agricultural and industrial strategy, this situation will not be reached until 1992 (reserves of 50 thousand million barrels) or the year 2000 (reserves of 75 thousand million barrels). More importantly, under the oil strategy, the structure of the economy would become warped and unfavourable for future growth: by 1981, oil would constitute 75 per cent of total exports.

There are basically three reasons why, despite these huge reserves, the critical level of oil production is reached so soon under the oil strategy. First is the sheer size of the Mexican economy compared with, say, Saudi Arabia, where similar reserves could last 50 or 100 years. Second, there is the assumed rate of growth of GDP of 8 per cent per annum. Third, the removal of protection and integration with the world economy substantially raises the import coefficient (the rate of growth of imports for a given percentage growth of GDP). This coefficient is assumed to have a value of 2.5 in the initial stages when the protection is removed,[14] which gradually falls over time. In the agricultural and industrial strategy, a high degree of protection limits the import coefficient to its historical level observed between 1960 and 1970.[15]

The full implications of the two strategies for long-term growth of output and employment are brought out when, after the oil production has peaked, the growth rate is allowed to vary subject to a common balance of payments target (assumed to be a current account deficit of 5 per cent of GDP). The results are reported in Tables 8.5 to 8.7. The simulations show that only under the agricultural and industrial strategy

Table 8.4: Structure of the current account of the balance of payments under alternative strategies of economic policy, in peak years of hydrocarbon production (percentages of total exports)

	1980	Oil strategy		Industrial and agricultural strategy	
		(50 MMB) 1986	(75 MMB) 1987	(50 MMB) 1992	(75 MMB) 2000
Exports	*100.0*	*100.0*	*100.0*	*100.0*	*100.0*
Agriculture	6.6	2.1	1.9	2.7	1.2
Mining	0	0.9	0.8	1.8	1.3
Hydrocarbons	47.9	74.5	75.0	29.3	0
Manufacturing	16.7	10.9	11.1	46.0	84.0
Non-factoral services	26.8	11.6	11.2	20.2	13.5
Imports	*106.8*	*102.9*	*102.7*	*105.3*	*104.0*
Agriculture	13.7	15.2	14.3	21.6	14.7
Mining	4.0	3.4	3.3	7.6	7.3
Hydrocarbons	2.0	1.2	1.2	2.7	36.4
Manufacturing	57.1	69.8	71.4	51.7	30.3
Non-factoral services	13.4	6.8	6.4	11.2	8.3
Factor payments	16.6	6.5	6.1	10.5	7.0

Notes: i. The years selected are those in which hydrocarbon reserves reach their critical level, or the technical limit of their annual extraction.
ii. Agricultural imports and exports include livestock and fisheries and semi-manufactures of food, beverages and tobacco.
iii. Manufacturing exports include value-added of the in-bond industry.
iv. Trade margins have been distributed among the different exports by branches of origin.
MMB = thousand millions (10^9) of barrels of crude-oil equivalent.
Source: Brailovsky (1981).

Table 8.5: Per capita product and accumulated product under alternative strategies of economic policy, 1980–2000[1] (United States dollars at 1980 prices)

		Per capita product		Accumulated product
		1980 (thousands)	2000	1980–2000 (thousand millions)
Oil strategy				
i. Reserves:	50 MMB	2,202	2,161	4,692
ii. Reserves:	75 MMB	2,202	2,529	5,241
iii. Reserves:	200 MMB	2,202	3,207	5,785
Industrial and agricultural strategy				
i. Reserves:	50 MMB	2,202	4,653	6,965
ii. Reserves:	75 MMB	2,202	5,987	7,618
iii. Reserves:	200 MMB	2,202	7,551	9,385

1. Assumes a population of 70 million in 1980 and 120 million in the year 2000.
MMB = thousand millions (10^9) of barrels of crude-oil equivalent.
Source: Brailovsky (1981).

Table 8.6: Employment growth under alternative strategies of economic policy, 1980–2000 (remunerated economically active population)

		1980	2000	1980–2000 (average annual growth rate in %)
		(millions of persons)		
Oil strategy				
i. Reserves:	50 MMB	15.4	20.0	1.3
ii. Reserves:	75 MMB	15.4	22.1	1.8
iii. Reserves:	200 MMB	15.4	25.0	2.5
Industrial and agricultural strategy				
i. Reserves:	50 MMB	15.4	28.2	3.1
ii. Reserves:	75 MMB	15.4	31.7	3.6
iii. Reserves:	200 MMB	15.4	35.9	4.2

MMB = thousand millions (10^9) of barrels of crude-oil equivalent.
Source: Brailovsky (1981).

Table 8.7: Structure of gross domestic product and of employment by branches of origin under alternative strategies of economic policy, 1980–2000 (percentages)

	1980	2000 Oil strategy		Industrial and agricultural strategy	
		50 MMB	75 MMB	50 MMB	75 MMB
Gross domestic product	100.0	100.0	100.0	100.0	100.0
Agriculture	6.9	8.0	6.2	4.5	3.5
Mining	1.2	1.9	1.6	1.2	0.9
Hydrocarbons	7.2	4.4	6.5	2.3	3.4
Manufacturing	21.2	24.7	19.7	34.4	33.2
Construction	8.4	11.0	11.9	15.3	16.8
Electricity	0.9	1.1	1.1	1.2	1.2
Services	54.1	48.9	53.0	41.1	41.0
Remunerated economically active	100.0	100.0	100.0	100.0	100.0
Agriculture	31.2	25.1	22.7	18.2	16.1
Mining	0.5	0.3	0.3	0.2	0.2
Hydrocarbons	0.8	0.6	0.7	0.5	0.5
Manufacturing	20.6	22.4	19.3	31.3	31.6
Construction	6.2	8.2	8.9	12.5	14.0
Electricity	0.6	0.6	0.6	0.7	0.7
Services	40.1	42.7	47.4	36.6	36.9

Note: To make these figures comparable with those of Table 1, manufacturing includes, and agriculture excludes, the processing of food, beverages and tobacco.
MMB = thousand millions (10^9) of barrels of crude-oil equivalent.
Source: Brailovsky (1981).

can employment expand at a rate adequate to absorb the new entrants to the labour force.[16] Under an oil strategy, even assuming the reserves to be a colossal 200 thousand million barrels, the long-term rate of growth of employment falls far short of the projected growth of labour force.[17]

The reasons for the superior performance of the agricultural and industrial strategy in these projections are: (a) protection, the consequent growth of internal market and the dynamic economies it generates in the manufacturing sector; (b) high rates of investment in agriculture and industry.[18] The latter have adverse short-term effects on the growth of consumption (which would need to be ameliorated by progressive taxation policies), but in the medium- to long-term, consumption, production and employment would all increase at a much faster rate.

In principle, the favourable effects of protection may also be obtained for the oil strategy by a policy of progressive and continuing devaluations of the currency. This, however, was seen to be an unviable option for two main reasons. First, it would generate unacceptable rates of inflation since the size of currency changes required would be rather large to meet the balance of payments constraint (see further discussion in Section 8.6). Second, under conditions of relative free convertibility of currency, such devaluations might cause financial instability and currency upheavals on the foreign exchange markets.

8.6   THE MODELLING OF THE IMPENDING ECONOMIC CRISIS AND OF THE SHORT- AND MEDIUM-TERM POLICY ISSUES

In the event, neither strategy was fully implemented. The economists at the Patrimonio had two significant victories: one real and the other symbolic. The real gain was that President Lopez Portillo in his State of the Union address to the Congress on 1 September 1980 fixed a limit on oil exports. He enunciated the government's oil policy which envisaged that sufficient oil would be produced to meet the needs for the domestic economy, but that oil exports should not exceed 1.5 million barrels per day. The symbolic victory was that the government accepted the Patrimonio's advice and did not join the General Agreement on Tariffs and Trade (GATT), a proposal which was being strongly advocated by most other economic ministries. Although this implied a policy of less close integration with the world economy, the government nevertheless continued vigorously with its policy of import liberalisation on which it had embarked almost from the beginning of the administration.

Tables 8.8 and 8.9 provide evidence on the actual behaviour of the economy: both the real (Table 8.8) and the financial economy (Table 8.9). As can be seen, between 1977 and 1981, the Mexican economy achieved an extraordinary rate of expansion of 8 per cent per annum at

Table 8.8: The performance of the real economy: Mexico, 1976–81 and 1971–76

	1976	1977	1978	1979	1980	1981	Average 1976-81	Average 1971-76
Growth of GDP[1] (% pa)	4.2	3.4	8.2	9.2	8.3	8.1	7.4	6.5
Growth of non-oil GDP[1] (% pa)	4.2	3.3	8.0	9.0	7.9	7.9	7.2	6.5
Growth of employment[2] (thousands)	154	285	416	503	622	627	491	na
Memorandum: growth of occupations[3] (thousands)							811[4]	440

1. At constant prices.
2. Refers to economically active population.
3. This figure is for the number of persons employed, but involves double counting of persons with multiple occupations, and is therefore higher than the figure for economically active population.
4. Average for 1976–80.
Sources: *Sistema de Cuentas Nacionales de México* (SPP, SEPAFIN Industrial Model).

Table 8.9: The financial performance of the Mexican economy, 1976–81 (all figures in thousands of millions of US$ except where otherwise stated)

	1976	1977	1978	1979	1980	1981
% change in GDP deflator	19.6	30.4	16.7	20.3	28.7	26.3
Balance of payments current account	– 3.06	– 1.62	– 2.69	– 4.85	– 6.76	– 11.7
(a) Balance of goods and non-factor services	– 1.19	0.36	– 0.31	– 1.54	– 1.80	– 4.1
(b) Balance of factor payments	– 1.87	– 1.98	– 2.38	– 3.31	– 4.95	– 7.6
Memorandum						
Interest on external public debt	1.26	1.54	2.02	2.88	3.95	5.5
Oil exports	0.54	1.02	1.79	3.86	10.30	14.4
Merchandise imports	5.42	5.15	7.37	11.38	17.17	23.1
% change unit value in US$ of manufactured imports	7.4	8.0	10.5	12.7	15.2	17.0
% change in unit value in US$ of oil exports	8.4	6.7	0.5	47.2	55.2	8.3

1. Provincial figures.
2. Figure is for all imports.
Sources: Sistema de Cuentas Nacionales de Méxcio, SPP, Informe Annual de Banco de México, various years.

a time of significant deceleration in world economic growth. Instead of increasing unemployment which most industrial countries experienced during this period, in Mexico, on average, at a conservative estimate, half a million new jobs were being created each year. Towards the end of the period, revised figures indicate that the government's employment target was more than being met.[19]

However, as Table 8.9 shows, the health of the financial economy was not so robust. After a sharp fall from its 1977 level of 30 per cent, the rate of inflation (measured by the GDP deflator) in 1980 was again 28.7 per cent cent and in 1981 26.3 per cent. But the most important indicator of the deterioration of the financial economy was the continuing increase in the current account deficit which by 1981 had reached a colossal figure of US $11.7 thousand million. This was despite the nearly 30-fold increase in oil revenues, which rose from US $0.5 thousand million in 1976 to US $14.4 thousand million in 1981. This disjuncture between the financial and the real economy was directly responsible for the economic collapse which followed in 1982.

The economic crisis was not unexpected. It was foreseen and predicted by economists at the Patrimonio as well as by orthodox economists much earlier. There were, however, very different analyses about the nature of the crises and how it could be overcome. The orthodox view was that the economy was overheated and that this was responsible for the inflation – and that since the Mexican rate of inflation was greater than the United States rate, the *peso* was overvalued and hence the consequent payment deficits. Thus, the conventional remedy was proposed: devaluation and deflation.

The Patrimonio economists had a rather different view of the causes of inflation and the current account deficit. Essentially they explained inflation in terms of the observed increases in costs, including those due to the government's own introduction of the value added tax, the increase in interest rates and wages. Nevertheless, they thought that the economic situation was extremely serious and argued that the economy was, indeed, overheated but in a very specific and clear sense: 'Given current trade policies, the overall rate of expansion of the economy is excessive in that it leads to a rate of increase of manufactured imports which cannot be sustained in the medium term' (Eatwell and Singh 1981). They noted the extraordinary increase in imports (See Table 8.9), as well as in the propensity to import.

The crude elasticity of imports with respect to manufacturing production had increased from its historical level of slightly less than unity observed during 1960–70 to about 2.5 in 1978, 4.5 in 1979 and nearly 6 in 1980. They, therefore, argued that the growth of output at a rate of 8 per cent per annum (the government objective to meet its employment goals) was still sustainable provided there was a strict control on imports. They also suggested a set of measures to contain inflation, the most important being an incomes policy.

To evaluate the *short- and medium-term* effects[20] of these alternative economic policies on inflation, exchange rate, production and employment, simulations were carried out on CIDE's macro-economic model of the Mexican economy. The following main policies were analysed:

1. a policy of deflation and a reduction in the rate of economic expansion;
2. a policy of devaluation and slower economic growth;
3. a policy of selective direct control on manufactured imports and maintenance of the growth rate of GDP at 8 per cent per annum.

The results of the simulations are reported in Tables 8.10, 8.11 and 8.12. In order to make the results of the alternative policies comparable, a common objective was set in each case: a reduction of the current account deficit from a level of about 4 per cent of GDP in 1980 to 3.5 per cent in 1981, 3 per cent in 1982 and 2.5 per cent from then onwards. In addition, certain assumptions with respect to Mexico's oil exports and inflation, and growth in the United States economy (Mexico's main trading partner), are common to all simulations.[21] In order to facilitate the interpretation of the results of the simulations, the econometric equations in the model imply the following principal coefficients for price (e_p) and income elasticities (e_q) for imports and exports.

	e_p	e_q
Industrial imports	− 0.85	2.9
Imports of services	− 0.72	1.56
Industrial exports	− 1.13	2.36
Exports of services	− 0.68	2.17[1]

1. An annual rate of growth of foreign demand of 3 per cent is assumed.

Source: Eatwell and Singh (1981).

Table 8.10: Simulations on the CIDE Model I Mexican Economy: 1981–90 (required output adjustment to meet current-account target; fixed exchange rate)

	1981	1982	1983	1985	1990
1. Consumer prices (% increase over previous year)	22.6	19.04	16.5	13.8	12.0
2. Rate of growth of real GDP (% pa)	6.7	5.6	− 1.5	2.1	2.3
3. Trade balance (US$ thousand million)					
(a) Agriculture	− 0.79	− 0.99	0.304	2.135	16.74
(b) Industry	− 20.14	− 28.6	− 31.4	− 45.9	− 112.4
(c) Oil	18.56	26.08	29.73	38.64	74.05
(d) Goods and services	− 1.1	− 2.38	− 0.947	− 1.08	− 5.99
(e) Current account	− 7.3	7.6	− 7.7	− 11.2	− 29.04
4. Exchange rate (*pesos* per US$)	22.95	22.95	22.95	22.95	22.95

Source: Eatwell and Singh (1981).

The e_p coefficients are applied to the *relative*, proportional variation between the respective domestic and foreign prices. The e_q imports coefficients are related to proportional changes in the Mexican GDP, while the e_q exports coefficients are associated with the corresponding foreign-demand indicator. It is important to point out that the income elasticity for industrial imports that was employed in the simulations was lower than the crude average elasticity registered during the previous three years (which was approximately 3.75).

Table 8.10 reports the results of the simulations[22] for the policy of deflation, ie the only instrument of adjustment used here to maintain the trade deficit within limits is variations in the rate of growth of output.[23] The nominal exchange rate is assumed to remain at the level reported for 1980. The results of a policy of devaluation together with a reduction in GDP growth are reported in Table 8.11. A 7 per cent annual rate of growth of production is assumed for 1981, and a 6 per

Table 8.11: Simulations on the CIDE Model II Mexican Economy: 1981–90 (required output and exchange-rate adjustment to meet current-account targets)

	1981	1982	1983	1985	1990
1. Consumer prices (% increase over previous year)	24.3	24.1	38.4	69.2	318.3
2. Rate of growth of real GDP at constant prices (% pa)	7.0	6.0	6.0	6.0	6.0
3. Trade balance (US$ thousand million)					
(a) Agriculture	− 0.83	− 1.12	− 1.48	− 2.46	− 4.96
(b) Industry	− 18.4	− 27.34	27.3	− 37.26	− 58.8
(c) Oil					
(d) Goods and services		Same as in simulation I			
(e) Current account					
4. Exchange rate	24.6	26.8	39.2	101.8	1,539.0

Source: Eatwell and Singh (1981).

Table 8.12: Simulations on the CIDE Model III Mexican Economy: 1981–90 (required adjustment by direct control of manufactured imports to meet current-account target; fixed exchange rate and growth rate of output)

	1981	1982	1983	1985	1990
1. Consumer prices (% increase over previous year)	21.0	17.7	15.4	12.9	11.3
2. Rate of growth of real GDP (% pa)	8.0	8.0	8.0	8.0	8.0
3. Trade balance (US$ thousand million)					
(a) Agriculture	−	Same as in simulation I			
(b) Industry	− 19.56	− 25.04	− 26.07	− 31.6	− 40.3
(c) Oil	−				
(d) Goods and services	−	Same as in simulation I			
(e) Current account	−				
4. Exchange rate	22.95	22.95	22.95	22.95	22.95
5. Rate of growth of volume of manufactured imports	26.0	11.0	0.0	− 2.0	− 2.0

Source: Eatwell and Singh (1981).

cent rate from 1982 onward. Given this assumption, the rest of the adjustment necessary for maintaining the balance of payments deficit within bounds is carried out by means of variation in the exchange rate. Since this scenario leads to a rapid drop in the value of the *peso* in relation to the dollar, as well as to an explosive rate of inflation, the projections are not extended to 1990 as in the previous case, but only to 1988.

Table 8.12 simulates the behaviour of the economy under a policy of direct and selective controls on manufactured imports. The adjustment in this simulation is carried out by means of the application of these controls whilst maintaining the rate of growth of GDP at 8 per cent per annum, throughout the entire period and without modifying the nominal exchange rate.[24] In order to satisfy the balance of payments restriction, imports would have to grow in real terms at the rates indicated in the last line of the table. The average of these rates is 12 per cent per year during the period 1980–83, becoming negative (at approximately – 2 per cent per annum) thereafter.

In summary,[25] the simulations of alternative economic policies in Tables 8.10–8.12 indicated that a policy of deflation alone to achieve the balance of payments target would lead to an appreciable reduction in the rate of economic expansion in the short term, and an extremely slow rate of GDP growth (about 2 per cent per annum) in the medium- and longer-terms (despite the contribution of oil). The effects on employment would be severe: instead of creating 800,000 new jobs each year to meet the government's employment target, fewer than 200,000 such jobs would be created. This policy was, however, compatible with relative price stability as it did not involve currency depreciation. Devaluation, coupled with some slowdown in economic expansion, yielded a relatively much higher rate of economic growth in the medium- and long-terms, but this was achieved at the heavy cost of hyper-inflation. On the other hand, a policy of import controls which limited the rate of growth of manufactured imports to 12 per cent up to 1983, and sought a moderate reduction in their levels subsequently, was seen to be not only compatible with a rate of economic growth of 8 per cent, but also exchange rate and (relative) price stability. This policy, if feasible on other grounds, was therefore superior on all counts to the orthodox policies examined here.

An important issue was whether, even if it were conceded that, from the demand side, a high rate of economic expansion was compatible with a balance of payments target by means of import controls, such controls would lead to a reduction in the rate of growth of GDP from the supply side, ie whether there would be supply-side bottlenecks to reduce production. A detailed analysis by the Patrimonio economists showed that the kinds of controls which were being proposed were compatible with economic expansion at the rate envisaged.[26] Significantly, the most recent evidence from Mexico points in the same direction. Reports indicate that the industrial economy is coping with the catastrophic fall in imports which has occurred in Mexico in 1983 far better than had been anticipated.[27]

Finally, as is obvious, the specific results of the alternative economic policies would be quite different if assumptions other than those mentioned earlier were made with respect to the projected rate of growth of the United States economy or its rate of inflation, or the rate of growth of agricultural production in Mexico, and so on. However, the essential point is that within the plausible limits of alternative assumptions that rankings of the three main policies of import controls, devaluation and deflation with respect to output, employment and inflation are unlikely to change.[28]

8.7   CONCLUSION

No attempt will be made to summarise the chapter here, but in conclusion we briefly note what we regard as the most important successes and failures of the Mexican macro-economic policy models. In our view, their main success was in articulating and quantifying an alternative approach to economic policy to that which traditionally prevailed in Mexican economic circles. Economic policy in Mexico had hitherto been dominated by the Treasury and the Central Bank where orthodoxy reigned supreme.[29] With the help of these macro-economic models, the Patrimonio economists were able to put forward well worked out, consistent radical alternatives with respect to short-, medium- and long-term policies which could not simply be ignored. On the contrary, even those who disagreed with these analyses felt obligated to spell out their reasons with care and greater clarity. We believe it would not be unfair to claim that these models, and the analyses which they gave rise to, helped change fundamentally the terms of the economic policy debate in Mexico. As Kornai (1977) rightly points out, for a country to carry out successful economic planning, the importance of such public policy debate cannot be exaggerated.[30]

At a more technical level, the models helped in anticipating and analysing the nature of the impending economic crisis. At that level, their main weakness was their inadequate treatment of the capital account of the balance of payments and any systematic analysis of the nature and size of the capital flight which may occur in a crisis. Other than the huge increase in imports, the capital flight towards the second half of 1981 and in 1982 played a highly significant role in precipitating the crises. However, for well-known reasons, such extraordinary events are difficult to model in detail.

NOTES

1. See Kaldor (1981).
2. The best analysis of this strategy is contained in Brailovsky (1981) and in the *National Industrial Plan*, produced by the Secretaría de Patrimonio y Fomento Industrial. For a critical general analysis of the World Bank strategy, see Singh (1981).
3. See Chapter 2.
4. For a comprehensive review, see Blitzer, Clark and Taylor (1977).
5. For a survey of these models, see Bhagwati and Chakravarti (1969) and Rudra (1975).

6. This does not mean that the supply side was neglected. The effects of increasing investment and of industrial policies on supply, and the dynamic feedback effects on productivity and international competitiveness, are integral parts of these models.

7. A full description and details of the econometric equations of the *CIDE* model may be obtained from the Centro de Investigación y Docencia Ecónomicas. For a fuller account of the multi-sectoral Industrial Model of Mexico, see the *National Industrial Plan* for an abbreviated version of this model, which was used in some of the simulations outlined in the next section, see the appendix to Brailovsky (1981).

8. In this section, I have drawn extensively on the analysis of Brailovsky (1981).

9. This must necessarily be a brief outline of a vast subject. See, further, Singh (1981a) and the references to the literature cited therein.

10. As Table 8.2 shows, commerce is an exception to this. In the structuralist argument, there are, however, special factors with respect to commerce which make the growth of this sector a function of manufacturing growth. For a detailed analysis, see Brailovsky (1981). See also Cripps and Tarling (1973).

11. For a description of the former, see the *National Industrial Plan*; the latter is described fully in an appendix to Brailovsky (1981).

12. It should be noted that the oil reserves in the following projections are never completely exhausted. Following the oil industry practice, they are assumed to be 'exhausted' or reach a critical level when they are less than 15 times the amount of annual extraction. This implies a policy decision to have available at any moment, for national security or other considerations, an adequate relative volume of hydrocarbons. See, further, Brailovsky (1981).

13. For a detailed analysis of Mexico's 'proven', 'probable' and 'potential' reserves in 1980, see Brailovsky (1981).

14. This is by no means an unreasonable figure in view of the actual recent experience of Mexico. See further Section 8.6 below.

15. In the initial stages, a higher value is assumed to accommodate higher rates of investment.

16. The long-term growth of employment in each sector in this model is determined by Verdoorn-type relationships described earlier, ie it depends on an autonomous factor and the increases in production.

17. It will be recalled from Section 8.2 that on account of demographic considerations the Mexican labour force is projected to grow at a rate of 3.5 per cent per annum over the period 1980–2000. Table 8.6 shows that under the oil strategy, even with oil reserves of 200 thousand million barrels, the rate of growth of employment is only 2.5 per cent per annum.

18. Investment as a proportion of GDP is initially assumed to increase by four percentage points. See Brailovsky (1981).

19. The government's minimal employment goal was to provide jobs for at least the new entrants to the labour force, ie that employment should grow at a rate of 3.5 per cent per annum.

20. This is in contrast to the analysis of Section 8.5 where the alternative *long-term* development strategies are considered.

21. For full details, see Eatwell and Singh (1981).

22. To clarify further the purpose of these simulations, the essential objective to be met in case of each of the three strategies examined here is a balance of payments target as described above. In the case of the strategy of deflation, the only instrument for achieving this objective is a variation in the rate of growth of GDP; with respect to the second strategy of devaluation

and slower economic growth there are two such instruments of adjustment, ie (a) variation in the exchange rate and (b) variation in the rate of
economic growth. Finally, in the import control strategy, both the
exchange rate and the variation in the rate of economic growth are ruled
out as instruments of adjustment. The rate of economic growth is fixed at
8 per cent per annum (which was the government's objective to meet its
employment goal). The only instrument of adjustment in this strategy to
meet the balance of payments objective was a reduction in the rate of
growth of imports.

23. Reductions in the rate of growth of output are achieved by a combination
of appropriate deflationary fiscal and monetary policies. Within the
context of CIDE's aggregative macro-econometric model being considered
here, the exact mix of the deflationary monetary and fiscal policies is not
as important as such in relation to meeting the specified balance of
payments target as the reduction in the rate of growth of GDP which these
policies help to bring about.

24. It is assumed that the policy of import controls does not lead to retaliation
from the United States and Mexico's other trading partners. This assumption in the case of Mexico is realistic for two reasons. First, by 1981, nearly
75 per cent of Mexican merchandise exports consisted of oil which the rest
of the world needs. It will be appreciated that even the Islamic Republic
of Iran continues to export today as much oil as it can produce, though
perhaps at some small discount. Secondly, Mexico had traditionally maintained a policy of strict import controls which was only partially relaxed
during the years 1977–81; this policy had not brought retaliation before.

   A referee has asked: 'How realistic is an 8 per cent rate of growth during
a period of world recession?' There are two points which may be made in
this connection. First, as noted in the text, this was the target rate of
growth required for meeting the government's employment objective.
Second, and more importantly, as Table 8.8 shows, despite a sharp
deceleration in world economic growth, the Mexican economy expanded
at the rate of 8 per cent per annum during the period 1977–81. The main
point of the import controls exercise was to show that despite the
unfavourable world economic conditions, and even while staying within
the government's limits on oil exports, such a rate of growth was compatible with the balance of payments equilibrium provided the *propensity* to
import was sharply reduced to its historic pre-oil-boom levels.

25. For a detailed discussion of the results of the simulation, see Eatwell and
Singh (1981).

26. Essentially, the Patrimonio economists advised a substantial reduction in
consumer-goods imports. Their discussions with government officials
suggested that investment-goods imports could also be rationalised and
significantly reduced with, if anything, positive rather than adverse effects
on production. At a practical policy level, the Patrimonio economists
proposed that commissions of government officials, with the help of the
relevant business firms and nationalised industries, should examine each
area of investment goods imports in order to reduce their overall rate of
growth to the level suggested by the simulations in the text. It was
envisaged that these commissions would also prepare planned import
substitution programmes for the medium and long term for each major
industry, so that industry and the economy could manage with moderate
reductions in overall imports which the model results suggested would be
necessary after the oil exports target had been reached.

27. See *Financial Times*, 12 Sep. 1983.

28. See Eatwell and Singh (1981).

29. See, for example, Aspra (1977) and Solis (1981) for typical contributions from this quarter.
30. Such debate is clearly not a sufficient condition for success.

BIBLIOGRAPHY

Aspra, L.A. 'Import substitution in Mexico: Past and present' in *World Development* 5, 1 and 2 (1977).
Barker, T. and Brailovsky, V. (eds) *Oil or industry?*, London, Academic Press (1981).
Bhagwati, J. and Chakravarti, S. 'Contributions to Indian economic analysis: A survey', *American Economic Review* (1969).
Blitzer, C.R., Clark, P.B. and Taylor, L. (eds.) *Economy-wide models and development planning*, Washington, DC, World Bank (1977).
Brailovsky, V. 'Industrialisation and oil in Mexico: A long-term perspective', in Barker and Brailovsky (1981).
Cripps, F. and Tarling, R.J. *Growth in advanced capitalist economies, 1950–70*, Occasional Paper 40, Cambridge, University of Cambridge, Department of Applied Economics (1973).
Eatwell, J. and Singh, A. 'Is the Mexican economy "overheated"?: An analysis of short- and medium-term issues in economic policy', in *Economia Mexicana* (1981).
Kaldor, N. *Strategic factors in economic development*, New York, Cornell University (1967).
Kaldor, N. 'The energy issues', in Barker and Brailovsky (1981).
Kornai, J. 'Models and policy: The dialogue between model builder and planner', in Blitzer, Clark and Taylor (eds) (1977).
Rudra, A. *Indian plan models*, New Delhi, Asia Publishing House (1975).
Singh, A. 'The Mexican economy at the crossroads: Policy options in a semi-industrial oil-exporting economy: A comment on Brailovsky', in Barker and Brailovsky (1981).
Singh, A. 'Third World industrialisation and the structure of the world economy', in Currie, D., *et al.* (eds): *Microeconomic analysis: Essays in microeconomics and economic development*, London, Croom Helm (1981a).
Solis, L. *Economic policy and reform in Mexico*, New York, Pergamon Press (1981).
World Bank. *Mexico, manufacturing sector: Situation, prospects and policies*, Washington, DC (1979).

Chapter Nine

Employment forecasting and the employment problem: Conclusion

Michael Hopkins, International Labour Office, Geneva, Switzerland.

9.1 INTRODUCTION

What is the future of work? Will unemployment continue to increase? Will students be able to use their diplomas? Is semi-skilled shipbuilding a declining profession? Will the effects of the introduction of the silicon chip create unemployment? Is trade protection necessary to preserve jobs? These are just a few of the questions that are being asked today, and that come under the umbrella of employment forecasting.

Indeed, the question has been raised whether the rapid increase in our knowledge, as represented by numerous research journals and monographs concerning forecasting, has not paid off in our ability to forecast. There is no doubt that forecasting socio-economic variables such as employment and unemployment is a difficult if not foolhardy task. But, in a sense, the whole of social science research is intended to help understand what will happen in the future, under certain conditions; thus the attempt to forecast and, in particular, to forecast employment is a natural extension of social science. Forecasting, as understood here, is not an attempt to predict the future but rather to look at alternatives under varying assumptions about events unknown (in advance). It is therefore akin to policy or scenario analysis where quantitative trends, under alternative assumptions about exogenous variables, are used to speculate about the future. Hence, forecasting examines a range of alternatives while prediction gives only one.

In this chapter, the treatment of employment in the preceding chapters is discussed in Section 9.2. This is followed in Section 9.3 by some suggestions on the sorts of variables that, ideally, should be included in employment forecasting models. Section 9.4 of the chapter examines the record of the OECD in employment forecasting, followed by a discussion in Section 9.5 of the employment policies in industrialised countries. Finally, some alternative scenarios to reduce unemployment are discussed and evaluated.

9.2 TREATMENT OF THE LABOUR MARKET IN THE MODELS PRESENTED

Since the chapters of this book were written, two years have passed, and we now know what happened to employment and unemployment in the industrialised countries in 1983, 1984 and 1985. Thus, we can look at the forecasting models anew and see how well their forecasts have fared. This we do in this section, as well as looking more closely at the treatment of employment itself in each of the models considered.

In Table 9.1 we present the actual unemployment rates in the countries covered for 1983–85 and the percentage changes in employment over the same period.

Table 9.1: Unemployment rates in selected OECD countries, 1983–85[1] (percentage of labour force according to national definitions)

Country	1983	1984	1985
Belgium	13.2 (−1.1)	13.3 (0.3)	13.8 (0)
Canada	11.9 (0.8)	11.3 (2.5)	11.0 (2.0)
France	8.1 (−0.8)	9.3 (−1.0)	10.5 (−0.8)
Germany, Federal Republic of	8.2 (−1.6)	8.3 (−0.2)	8.3 (0)
Italy	9.9 (0.3)	10.4 (0.4)	10.8 (0.3)
Japan	2.6 (1.7)	2.7 (0.6)	2.5 (1.5)
Netherlands	15.0 (−2.1)	15.6 (−0.6)	15.3 (0.8)
United Kingdom	11.6 (−0.6)	11.7 (1.4)	12.0 (1.0)
United States	9.6 (1.3)	7.5 (4.1)	7.3 (2.0)

1. Figures in brackets denote percentage changes in employment from the previous period, seasonally adjusted at annual rates.
Source: OECD, *Employment Outlook* (Paris), September 1985.

The high unemployment levels of 1983 were repeated in both 1984 and 1985. A plateau seems to have been reached in 1983, however, with only France and the United Kingdom of the countries displayed in Table 9.1 recording any significant increases in unemployment between 1983 and 1985. Evidence that a turning-point in the growth of unemployment may have been reached in 1985 is given by the fact that seasonally adjusted employment decreased in five of the nine countries in 1983, in three of the nine countries in 1984 and in only one (France) in 1985.

9.2.1 The United Kingdom

In the United Kingdom (Chapter 2), Barker presented three 'baseline' scenarios performed with the Cambridge economic model in 1978, 1982 and 1983. These are displayed in Table 9.2, along with actual data taken from The OECD's *Employment Outlook*.

As can be seen, the unemployment forecasts have been rather close to what actually happened. Because of slightly different definitions of

Table 9.2: United Kingdom unemployment forecasts and actual figures

CEF year of forecast	Unemployment in year of forecast (millions)	Baseline unemployment forecasts (millions unemployed)			
		1983	1984	1985	1990
1978	1.2	2.5	2.8	2.7	–
1982	2.8	3.2	3.2	3.2	3.3
1983	3.0	3.3	3.5	3.7	4.3
Actual figures		3.0	3.03	3.1	–

Source: Chapter II and OECD: *Employment Outlook*, Sept. 1985.

unemployment and because the 1983 CEF forecast was made in June of that year an overestimate of 300,000 unemployed was made for 1983. If the CEF forecasts are adjusted downwards by this amount, we can see that the CEF slightly underestimated the rise in unemployment in its earlier forecasts and slightly overestimated them in their later ones. Thus under- and then over-shooting probably occurred because, in the first case, unemployment levels were much lower (1.2 million) and in the second case unemployment was rising rapidly.

In the CEF model in Chapter 2, the working population is exogenously defined, and labour demand is determined from sets of equations giving total hours worked. The change in total hours worked is a function of the change in output, the ratio of investment to output and the change in levels of unemployment. Unemployment is, then, a residual of number of hours offered less the number of hours demanded. However, the labour force and the pattern (and success) of wage bargaining vary enormously by skill, occupation, sex, age, region, income, broader aspects of inequality, differences in employment, unemployment and wages. The model does not reflect these differences. On the labour supply side, labour is predetermined in full-time units – but there are alternative patterns of lifetime and family labour supply which would generate different income and employment profiles. These affect the macro-economic aspects but are not taken into account in the model. Furthermore, concerning non-wage incomes, the consequences for overall wage/non-wage shares of the alternative strategies are not spelled out. There is a lot of discussion of the role of incomes policy and wage control, but the other side of the mark-up – prices – are unsatisfactorily treated in the wage function.

9.2.2   France

In the DMS model of France, described in Chapter 3, population is exogenous, but the determination of labour supply is endogenous. This is accomplished *ex ante* on demographic grounds and then adjusted *ex post facto* on economic grounds. The demand for employment is determined in two ways depending upon the sector of economic activity. Thus, in the industrial sectors, a detailed formulation is used with employment being determined from an inverse clay-clay production function where various types of capital vintages are used. On the other hand, in the non-industrial sectors, labour productivity is exogenously projected and when applied to endogenously calculated gross output levels gives labour demand. Hence labour demand in the DMS model of France is closely related to the level of effective demand in the economy. Finally, unemployment is obtained as the difference between labour supply and demand. An innovation in this model is that inertia is attributed to change in employment levels so that 'effective' levels of employment slowly adjust to the 'efficient' levels of employment that satisfy the production functions.

Under a number of alternative scenarios, the model projects to 1988 where it is anticipated that unemployment in the French economy will lie between 9.2 and 12.0 per cent. The most recent OECD unemployment projections for France (September 1985) project only as far as 1986 and predict 11.8 per cent unemployment. Recorded levels were 9.3 per cent in 1984. Hence the DMS figures – based on projections done in 1983 – compare favourably.

Most model results show the basic trade-off in French economic policy, ie a choice between an improved balance of payments position and more employment. Until the end of 1982 the employment focus was dominant, with the result that unemployment in France hardly increased and is much lower than in most other EEC countries.

The characteristic feature of most French models is that they react favourably to wage increases. Wage increases lead to more demand and through the accelerator principle to more investment. In the current economic situation of France we see, however, that this is not the case. As a result, model results give a biased picture of reality. This is particularly true of the simulation on the reduction of working time with full wage compensation.

9.2.3 Belgium

In Chapter 4 two models are used to calculate unemployment levels for the Belgian economy. The first – Maribel – is an aggregated model with only three economic sectors, while the second, SERENA, is fairly disaggregated with seven economic sectors and three regions. In both models employment in the public sector is a policy variable, whereas in the enterprise sector employment is endogenous. Both models treat labour demand as inverse production functions, similar to the French DMS model. Labour supply is exogenous and unemployment is determined residually. Both models are used in the chapter to explore the impact of shorter working time on employment levels. The author of Chapter 4 uses yet another model to project changes in employment levels up

214 Michael J.D. Hopkins

to the year 1990 – this time using the most simple of all labour market models by projecting output and labour productivity rates exogenously. The employment growth rate is then the former variable divided by the latter. Aggregate employment was predicted to fall by 2.3 per cent in the base projection from 1983 to 1984 and by 1.9 per cent in a simulated high-growth scenario. Employment actually grew in Belgium by 0.3 per cent between 1983 and 1984, according to OECD statistics, making a mockery of the simple projection tool used.

The models in Vanden Boer's chapter were used for policy purposes in the field of reductions in working time. This assumes homogeneity in the nature of two of the major elements involved: labour and time. In a model based on the assumption of labour homogeneity, it implies *a priori* elimination of any bottleneck problems, which is a courageous hypothesis. This is indeed recognised by Vanden Boer in his chapter, but it is worth emphasising, nevertheless, that work cannot be 'redistributed' like a commodity, for this as well as for other reasons. Time is not homogeneous either, and hence a 'marginalistic' approach cannot be applied there. This is for two reasons.

First, there is probably no continuity between variations in the duration of working time on the one hand and the volume of employment created on the other; there are probably jumps and thresholds. Below a certain quantum, a reduction in working time will probably have no effect. To be concrete, let us say that a reduction of ten minutes a day in the duration of work will probably have no consequence on employment in most cases and people will certainly be reluctant to accept a cut in their wages for a change that would not really alter their lives; they would not feel compensated for it. Yet it is a reduction that amounts to 2.5 per cent of the total duration of work if the 40-hour-week system is in force. The models presented do not appear to take this kind of consideration into account and, for example, one can wonder whether the exercise carried out by the Belgian Planning Office with the Maribel model to evaluate the consequences of reductions in working time of 1 per cent or 3 per cent a year would lead to very reliable conclusions, as long as the change studied remains marginal.

A second important element should be considered when discussing the effects of a reduction in the duration of the working time. This resides in the modalities according to which such a reduction is introduced. It is not a matter of indifference whether the reduction is implemented on a daily basis, on a weekly basis (eg through a reduction of the working week) or on an annual basis (ie through an extension of annual leave entitlements). The various formulas will certainly differ from the point of view of acceptability of a simultaneous cut in wages, which is a basic factor in determining whether the effect on employment will be positive or negative as it affects the unit cost of labour for enterprises. This also seems to be ignored by the models.

To sum up, this leads to two propositions:

a.   a small reduction in working time will probably exacerbate infla-
     tion and create practically no jobs;
b.   a substantial reduction in working time will probably have a
     positive effect on employment – but the accent has to be placed
     on the possible effect on the submerged economy – and supposes
     radical changes in life-styles.

Models that could throw some light on this and give more precise
indications than 'a small reduction', 'a large reduction', and so on,
would be most useful. However, they would have to integrate
psychological behavioural coefficients that have been omitted so far.

9.2.4   **The Netherlands**

In the labour market part of the model for the Netherlands, described
in Chapter 5, the main assumption is that wages do not adjust quickly
to changing demand and supply conditions in order to achieve
continuous equilibrium. Labour supply is largely determined by
demographic factors, except in the case when there is excess supply
which then produces a certain number of 'discouraged' workers. Labour
demand is linked both to labour required, when production is at
capacity, and to the utilisation rate (in times of underutilisation of
labour, enterprises hold on to a cyclical labour reserve).

The FREIA model shows the usefulness of models as a tool of policy
analysis. The simulations run with the model embody across-the-board
changes in particular variables. Policy-makers fortunately have
somewhat more scope for adapting their policy interventions. They are
able to differentiate to some extent among the groups to be affected and
introduce certain qualitative variations. There is also a need to take
account of institutional and behavioural constraints.

This is important when one considers that the Netherlands is a small,
open and increasingly post-industrial society. It has gone from relatively
low unemployment to one of the highest rates in the OECD. It is
confronted with the problem of how to bring down high unemployment in the face of large government budget deficits and a high
underutilisation rate of production capacity.

The chapter is highly pessimistic and suggests that there appear to be
few options. It states that, as a consequence of the large deficits, an
expansionary policy is hardly possible. While there clearly is some
reason for this negative outlook, the paper in its policy analysis does not
appear to take enough account of a number of advantages in the
Netherlands' situation. These include one of the lowest inflation rates
in the OECD, energy self-sufficiency, a good international product
reputation and a skilled and well-educated labour force.

Turning now to the simulations, the increase in public expenditure by
0.5 per cent of national income, equally distributed over government

consumption of goods and services, and income transfers to households appears to be least appealing in terms of its employment effect. There may be some basis for pessimism here, particularly when one also notes that the Netherlands has the second highest rate of government expenditure in the OECD. Nevertheless, there may be more scope for moving the government away from income-maintenance type of expenditure to investment in infrastructure and other economic services that are job creating.

The second simulation concerns increasing investment subsidies to the amount of 0.5 per cent of national income. This policy option addresses a number of the country's problems such as stagnant production growth, reduced exports and ageing capital equipment. It is important to note in this regard that the Netherlands is reported to have had a shortage of economically efficient productive capacity. There remains the question of how to increase the employment effects of this policy alternative. One possibility would be greater targeting, ie concentration on small and medium-sized enterprises and, more basically, favouring industries with greater growth potential over declining industries. Particular attention might be given to export-oriented industries. There also might be potential for offering investment subsidies, sometimes in combination with employment subsidies, particularly wage subsidies.

The third simulation pertains to the once-and-for-all 2 per cent reduction of the wage rate of enterprises in 1983. Such an option, of course, is only feasible to the extent that the trade unions will accept such a wage reduction. Here it should be noted that labour experienced a 3 per cent fall in real wages in 1980–81 and no change at all in real wages for the period 1978–82. The paper itself points to the decline of private consumption associated with this policy choice, which must be a source of some concern.

A sub-option presented is a 2.5 per cent wage reduction during a four-year period, in combination with an annual reduction of taxes on wage income of 0.5 per cent net annual product. It is not fully clear how this particular combination was arrived at and why a somewhat higher wage restraint over four years, in combination with annual tax reductions, would be any more acceptable to workers.

A 10 per cent reduction of the number of days worked per year spread out equally over four years represents the final simulation. Here the chapter could be clearer in the form that a shorter working year is to take. For instance, will it take the form of a shorter working week or alternatively longer holidays? If it is the former it is useful to note that this policy in France has to date been unimpressive in its employment creation results. There are, of course, many ways of reducing labour supply or spreading available work, eg early retirement, job-sharing and more recourse to part-time jobs. Their varying impacts on employment and labour productivity remain to be carefully examined. The paper rightly points to our insufficient knowledge of the effects of short working time at the micro-economic level. This represents a fruitful area for future in-depth policy analysis.

9.2.5 OECD

The OECD labour market forecasts presented in Chapter 6 consist in the main of forecasts of aggregate levels of employment. Labour supply is exogenous. Employment is determined in terms of hours worked. In turn, this latter variable is a function of a lagged time trend of hours worked, the deviation from normal capacity utilisation, the deviation from average output growth and the share of non-wage labour costs in the compensation of employees in the business sector.

The OECD model, much more than most national and international models, is used essentially as a framework for organising the views of economists and others not involved in the estimation and construction of the model. These views come both from within the OECD secretariat and from the relevant departments in the member governments. The process of reconciling these views in the overall framework of the model has a major influence on the forecasts, with the model providing consistency and relationships held to be non-controversial.

The results presented in the chapter are from a model which had not gone through that process at that time. The model has been specified and estimated but the main emphasis of the paper is on its simulation properties.

This extension to the OECD model is of great interest to those concerned with unemployment in the OECD area as it introduces a set of supply blocks into the national models. It endogenises employment, unemployment, hours worked and investment, taking the labour force and government employment as exogenous. This is apparently a considerable advance since, before this, employment was forecast on a much more *ad hoc* basis in INTERLINK and the OECD was in a weaker position to analyse and describe co-ordinated policies between member governments to reduce unemployment.

9.2.5.1 *Remarks on the model estimated*

The model is characterised by having many unobserved or 'synthetic' variables, by being highly non-linear, by assuming constant returns to scale and by being very aggregated. We shall take these factors and their implications one by one.

Amongst the unobserved variables are: d, the scrapping rate; $ETOPT$, $ENOPT$, the optimal levels of labour and energy inputs; $POTB$, potential output; and GAP, capacity utilisation. Several equations are estimated, using time series of these unobserved variables. However, since the data are limited, it is very important to ensure that the derived variables are sensible in relation to other indicators and *a priori* expectations. It would have been helpful to see how the estimates of capacity utilisation, for example, compared with survey data and peak-to-peak estimates.

The model is also non-linear and in this sort of situation it is often possible that a variety of different sets of estimates can be obtained with more or less equal statistical acceptability measured by a log-likelihood ratio. It becomes essential to ensure that the overall properties of the model are sensible.

The CES production function chosen assumes constant returns to scale without empirical justification, although again it will make a major difference to the results when explaining employment and investment over the cycle. It is particularly important to recognise that elasticities of employment with respect to output, which are often estimated at 0.5 or less for the United Kingdom and France, for example, can imply substantial economies of scale, so that the imposition of constant economies of scale may well bias the results.

Finally, the model is estimated for whole economies. Even at the industry level the maximisation assumption seems extreme; here it is applied to the whole United States economy. For the United Kingdom the assumption prompts the question of how North Sea oil is treated since the investment and output are significant in relation to the totals for the economy; they are substantially displaced in time with investment coming first, and the labour-output and other ratios are orders of magnitude different from other sectors. (In fact, it turns out that the oil sector has been treated as exogenous.)

In view of these difficulties the results should be seen as a means of organising the data into a few summary parameters with the organisation determined by economic theory and econometric experience. With new observations and with changes in output, labour or investment mix, we would expect the estimates to change. This also casts doubt upon the differences between substitution elasticities measured for different countries. For example, the capital-energy elasticity varies from 0.97 for Japan to 0.16 for France. Are such differences statistically significant? There are similar differences in the substitution between the capital-energy bundle and labour for different countries. If the elasticities are to be used for comparing different scenarios over one period of time, then the high substitution elasticities measured from time-series data may not be appropriate. They may partly reflect embodied technical change which does not quickly (if at all) respond to different relative prices.

9.2.5.2 *Policies to increase employment*

The model identifies two means of increasing employment:

a. greater utilisation of existing capacity although adjustment lags delay response; and

b. more investment such that the extra labour employed on new capacity is greater than the jobs lost from scrapped capacity.

We would add one more policy which is hidden in the aggregative approach:

c. a change in the mix of output or investment. Since labour-output ratios differ dramatically between industries, different reflationary mixes, emphasising investment as against consumption, for example, can have different effects on employment.

9.2.5.3 *The simulations*

Given the non-linearities and profusion of unobserved variables, the simulations are invaluable for assessing the economics and plausibility of the model. All are unlinked (ie each country model is run independently) and all assume a fixed exchange rate. It is sensible to ensure that the control-run values of the unobserved variables are reasonably plausible, especially since the model is non-linear.

The 'consensus' simulation clearly gives a major boost to employment in the OECD area. It would be interesting to see if the wage restraint/income tax reduction combination could be replaced by a reduction in employment taxes (typically national insurance contributions) and so prove equally effective without the problem of persuading governments, trade unions and employers to accept incomes policies.

The base scenario forecast is given in Table 9.3 below, together with the corresponding actual OECD employment figures.

From the table it can be seen that the forecasting ability of the OECD *Interlink* project – as it was in 1983 – is far from perfect. Indeed the model significantly underestimated the rise in employment in the United States and Canada and missed the increase in employment in the United Kingdom, at least at the end of 1983 and the beginning of 1984. On average, the forecasts were 1.2 percentage points away from the actual change in employment levels. The forecasts were relatively good for France, the Federal Republic of Germany and Japan and better for the end of 1984/beginning of 1985 than the end of 1983/beginning of 1984 for all countries examined. This is because the larger the change in aggregate employment over what has happened before, the less robust is the model to spot the changes. These are general problems for all models, namely to spot turning-points when they occur and to forecast over future periods when the past has been no guide.

Table 9.3: OECD employment baseline scenario compared to OECD forecasts (percentage increase from previous period)

Country	Year								
	1983:2		1984:1		1984:2		1985:1		
	Actual	Fore-cast	Actual	Fore-cast	Actual	Fore-cast	Actual	Fore-cast	Country MAD[1]
Canada	4.3	0.6	4.3	1.1	3.1	1.3	1.5	1.2	2.2
France	− 0.8	− 0.5	− 1.0	− 0.4	− 0.9	− 0.3	0.8	− 0.4	0.7
Germany, Fed. Rep. of	− 0.6	− 0.3	0.5	− 0.2	− 0.2	− 0.2	− 0.0	− 0.2	0.3
Japan	0.3	0.6	1.3	0.6	1.7	0.6	1.5	0.6	0.8
United Kingdom	1.1	− 0.5	1.0	− 0.1	1.1	0.1	1.0	0	1.2
United States	4.9	0.8	4.3	1.1	2.4	1.3	2.0	1.2	2.3
Column MAD =	1.7		1.6		0.9		0.7		
					Overall MAD =				1.2

1. MAD = Mean average absolute deviation.

9.2.6   LINK

The LINK project forecasts described in Chapter 7 are based on national models, each of which has its own labour market specification; thus it was not possible to describe them all in the chapter. In general, however, employment is modelled as a function of output, relative factor prices and a lagged time trend. The results of the baseline forecast for unemployment are given in Table 9.4, together with the actual unemployment figures taken from the OECD: *Employment Outlook*.

As can be seen from Table 9.4, the LINK forecasts of unemployment change are rather poor. This is not altogether surprising for three main reasons. First, because of the statistical artefact whereby the unemployment variable is the difference of two large numbers (labour supply and labour demand), percentage changes are likely to be volatile even in times of low and stable unemployment levels. Second, the forecasts did not allow for the more than expected rapid rise in output levels in the post-recession year of 1984. Third, the LINK models, in general, expected more change in unemployment levels than actually occurred and this was probably because of the poor modelling of the labour market. In general, none of the models in LINK treats labour markets with more than rudimentary attention and this helps to explain their poor forecasting performance.

Table 9.4: LINK: unemployment change forecasts compared to OECD actual figures for 1984 and 1985 (percentages)

Country[1]	Actual unemployed (%)			Forecasts (% change in model of unemployment)		Actual (% change of unemployment)		ABS (forecast-actual)		MAD[2]
	1983	1984	1985	1984	1985	1984	1985	1984	1985	
Australia	9.9	8.9	8.25	4.2	-3.7	-10.1	-7.3	14.3	3.6	9.0
Austria	4.1	4.1	4.0	10.9	4.6	0.0	-2.4	10.8	7.0	8.9
Belgium	13.2	13.3	13.75	14.5	-0.2	0.8	3.4	13.7	3.6	8.7
Canada	11.9	11.3	11.0	-4.1	-7.8	-5.0	-2.7	0.9	5.1	3.0
Denmark	10.5	10.1	9.25	5.3	-2.7	-3.8	-8.4	9.1	5.7	7.4
Finland	6.1	6.1	5.75	-0.1	-1.4	0	-5.7	0.1	4.3	2.2
France	8.1	9.3	10.5	6.6	5.8	14.8	12.9	8.2	7.1	7.7
Germany, Federal Republic of	8.2	8.3	8.25	6.6	-2.5	1.2	-0.6	5.4	1.9	3.6
Iceland	1.1	1.3	1.0	-18.2	0.0	18.2	-23.1	36.4	23.1	29.7
Italy	9.9	10.4	10.75	1.7	-2.8	5.1	3.4	3.4	6.2	4.8
Japan	2.6	2.7	2.5	-5.0	-2.6	3.8	-7.4	8.8	4.8	6.8
Norway	3.3	3.0	2.75	-32.5	-6.2	-9.1	-8.3	23.4	2.1	12.8
Portugal	10.8	10.5	11.5	-0.1	-5.1	-2.8	9.5	2.7	14.6	8.7
Spain	17.8	20.6	21.5	-0.7	-2.6	15.7	4.4	16.4	7.0	11.7
Sweden	3.4	3.1	2.75	-8.6	-22.4	-8.8	-11.3	0.2	11.1	5.7
Switzerland	0.9	1.1	1.00	0.0	0.7	22.2	-9.1	22.2	9.8	16.0
Turkey	12.0	12.4	12.75	-4.0	0.3	3.3	2.8	7.3	2.5	4.9
United Kingdom	11.6	11.7	12.0	2.7	-7.3	0.9	2.6	1.8	9.9	5.9
United States	9.6	7.5	7.25	-10.6	-9.3	-21.9	-3.3	11.3	6.0	8.6
									MAD average =	8.7

1. Yugoslavia is omitted from this table; it is not an OECD country and recent unemployment figures are not available.
2. MAD = mean average absolute deviation.

9.2.7 **Mexico**

The case study of Mexico (Chapter 8) has been included in this volume because it is a semi-industrialised economy and because the same philosophy of model-building that was applied in the case of the United Kingdom was also adopted in that case study. The model differs from the OECD and LINK models in that it is a policy model, ie it purports to illustrate the relative merits of alternative strategies of development rather than predict absolute levels of employment (for example) *per se*. However, employment is treated extremely simply in the model as a function of output and productivity. Thus, absolute employment levels are largely a function of economic growth.

In order to maximise economic growth (and hence employment) the CEPG advised – and this they backed up with their model – a strategy of import protection coupled with a huge investment drive for industrialisation in order to reach a growth rate in the 1980s of 8 per cent per annum. They strongly advised against the IMF/World Bank strategy of devaluation followed by reductions in public expenditure coupled with an export drive (of oil and other products). In the event neither strategy was completely adopted. Mexico's growth rate fell from an average of 6 per cent per annum during 1970–80 to zero between 1980 and 1984. Further, real wages fell over 1981–85 by nearly a half in a country where only 50 per cent of the 25 million workforce is fully employed. The *peso* in 1986 represented only one-twelfth of its value against the dollar compared to 1982, thereby 'speeding the erosion of middle-class confidence in the regime'. Public spending cuts, and the removal of many subsidies that had previously cushioned the Mexican poor, had aggravated tensions already present before the 1982 crisis.[1]

With the 1985–86 massive drop in oil prices, Mexican GDP growth rate will undoubtedly not recover in the coming years. Thus, the CEPG strategy is partially vindicated in that the adoption of an industrialisation strategy and a move away from almost total dependence on oil could have prepared Mexico well for the shocks to come. Such a view is vigorously opposed by Bela Belassa in his critique of the CEPG advice, where he argues that Mexico's basic problem was an overvalued currency coupled with inefficient public investment.[2]

9.3   WHAT VARIABLES TO FORECAST AND FOR WHOM?

The conceptual basis which determines the identification of employment-related variables, the indicators used to measure them and the data that must be collected in order to see how employment changes over time is a matter for controversy and uncertainty. In Table 9.5, a list of employment variables of interest to forecasting is given, followed by a list of some of the major influences on them.

Table 9.5: Employment and its determinants

Employment variables
Unemployment (visible and invisible)
Underemployment (visible and invisible)
Employment
Labour supply
Labour productivity
Labour demand
Labour supply
Labour mobility
Part-time work
Social costs
Wages
Internal and international labour force migration
(All disaggregated by skill, occupation, education, age, sex, sector, region)

Some major influences
Government economic and social policy
Inflation
Trade
Economic growth
Consumption (public and private)
Investment (public and private)
Technology and innovation
Psychological variables such as attitudes to work, stress
Distribution of income and wealth
Land distribution and ownership
Interest rates
Population structure, distribution and growth
Level of human needs satisfaction
Degree of organisation of workforce and power of competing interest groups
Labour market structure and labour flexibility
Size of industry
National physical and human resource base

The list of major influences on employment could be extended almost *ad infinitum*, and some (eg work attitudes, government policy) are more difficult to quantify than others (interest rates, growth, etc). For forecasting purposes the implied interdependence in Table 9.5 (for example, employment is dependent on economic growth amongst other things yet economic growth is highly related to the consumption of workers who obtain their income from employment) have given rise to econometric models as the main tool in both understanding inter-relationships and forecasting their evolution. As Makridakis and Wheelwright[3] remark, the main advantage of econometric models lies in their ability to deal with interdependence. They state, too, that it is important to distinguish between econometric models used for policy purposes and econometric models used for forecasting. This is because, they argue, the former use is for understanding and the latter for prediction. This they justify because they believe that economic models perform considerably better than a naive forecast but not much better than a simple model based on a few simple equations. The little experience obtained, to date, with economic forecasting tools has probably served to back up their argument. Nevertheless, it is difficult to understand how predictive forecasting can improve without better understanding and, hence, conceptually more sophisticated models. None of the models presented in this book, as has been seen in the preceding section, include more than 5 per cent of the variables listed. None models the supply side of labour, and demand is usually determined as an econometric function of wages and economic output. The lack of attention paid to the labour market, in the influential models presented in this book, may help to explain the lack of alternatives to cope with the continuing employment problem in industrialised countries.

As well as methodology, important in employment forecasting are geographical coverage (world, nation, region, economic sector, etc), time horizon (short term – up to one year; medium term – one to five years; and long term – more than five years) and potential users. This is illustrated in Table 9.6 and has been based upon a chart originally drawn up by Vincens.[4]

In Table 9.6 it can be seen that the users of employment forecasting are governments, households, enterprises, unions and financial institutions. Associated with each of these users in the table are a number of stylised questions in which each user may be interested.

Implicit in Table 9.6 is one major area of employment forecasting activity: manpower forecasting.[5] This attempts to forecast manpower requirements at some future point in time in order to determine educational and training strategies. Employment forecasting and manpower forecasting are two sides of the same coin. Manpower forecasting usually attempts to fit people with certain skills and education into slots commensurate with their characteristics in the labour market at some time in the future. Any mismatch is then presumed to be dealt with through changes in the education and training system. Employment forecasting is concerned with labour market policies that avoid the misuse of manpower as happens in the case of unemployment, for example. Employment forecasting implies, therefore, a concern with wider macro-economic issues than mismatch on the educational skill make-up of the labour market. However, to understand the demand and supply of labour at some future point in time of interest to manpower forecasting requires an understanding of macro-economic factors. Hence, the difference between employment and manpower forecasting is more apparent than real.

9.4   RELIABILITY OF FORECASTS

We saw in Section 9.2 that the forecasting record of the major models

Table 9.6: Usual categories for employment forecasting

Users	Areas of action involving employment forecasting	Short term (up to 1 year)	Medium term (1–5 years)	Long term (above 5 years)
Government	– Full employment policy	x	x	x
	– Education and training expenses		x	x
	– Policies designed to use human resources efficiently and to improve the functioning of the labour market	x	x	x
Households	– Choice of education and training		x	x
	– Choice of a profession		x	x
	– Choice of a place to work	x	x	x
Enterprises	– Administration of personnel	x	x	x
	– Choice of most productive capital/technology/labour mix		x	x
Unions	– Strategy of negotiation	x	x	x
	– Defence of interests in salaries and conditions of work	x	x	x
Financial institutions	– Evaluation of wage settlements on country lending policy	x	x	
	– Evaluation of short- versus long-term effects on loans designed for human resource development	x		x

has been mixed: the United Kingdom forecasts of unemployment were close to what actually happened; the French model performed well; the Belgian forecasts were poor; the Netherlands model illustrated well current problems in employment in that country; the OECD *Interlink* projections were far from perfect; and the LINK projections were poor. In general, it would seem that the nationally constructed models are rather more accurate (except in Belgium, where a very simple model was used) than the internationally constructed ones. Clearly, this is because more time, care and effort can be devoted to national single-case models than to international multi-case studies. What all the models have in common is the difficulty in identifying turning-points.

This section takes a slightly different tack and looks at the relative merits of a naive method of employment forecasting versus a major modelling effort. This is done for the OECD employment forecasts because, arguably, these are the most well known and because they are easily and regularly accessible through the OECD's *Economic Outlook*.

9.4.1   OECD employment forecasting record

The short-term macro-economic forecasts of the OECD for industrialised countries are some of the most widely discussed and, in a sense, are typical of what forecasters in the economic sphere have offered to date. A similar exercise to assess accuracy has been performed by David Smyth[6] for OECD economic forecasts for the year ahead for seven major OECD countries, the United States, Japan, the Federal Republic of Germany, France, Italy, the United Kingdom and Canada for real gross national product, inflation and the current balance of payments.

A similar methodology is used here to that of Smyth in order to assess the accuracy of OECD forecasts one year ahead for the unemployment rate and for the percentage increase in aggregate levels of employment. Smyth did not examine employment in his analysis. The forecasts chosen for analysis are those made in the December issue of the OECD publication, *Economic Outlook*, for the following year. Apparently, since unemployment became an important issue for the OECD only towards the end of the 1970s, no one table before 1981 in *Economic Outlook* contains unemployment forecasts for the year ahead. However, figures for unemployment forecasts (the raw data are presented in Table 9.7) are generally given in *Economic Outlook* for individual countries in a descriptive section on prospects. Unlike Smyth, the period 1975–82, following the oil price rises, was chosen for analysis both because of the increased interest in employment issues in that period (in fact, OECD only started giving major sections on employ-ment in *Economic Outlook* from 1974 onwards) and because it avoids the first OPEC oil price rise that Smyth found to have negatively affected the OECD projections around that period.

Table 9.7: Raw data used for analysis of OECD short-term employment forecasting performance

Country	1975			1976			1977			1978		
	Actual (A_t)	Forecast (P_t)	Naive (P_t)	Actual	Forecast	Naive	Actual	Forecast	Naiva	Actual	Forecast	Naive
Topic – Unemployment (national unadjusted %)												
United States	(8.5)	–	5.6	7.7	8.0	8.5	7.0	7.25	7.7	6.0	6.5	7.0
Japan	(1.9)	–	1.4	2.0	1.9	1.9	2.0	1.75	2.0	2.2	2.9	2.0
Germany, Federal Republic of	4.9	4.0	2.7	(4.7)	–	4.9)	4.6	6.0	4.7	4.4	5.25	4.6
France	4.0	3.5	2.3	4.2	5.5	4.0	4.8	5.0	4.2	5.1	6.25	4.8
United Kingdom	3.9	3.75	2.5	5.4	6.5	3.9	5.7	6.5	5.4	5.6	6.5	5.7
Canada	7.1	6.5	5.4	7.2	7.5	7.1	8.1	7.5	7.2	8.4	8.75	8.1
Italy	3.3	4.5	2.9	3.7	4.25	3.3	(7.2)	–	3.7)	7.2	9.0	7.2
Topic – Employment (% change over previous year)												
United States	(−1.3)	–	–)	3.2	2.0	−1.25	3.5	2.5	3.25	4.2	2.75	3.25
Japan	(−0.4)	–	–)	0.9	1.0	−0.5	1.3	1.0	0.5	1.2	0.75	1.25
Germany, Federal Republic of	(−3.3)	–	–)	−0.9	−1.25	−3.75	−0.3	−0.75	−1.25	0.6	−0.75	−0.5
France	(−1.2)	–	–)	0.1	−0.5	−0.5	0.1	−0.5	0.0	0.2	−0.5	−0.5
United Kingdom	(−0.7)	–	–)	−0.8	−2.75	−2.25	0.4	−0.5	−1.0	0.4	−0.5	0
Canada	(1.9)	–	–)	2.2	2.0	1.75	1.9	2.25	2.5	3.3	1.5	1.75
Italy	(0.5)	–	–)	0.7	−2.0	0.0	1.0	−0.25	−0.75	0.6	0.5	1.25

Table 9.7: Continued

Country	1979 Actual (A_t)	1979 Forecast (P_t)	1979 Naive (P_t)	1980 Actual	1980 Forecast	1980 Naive	1981 Actual	1981 Forecast	1981 Naive	1982 Actual	1982 Forecast	1982 Naive
Topic – Unemployment												
United States	(5.9)	–	(6.0)	7.2	7.5	5.9	7.6	8.0	7.2	9.5	9.0	7.6
Japan	(2.2)	2.5	(2.2)	2.0	2.2	2.2	2.2	2.0	2.0	2.25	2.25	2.2
Germany, Federal Republic of	3.7	4.4	4.4	3.4	3.75	3.7	4.8	4.25	3.4	7.0	6.0	4.8
France	5.9	5.1	5.1	(6.3)	–	(5.9)	7.3	7.6	6.3	8.5	8.5	7.3
United Kingdom	5.1	5.6	5.6	7.0	6.75	5.1	10.6	10.6	7.0	12.25	12.0	10.6
Canada	7.2	8.4	8.4	7.5	8.0	7.2	7.6	8.3	7.5	11.0	8.25	7.6
Italy	7.5	7.2	7.2	7.6	9.0	7.5	8.5	8.6	7.6	9.25	9.0	8.5
Topic – Employment												
United States	2.7	1.25	4.0	0.3	0.0	2.5	1.1	0.75	0.25	-0.75	-0.5	1.0
Japan	1.4	1.0	1.5	1.0	1.0	1.5	0.8	1.0	1.0	1.0	1.0	0.75
Germany, Federal Republic of	1.3	0.25	-0.25	0.9	-0.25	0.5	-0.8	-1.0	0.75	-1.75	-1.0	-1.0
France	-0.1	0.25	0	0.2	0	0	-0.7	-0.5	0	-0.75	0.25	-1.0
United Kingdom	0.4	0	0.5	-2.3	-1.0	0.5	-4.8	-3.5	-2.25	-3.0	-2.0	-4.75
Canada	4.0	2.5	3.0	2.8	1.5	3.75	2.6	0.75	2.5	-3.0	1.5	3.0
Italy	1.1	0.5	0	1.5	0.5	0.5	0.4	0	0.5	0	-0.5	0.25

Note: Brackets indicate that the data were not used in the analysis because of missing values; naive = previous years.
Source: OECD: *Economic Outlook*, December issues, 1974–82.

9.4.2 OECD methodology

Forecasting in the OECD is a mixture of macro-economic modelling and expert judgement. Economic variables are forecast using the *Interlink* model, which is essentially an accounting framework that ensures consistency amongst a number of econometrically estimated national models.[7] From available documents it is not altogether clear how employment and unemployment are treated. There is no mention of employment variables in the technical description of *Interlink*.[8] In consecutive issues of *Economic Outlook* one finds that employment is being treated with a growing relative degree of sophistication. Look, for example, at the following statements from *Economic Outlook*:

- 'The forecast change in the level of demand leads to forecasts for employment' (Dec. 1976).
- 'The initial change in the level of demand, together with the extrapolation of demographic trends, leads to forecasts for employment' (Dec. 1980).
- 'Changes in the level of demand, together with a judgement of the effect of demographic trends on participation rates, leads to forecasts for employment and unemployment' (Dec. 1982).

Note that unemployment only entered in later years in these summary technical descriptions even though forecasts of unemployment had actually been made in earlier years.

In general, each country provides national forecasts whose economic variables are made consistent by the *Interlink* model.

An early description (1965) of the employment forecasts for Canada are typical of the work performed in the OECD countries.[9] There the assessment of the outlook for the employment and unemployment situation centres on the relationship between changes in output, productivity and the labour force. The question, broadly, is whether the projected levels of output and demand as anticipated in the GNP forecast are likely to be sufficient to absorb fully the expected increase in the labour supply, given certain assumptions as regards productivity in the year ahead. In reaching a judgement on this question, a forecast is made of the anticipated increase in the labour force in the light of expectations concerning the natural increase of the population, the level of net immigration and participation rates. In the short run, participation rates, and hence the labour force, are primarily influenced by the cyclical demand for labour. Consequently, an assessment is usually made first of labour demand by (at least) major industries. This information, plus the knowledge of how various groups of workers behave in the labour market over the cycle, forms the background for making necessary judgements about participation rates. In addition, a key consideration is the course of productivity in the year ahead. Past trends in productivity provide the basic guidelines for the estimate in this area, but modifications are made in the light of the position of the economy in relation to the stage of the business cycle. This is because cyclical upturns had been marked in the past by sharp gains in productivity or a retardation in the rate of productivity growth.

All of these projections are drawn together in a consistent framework and the forecast of the change in employment levels is then determined as the result of two interacting factors – the anticipated change in the physical volume of output and the anticipated change in the production-employment ratio, ie productivity. The forecast of unemployment is determined as the difference between the total labour supply estimated as above and the forecasted level of employment.

This simple approach dominated other national forecasts at least until the early 1980s.[10]

9.4.3   Technique of analysis

The forecasts of unemployment and percentage change in aggregate employment are made in December of $t-1$ for year t (in fact, the OECD also produce forecasts for the year ahead in June of each year but this data has not been included here). What is compared here is the actual value A_t to the predicted value P_t for the year t. The predicted value for each variable comes from the December $(t-1)$ *Economic Outlook*. The actual value A_t comes from the December $(t+1)$ *Economic Outlook* (nearly always true but sometimes it is not available and the December t value is used instead) because the estimate then is thought to be closer to the actual value than the estimate of the actual value for year t given in the December *Economic Outlook* in the year t. This procedure is consistent with that of Smyth.

Perfect forecasting requires $P_t = A_t$ for all t. Following Smyth,[11] measures of the closeness of P_t and A_t are used, namely *MAE*, the mean-absolute error of the forecasts, and *RMSE*, the root-mean square error. These are defined as:

$$MAE = \frac{1}{n} \left| P_t - A_t \right| \qquad \text{where } n = \text{number of countries}$$

$$RMSE = \sqrt{\frac{1}{n}(P_t - A_t)^2}$$

9.4.4   Accuracy of the forecasts

Table 9.8 gives the summary statistics for the analysis. In order to evaluate the OECD forecasts not just in isolation but in conjunction with other forecasts, the accuracy of each set of forecasts is evaluated against those generated by a naive model. Again, following Smyth, the estimated value for $t-1$ available in *Economic Outlook* at time $t-1$ for both employment and unemployment was used as the naive forecast for time t, ie in the naive model $P_t = P_{t-1}$. In Table 9.8, $\overline{A}$, $\overline{P}$ and $\overline{P}_N$ are the means of the actual, the OECD-predicted series and the naive forecasts respectively; S_A, S_P, S_{PN} are the standard deviations. The measures *MAE* and *RMSE* were calculated for the difference between the actual and OECD-predicted values and for the difference between the actual and the naive forecasts. The t-values represent a test of the difference in means of the actual and OECD predicted values, and the difference in means of the actual and naive forecasts. The results reported in successive columns in Table 9.8 are for all the unemployment forecasts pooled and all the employment forecasts pooled.

Table 9.8: Summary statistics

Value	Unemployment (% of labour force, national definition)	Employment (% change from previous year)
$\overline{A}$	5.98	0.60
$\overline{P}$	6.20	0.19
$\overline{P}_N$	5.38	0.50
$S_{\overline{A}}$	2.52	1.78
S_P	2.43	1.32
S_{P_N}	2.26	1.76
MAE	0.61	0.78
RMSE	0.79	0.98
MAE_N	0.88	0.90
$RMSE_N$	1.13	1.22
N	50	49
$^t\overline{A} - \overline{P}$, n = 50	−0.09	0.23
$^t\overline{A} - \overline{P}_N$, n = 50	0.24	0.06
	($^t5\% = 2.0$)	

For unemployment it can be seen that the test showed, on average, that the OECD forecasts were quite good and better than the naive forecasts. The t-test of the null hypothesis that the OECD-predicted values were the same as the actual values could not be rejected. However, the same t-test results also applied to the naive forecasts, which, although they performed worse than the OECD, suggests that the OECD did not have a particularly difficult job in predicting unemployment because the unemployment level of the current years gave a good estimate of the subsequent year.

For changes in the aggregate level of employment the naive prediction performed better than the OECD predictions on average when means are compared. However, the standard deviation of the naive forecasts was larger than the OECD prediction, and the two tests of performance showed that the OECD performed better, but only just, than the naive projections. This suggests, and a glance at the data in Table 9.7 confirms this, that the OECD forecasts were better than the naive forecasts at predicting the changes in sign (ie the turning-point) but were not as good as the naive forecasts at predicting magnitudes of change. Again the test of means showed that the null hypothesis of similarity between predicted and actual values of employment could not be rejected.

9.4.5   Changes in performance over time

As can be seen from the quotations concerning methodology above, the OECD has been gradually improving the methods used for employment forecasting. Again following Smyth, one can usefully ask whether the OECD employment forecasting performance has improved over time and/or whether forecasting is becoming easier or more difficult. These questions are examined by calculating some rank correlation coefficients which are given in Table 9.9.

Table 9.9: Rank correlation (Spearman's ϱ) coefficients

Rank correlation between	Unemployment		Employment	
	MAE	RMSE	MAE	RMSE
OECD forecast and time	− 0.17	− 0.19	− 0.04	0.11
Naive forecast and time	− 0.33	− 0.12	0.11	0.11

Note: t-tests not significant for any of the coefficients.

The ranks were arrived at by calculating the measures, *MAE* and *RMSE*, for the difference between actual and predicted values for each year. Country information was pooled for each year. Then the largest rank was given to the largest figure and correlated with the ranks for time, giving the rank 1 to 1975, 2 to 1976 and so on. If the forecasting performance was improving over time, one should expect a negative rank correlation coefficient between the OECD forecasts and time. If forecasting was becoming easier over time one should also expect a negative rank correlation coefficient. As it happened none of the correlation coefficients were significantly different from zero, even though the signs were in the expected direction, namely negative for the unemployment forecasts suggesting that the OECD performance was improving over time. Yet, whether this was due to improved methodology or whether forecasting was becoming easier (because the naive forecasts also improved over time) could not be untangled from the evidence presented. For employment only one (just) negative correlation coefficient out of four was found suggesting that the OECD performance got neither better nor worse over a period in which year-to-year difficulties in forecasting remained about the same.

9.4.6 Summary

In summary, one can deduce that the OECD unemployment forecasts are quite accurate and generally outperform a naive model. However, it did not seem to be too difficult to give good forecasts over the period, due to the generally increasing trend of unemployment in the 1970s and early 1980s. The OECD performance of forecasting unemployment rates improved over time, although whether this was due to improved methodology or because forecasting became easier over time could not be deduced. Forecasts of aggregate employment levels were not much better than the naive forecasts. These conclusions are very similar to those of Smyth, namely:

> . . . the OECD annual forecasts do outperform those generated by a random walk process for GNP but this is due to the breakdown of the random walk model during the 1974–76 period in response to the OPEC oil price rise. The OECD price and current balance forecasts are not significantly superior to those obtained by the random walk model. The OECD's forecasting performance has neither improved nor deteriorated over time.[12]

What confidence do these results give us for employment forecasting? Most people, when asked, doubt the usefulness of forecasting because they believe it to be unreliable. The above exercise has, at least, shown that informed forecasting – informed because that is what the OECD forecasts are – performed slightly better than a naive model. Unfortunately, there is no guarantee that more informed forecasting based on better, and thus more elaborate, models will lead to better forecasts. Therein lies the dilemma. Informed forecasting performs better than naive forecasting but how much investment should be made in the former? This is not easy to answer. The modelling process, namely the testing of hypotheses against data, leads to a better understanding of how economies function. Such understanding is intended to lead to improved economic policy and, in our case, creating employment and eliminating unemployment. That OECD forecasting is improving, albeit slightly, over time suggests, therefore, that some investment in further work is worthwhile in order to improve our understanding of economic systems even if this may not lead to significant improvement in our ability to forecast.

9.5 EMPLOYMENT POLICIES IN INDUSTRIALISED COUNTRIES

9.5.1 Is unemployment a problem?

It could be argued that high rates of unemployment and its further continuation are acceptable to the industrialised mixed economies compared to the lower rates of the 1960s and early 1970s for a number of reasons. Social security payments alleviate hardship; high unemployment allows a restructuring of industry through a 'shake-out' of inefficient jobs, contributes to a downward pressure on wages of those employed and forces productivity improvements. From a human point of view, however, these 'virtues' of unemployment must be rejected because of the alienation and loss of welfare that unemployment generates.[13]

Alienation comes from a number of sources. First, the sense of belonging and the feeling of contributing to society is seriously shaken, particularly for the long-term unemployed, because of the rejection involved. 'What counts is not the achievement of satisfaction that flows from action but the status of the social relationship that commands production – that is, the job, situation, post or appointment.'[14] Second, different social groups are affected in different ways – young people who feel rejected by society before they have had the chance to make any contribution, women for whom the move towards liberation is given a sharp rebuke, and old people nearing retirement who are effectively told that they are useless at a critical period in their lives.

Loss of welfare comes from two sources. First, the social security benefits that are received always fall short of previous wages and also tend to decline as the length of unemployment increases. Second, those who remain in employment will not only have a higher income than those unemployed, but their wages are likely to be increased because of productivity gains due to the 'shake-out' of inefficient jobs. Hence, the unemployed are doubly hit: they become materially worse off, and as the distribution of income worsens they become relatively worse off as well.

In the eyes of some, unemployment has become respectable. Undoubtedly, leisure activities may increase (or rather are forced to increase in many cases), and many argue that this can help to stimulate untapped creativity that would otherwise be stifled by time-consuming, uninteresting work. As Bertrand Russell stated: 'I think that there is far too much work done in the world, that immense harm is caused by the belief that work is virtuous', and '. . . the road to happiness and prosperity lies in an organised diminution of work.'[15] Also, high levels of unemployment can stimulate a discussion on the alternatives to work; and on why work is necessary when machines can perform unenviable tasks. However, the discussion is surely on the creation and distribution of surplus, because if people do not work they receive only a pitiful part of the surplus generated by highly productive industry (which requires increasingly fewer workers). As Russell argues:

Modern methods of production have given us the possibility of ease and security for all; we have chosen, instead, to have overwork for some and starvation for others. Hitherto we have continued to be as energetic as we were before there were machines; in this we have been foolish, but there is no reason to go on being foolish forever.[16]

It is tempting to imagine a world where unpleasant work has been eliminated and what work is done is done for the satisfaction of human needs rather than for its own sake, but that is a far cry from the harsh realities of the politician's desire for growth and the economist's regression analysis.

9.5.2 The causes

The current and prospective decline in employment has its roots in the anti-inflation policies of the 1970s. In turn, the inflation of the 1970s had its roots in war – from the need to finance the massive deficits run by the United States to finance the Vietnam war, to the Yom Kippur war that led to the formation of OPEC in the early seventies. The inflation was caused by higher oil prices, leading to a dampening of world trade which, in a period of economic growth, led to severe balance of payments difficulties. Coupled with this imported inflation was some cost-push inflation as workers attempted to force pay rises over and above the anticipated rate of inflation.

Inflation was successfully controlled through tight monetary policy that used monetary targets as the main navigational aid to monetary policy. Unfortunately, the main controlling instrument of the money supply was the rate of interest. High rates of interest led to reduced investment and a depression in output, causing the collapse of many industries (particularly steel and textiles) and high levels of unemployment.[17] A vicious twist to the monetary squeeze led to the serious misalignment of certain key exchange rates (and not only the dollar and the pound) and hence substantial non-oil trading deficits. This was compensated somewhat by an inflow of funds attracted by high interest rates. People moved funds into deposit accounts due to the attraction of high interest rates while industry was being forced by the recession to increase bank borrowings. Consequently, banks had to raise rates to attract deposits. This was a classic problem of excess demand for money from people trying to switch out of goods into money. Ironically, therefore, if interest rates had been lower the money supply (M3) would not have risen so rapidly. Consequently, investment in industry fell, followed by lower growth rates and a reduced demand for labour. Hence the major adjustment of the strict monetary policy fell on the labour market. This approach by economists [18] (severely criticised by non-money supply-side economists of the time) had extremely serious consequences in terms of unemployment. One notes that Japan avoided this situation and therefore its labour market effects.

Another school of thought, loosely termed as structuralist, stressed that major structural rigidities in the Western market system led to the current depression. Marxists[19] argue that the evidence points to a fall in profits prior to the mid-1970s (and consequently falls in investment, growth and employment) because of a fall in the rate of exploitation, rather than a rise in the organic composition of capital. Structuralists, who might also be sympathetic to the Marxist analysis, agree, according to Willke,[20] on three basic assumptions. First, product and labour markets are heterogeneous and hence prices and wages are sticky; quantities, then, adjust faster than prices and in a downward direction. Second, disequilibrium transactions take place, and third, the adaptation of prices and wages to demand and supply is non-linear. Solutions to unemployment, then, run from policies of self-reliance and vigorous market interventions to full-scale socialisation of the economy. Focus is given more to the distribution of power, the ownership of capital and the struggle between classes rather than to the aggregate generalisations of neo-Keynesian macro-economists.

Undoubtedly a push towards increasing demand through Keynesian policies could, at the macro-economic level, go part of the way in restoring employment.[21] However, it would be naive to expect interest groups, who see advantages in high unemployment to weaken union power and force down wages, to be readily concerned, as the structuralists have so rightly seen.

Another school of structuralist thought consists of those who see recession, depression and growth as part of long-wave cycles – the Kondratiev cycles being the most celebrated.[22] Mensch, for example, argues that basic innovations (innovations are the implementation, after a time lag, of inventions) have been clustered in decades of deep depression, specifically around 1835, 1886 and 1936; and that these basic innovations provide the main impetus for the next big upswing of the economy.[23] During such deep depressions, entrepreneurs are obliged to search for more radical solutions, which were 'crowded out' when business was booming. This idea is attractive since it suggests that demand-led growth could be stimulated by new innovations which are being created in the early 1980s. Mensch argues that the economic policy of deficit spending is not the most satisfactory. Existing products do not have a positive multiplier effect, because they do not affect the essential problems of stagnation, which are the lack of basic innovations and the saturation of demand in the leading sectors. In summary, then, the fundamental solution to demand saturation is an aggressive innovation policy. However, this suggests that all that is necessary is to await a technological-led boom. Freeman, Clark and Soete are not entirely in agreement with Mensch's view and, although they believe that some evidence is available to suggest some 'bunching' of innovations, they argue that innovations can occur as much as a result of an upswing as a cause of it.[24] Nevertheless, they believe that while well-conceived technology policies can play an important part in combating unemployment, technology policies alone cannot be successful in solving the fundamental social, economic and political problems that exist.

9.5.3 Labour market policy

Three main approaches can be distinguished. First, there are certain economists who view unemployment as the result of the malfunctioning of labour markets and then suggest actions phrased solely in terms of labour market policy. These 'malfunctionist' labour market analysts characterise the unemployed by a number of categories. For example, the OECD disaggregates unemployment into three major categories: *demand-deficient unemployment*, resulting from lack of effective aggregate demand for output; *frictional (or search) unemployment*, reflecting 'normal' turnover at optimal capacity utilisation; and *structural unemployment*, defined as the difference between total unemployment and frictional unemployment.[25] The latter is also often referred to as the 'hard-core' unemployed. Identifying statistics in this way is, of course, useful for analysis; however, there is a danger that fragmenting unemployment in this way may allow it to appear acceptable and hence lower concern about it. One can see this from the way that commentators (particularly in the United States) tend, as unemployment increases, to increase the numbers in structural unemployment. This hardly follows from the definition given above.

A second approach has been in the area of conjunctural measures designed to mop up the most serious aspects of unemployment. It has been argued that unemployment arises for three main reasons not totally connected with the demand deficiency identified in Section 9.5.2 above. First, unemployment can arise from workers pricing themselves out of jobs through excessive wage claims (there is truth in this but the evidence is not strong).[26] Second, it may stem from increases in labour supply factors such as an increase in the female participation rate or a baby boom (in fact, the OECD labour force as a percentage of the population aged 15–64 years decreased slightly from 69.9 per cent to 68.6 per cent from 1960 to 1980, although the labour force grew by 1.1 per cent per annum in the same period, with a tendency to grow faster by 1.3 per cent during the years 1973–80; however, it slowed in 1981 and 1982 to 1.1 and 1.0 per cent respectively). Third, unemployment may result from capital intensiveness associated with technological change and the consequent increase in labour productivity. Between 1960 and 1980, employment in absolute terms declined in agriculture in all OECD countries, and in industry for the United Kingdom only, but it declined in relative terms for all other OECD countries, and increased in services. However, with new technologies more likely to hit the service sector in the future than in the past, the prospects of some technological unemployment are high in the short term. Accelerated productivity is bound to worsen unemployment in the short run but, in the long term, comparison between EEC countries does not show any clear association between changes in productivity and employment.[27] Further, productivity growth and employment changes are linked and conditioned by the whole structure of the economic system and its pattern of evolution.

A third labour market approach has been to apply specific labour market policies. However, according to the OECD, most OECD governments have not devoted major new resources to selective labour market policies,[28] although they have, in many cases, responded by targeting programmes more closely on the long-term unemployed. Thus, there has been less emphasis on policies in favour of youth, women or older workers as groups of unemployed, the effort concentrating rather on the longer-term unemployed within these groups. These policies have been concentrated in three main areas, namely an in-depth review of individuals affected, intervention by subsidising employment, and early retirement.[29]

The object of the first policy was to assess the qualifications and/or handicaps of unemployed people, and then to propose some action such as referral to suitable employment. This cumbersome procedure is likely to provide work mainly for the people running the scheme and can be dismissed easily enough. The second, comprising schemes subsidising employment, has been tried in many countries and presumably attempts to reallocate social expenditure from direct payment to the unemployed to employing enterprises. The recognition aspect of such a programme is welcome; however, it is unlikely that recipients find themselves materially better off, particularly at the 'poverty trap' end of the spectrum. The third measure, early retirement, forms part of a wider class of instruments designed to reduce labour supply, such as a reduction in the number of hours worked, longer vacations, part-time working, and job-sharing. On the face of it, such measures seem attractive; however, they all increase costs either for the public purse or for private employers and are unlikely to be readily accepted or to change unemployment levels by more than 1 or 2 per cent.[30]

Other labour market measures are concerned with improving the quality of the labour force through vocational education and training. When this helps workers to adjust, within an industry, from one technology to a more advanced one, or to a new industry, retraining can be seen as positive. However, one wonders how far such training is to fit workers to production rather than organising production in order to satisfy human needs.

9.6   SOME ALTERNATIVE SCENARIOS TO REDUCE UNEMPLOYMENT

There are, of course, many alternative scenarios that have been suggested as total or partial solutions to unemployment in industrialised countries,[31] and obviously, political considerations have a role to play here.[32]

It may be argued that there are three broad, not necessarily mutually exclusive alternatives to the current high levels of unemployment that are, or could be, considered. They can be summarised as: (i) neo-classical; (ii) neo-Keynesian; and (iii) structural.

9.6.1   The neo-classical alternative

In a sense, this alternative is the one currently being tried by major Western leaders. Its basic model is that of Adam Smith and the free market, ie the invisible hand of market forces works and works fairly well when unfettered by controls – and by this is meant, in general, State controls. As regards the problem of unemployment, exponents of this approach believe that a return to full employment will come about through a relative reduction in the costs of production, particularly labour costs, therefore raising the marginal efficiency of capital. From this, investors will be able to obtain high returns on their investments, leading to increased investment, growth and, finally, labour absorption. Concurrently, in order to encourage investment, there must be no exchange controls, and floating exchange rates, free trade and the cost of money (interest rates) must be influenced by demand and supply factors subject to overall monetary and fiscal targets. The influence of the State must be reduced through reductions in public expenditure, including lower social benefits, allowing income tax to be reduced, and hence increase the incentive to work. In this alternative, little emphasis is placed on labour market policy. Similarly, profits tax must be reduced or eliminated, as an incentive to invest. As far as social policy goes, education, health care, social insurance, and so on, should be taken over as far as possible by the private sector in order to make them (particularly education) more sensitive to the needs of industry.

9.6.2   The neo-Keynesian alternative

This alternative,[33] like the first one, seeks to stimulate economic growth in order to absorb labour. Economic growth is to arise through the stimulation of effective demand. In order to prevent cost-pushed inflation, a negotiated incomes policy is to be achieved through a contract between workers and management. Workers are to agree to accept wage rises not exceeding the rate of inflation plus any anticipated productivity increase. Monetary targets are to be relaxed in order to allow interest rates to fall coupled with some fiscal expansion.

However, there must be some control of the money supply – not an unbridled rate of expansion – coupled with fiscal and exchange rate policy. The exchange rate should be managed in order to reflect relative costs. There are to be selective import controls in order to prevent massive deterioration in the balance of payments that could arise from imports flooding in to meet the increased demand. This is because apparent losses of comparative advantage tend to become self-perpetuating since a sector which appears to have lost its comparative advantage (due to real exchange-rate overvaluation, say) will eventually lose its comparative advantage due to disinvestment. Generalised across a wider spectrum of the economy, the result is de-industrialisation.

On the international front, multilateral policies are needed to co-ordinate unilateral policies with respect to exchange rates, monetary and fiscal expansion, a large increase in IMF quotas and a sharp increase in aid coupled with strengthened international commercial bank lending to Third World countries.

9.6.3 The structural alternative

The word 'structural' is perhaps the most overworked and yet ill-defined word in the economists' vocabulary. Structural problems, as understood here, are the rigidities in the socio-economic system that prevent the social and economic change required so that the system moves towards satisfying human needs. Some of the economic aspects are, in this alternative, similar to those of the neo-Keynesian school. The major difference is the emphasis on human beings and their needs rather than on economic growth *per se*, ie on the level and quality of life rather than the means.[34] Keynes himself foresaw a time when 'we should once more value ends above means and prefer the good to the useful. We shall honour those who can teach us how to pluck the hour and the day virtuously and well . . .'.[35] Focusing on ends rather than means implies a greater questioning of what human needs are and what the purpose of economic growth is. Such an approach cannot accept unemployment or its close correlate, the rejection by society of a part of its population; nor can it accept great inequalities in the distribution of income and wealth. This is because a focus on satisfying human needs does not mean just satisfying the needs of a few – all have to be included.

Satisfying needs, in economic terms, entails stimulating effective demand. The same ground rules apply as in 9.6.2 above; however, a greater role is seen for planning – workers and employers cannot achieve agreement on wage settlements if productivity and inflation trends are unknown. Planners will have to use economic models to do this. But the difference from a centrally planned system is that the determination of needs and the application of planning decisions must be accomplished in a genuinely democratic and participatory society.

In addition to economic management, a social and cultural package is required that rethinks the role of employment in the lifetime of an individual. For example, individuals spend their lives in three main stages: in school or college, in or out of the labour market and in retirement. These usually follow sequentially. However, if human needs are the focus of socio-economic policy, education and retirement (or sabbatical leave) could be taken *à la carte*, as it were.[36]

The definition of human needs is no easy matter. On the other hand, the definition and measurement of economic activity is not easy either, yet there is no absence of attempts. Without wishing to go into any further detail, suffice it to say that the process and discussion that would be generated if the focus on economic growth could be widened to include intense discussion on the achievement of human needs could have its own momentum in helping society to decide on its priorities and eventually to achieve them.

9.7 AN EVALUATION OF THE SCENARIOS SUGGESTED

Each of the chapters in this book offered alternative scenarios to the problem of unemployment, and nearly all fell somewhere in between the neo-classical scenario and the neo-Keynesian scenario described in the previous section. None considered structural alternatives.

The United Kingdom study evaluates three broad scenarios, namely a tight financial strategy coupled with some easing of the public sector borrowing requirement, a protectionist strategy coupled with a concurrent domestic reflation, and a high investment strategy for industry coupled with an export drive and an incomes policy. Although the last scenario is preferred, it very much depends on a co-ordinated reflation policy with Britain's main trading partners. In the absence of this occurring, a protectionist strategy is preferred. Unfortunately, the extent to which retaliation by the United Kingdom's trading partners would harm her exports is treated only sparingly in the work. Further, the extent to which the oil-based economy of the United Kingdom, coupled with a high interest rate, and consequently, a high exchange rate, influenced a sharp decline in the country's industrial base was not treated in the chapter. To be fair to the author, the Cambridge Economic Policy Group (CEPG) at Cambridge has been a consistent critic of the Conservative economic strategy, and the current problems faced by the British economy would seem to back them up to an extent. On the other hand, the fall in relative costs in the United Kingdom and the 'shake-out' of industry may have made British industry more efficient than before, and this could bring long-term benefits to the British economy. Again, the model did not consider this. Unsurprisingly, when the CEPG applied their model and a similar set of scenarios to the case of Mexico in Chapter 8, the same conclusions emerge. Again, the CEPG missed an extensive discussion on the dominant role of high exchange rates.

In the chapter on France, the best result for employment occurred when there was intensive investment in industry in order to ease the pressure on the balance of payments. In the event, the ninth French plan (1984–88) adopted this approach with massive capital stock modernisation coupled with an attempt to halt the increase in the per capita purchasing power of the average wage. Nevertheless, persistent high levels of unemployment still exist in France and only partial success has been achieved, namely a strong currency and a healthy balance of payments. The experience of France in the early years of Mitterand's presidency was not discussed in the chapter, yet the reflation by France in that period contributed to growth in its neighbours, particularly the Federal Republic of Germany. Unfortunately, France's lone attempt to reflate its economy in the absence of co-operation from its trading partners led to a balance of payments crisis and a quick reversal of the strategy.

Strong pessimism emanates from the two smaller country studies. None of the three alternatives considered in the Netherlands study, (ie expansion through borrowing on the capital market, reduction in wages and reduction in working time) made more than a minor impact on the rate of unemployment. The Belgian study considered only reductions in working time and was fairly optimistic about such a policy. It ignored, however, the behavioural response of workers who may well be interested in shorter hours but not in lower compensation. It ignored, too, the type and quantity of reduction required. A small reduction may add to inflation and very little else; on the other hand, a large reduction poses major questions on alternative work patterns and lifestyles. A large reduction may well mean that Belgium would become highly uncompetitive on world markets unless other countries followed suit. Both studies therefore make a plea for internationally co-ordinated reflation policies, similar to those proposed in the United Kingdom study.

Similarly, the OECD chapter gives high marks to a 'consensus' scenario combining income tax reduction with wage restraint and an accommodating monetary policy. It is believed that this strategy has the most chance of success if the resulting increase in enterprise income leads to increased expenditure, and if labour does not respond to this pick-up demand (and employment) by wage demands in excess of productivity increases. Advocacy of this view also comes from the LINK chapter with the addition – ignored in all the other work in this volume – that a substantial recovery in the OECD is almost synonymous with a corresponding recovery in the Third World. However, the reverse is considered not to be true, ie a recovery in the Third World will not substantially contribute to recovery in the OECD world. Such linkages have not been treated in the LINK project, and thus this result must remain speculative. In other words, the LINK model has not untangled the 'chicken and egg' problem that occurs because of interdependency; does growth in the Third World stimulate growth in the OECD followed by an increased stimulus to Third World growth, or, as Pauly believes, does the chain start with growth in the OECD followed by a stimulus/response in the Third World?

9.8 CONCLUSION

This concluding chapter was divided into two broad parts. First, it asked what employment forecasting was all about, and then attempted to test the forecasting performance of some well-known unemployment forecasts. It concluded that the unemployment forecasts, at least for the OECD countries, seem to be reasonably reliable and that high levels of unemployment will not disappear within the immediate future. The second part of the chapter presented some of the major underlying causes of the high levels of unemployment that now exist in industrialised market economies. On the basis of the diagnoses and the issues associated with it, a number of alternative scenarios were presented.

To date, models concerned with the employment issue have been concerned with the policy issues associated with the first two alternative scenarios presented (characterised as neo-classical and neo-Keynesian). The third scenario (characterised as a structural alternative) is normative compared to the other scenarios, ie it talks about ends rather than means. Although this has not been done, there is no major reason why the third scenario cannot be tested using a model.

Many people question the usefulness of models and quantification in aiding policy formulation and design. This is very healthy, but few model builders would argue that models should be used for policy-making and nothing else. Nevertheless, large-scale macro-economic models have been influential in industrialised countries in pointing to forthcoming problems through their forecasting function and, therefore, cannot be ignored. Less successful, however, has been their role in testing alternative policy packages that do not depend upon conventional conservative economic thought, and/or that include a wider set of variables as depicted earlier in the chapter in Table 9.5. New models need to be developed that break away from the general equilibrium, neo-classical Walrasian mould, so that they include not only disequilibrium situations but also variables of great importance that have often been considered unquantifiable, such as the satisfaction of human needs, the role of bargaining power in determining economic phenomena such as wages and prices, the role of innovation, and political and institutional barriers. Imagination is needed because, even though models do not take decisions on how economies should be run, they have an influence in informing the various competing social groups on the feasibility of alternatives. Model-builders must be careful, therefore, not to ignore more unconventional alternatives nor exclude variables purely because they are difficult to quantify.

9.8.1   Is there a need for policy intervention?

In a recession with high levels of unemployment which it may be argued that the countries of the North are still experiencing, a vicious circle develops: investment is low because *expected* demand is low, and *actual* demand is low because investment, which is also part of actual demand, is low. Concerted action by the major industrialised countries to reflate their economies could provide a major stimulus to the reduction of unemployment in the North, increased world trade and development in the South.

There are a number of reasons why this 'pump-priming', ie government response to incipient recession due to a prospective fall in private investment (or other component of demand) by borrowing in order to reduce taxation or increasing its own expenditure (or both), has not been tried so far in the 1980s. First, the governments of the major industrialised countries (except France for a while and Japan) all proclaimed the virtues of free markets and the 'invisible' hand of market forces. Hence co-ordinated 'pump-priming' was not attractive as it implied government interference in markets.

Second, and related to the first point, demand management is seen to be inappropriate because of supply side constraints. According to this view, unemployment is high because of rigidities in the economic system. These rigidities stem from both governments and trade unions. Governments are considered to be a major source of rigidity because, through their own civil service employment and publicly owned companies and services, they attenuate market forces. Further, government assistance to companies in difficulty reduces the pressure of market forces; while job security legislation and related measures allow the effects of market forces to be ignored. Trade unions are considered to be a source of rigidity because their strength overrides market forces in wage negotiations and thereby brings about inflation or unemployment, or both. On the other hand, rigidities in corporate behaviour that come about because of the mere size and/or monopolistic or oligopolistic behaviour of enterprises are not usually considered to be as important as the other above-mentioned sources.

Third, it is believed that public 'pump-priming' would not lead to higher private investment because profits would not increase due to the aforementioned rigidities in the labour market, ie the strength of the trade unions would lead either to overmanning or real wage increase, or both. Hence, the injection of public funds through deficit spending would lead, eventually, to inflation. With inflation, private companies would be unwilling to invest in productive activities because their real return on investment would be eroded.

Fourth, 'pump-priming' would require additional financial resources that might not necessarily be available. If all industrialised countries reflated at the same time, either the price of money would increase or there would be additional inflation or a combination of both.

Fifth, because of the recession, existing capacity levels would be stretched with additional demand and this would lead to a higher balance of payments deficit or, again, more inflation or a combination of both.

In sum, therefore, the main reason for the lack of concerted 'pump-priming' by *all* major industrialised countries has been the fear of inflation. Unless it can be shown that reflation by the major countries will lead to more or less inflation-free growth, the fear of renewed inflation will continue to outweigh the fear of unemployment.

The consensus, however, of most of the studies in this book is that a co-operative reflation is the best way to increase employment. However, if co-operation proves too difficult, then a second-best alternative would be protectionism for large countries until their economies recovered. However, this does not provide much hope for small countries such as Belgium and the Netherlands, and their prospects must remain bleak.

NOTES

1. *Financial Times*, 24 Feb. (1986).
2. Belassa, B. 'The Cambridge group and the developing countries', in *World Economy*, 8, 3 (1985).
3. Makridakis, S. and Wheelwright, S. *Forecasting methods and application*, New York, John Wiley and Sons (1978).
4. Vincens, J. *La prévision de l'emploi*, Paris, Presses Universitaires de France (1970).
5. Also referred to as human resource planning, employment planning, active labour market policies, etc. See Richter, L. *What is manpower planning all about? A review of definitions*, Geneva, ILO (1981).
6. Smyth, D.J. 'Short-run macro-economic forecasting: the OECD experience', in *Journal of Forecasting* 2, 1 (1983). An application of the same tests that Smyth used were applied, independently, to sets of macro-economic forecasts of the French economy. See Fonteneau, A. 'La fiabilité des prévisions macroéconomique à court terme: 12 ans d'expérience francaises (1970–1981)', in *Revue de l'OFCE* 2 (1982).
7. A summary description of the OECD forecasting techniques is given in the appendix to *Economic Outlook*; more details are available in OECD, 'The OECD International Linkage Model', in *Economic Outlook Occasional Studies* (1979). See also Chapter 8 in this book.
8. OECD, ibid.
9. See OECD, *Techniques of economic forecasting*, Paris (1965).
10. New work has recently been carried out within the OECD on improving the labour market and creating new models.

11. Smyth also uses other methods as much to examine the robustness of the measures as to test the validity of OECD forecasts. The conclusions do not change much with alternative methods and hence only two tests were used here. Then the overall difference in results was small even though slightly different aspects of the data sets were brought out, depending on the test used. The major difference between the two measures is that the RMSE gives more weight to large differences than to small ones, hence one bad forecast will influence RMSE far more than the MAE.

12. Smyth, op. cit.

13. For an analysis for the United Kingdom, see Hakin, C. 'The social consequences of high unemployment', in *Journal of Social Policy*, 11, 4, October (1982).

14. Illich, Ivan. *The right to useful unemployment*, London, Marion Boyars, p.83 (1978).

15. Russell, Bertrand *In praise of idleness*, London, Unwin Paperbacks (1976).

16. Ibid.

17. See also Barker, T. 'Long-term recovery: A Return to full employment', in *Lloyds Bank Review* 143 (1982); and van Ginneken, W. *Unemployment in France, the Federal Republic of Germany and the Netherlands*, Geneva, ILO (1982).

18. Monetary control was seized upon by politicians who saw it as a way to attack a number of 'holy cows', such as strong unions, low productivity, increased competition, etc.

19. Harrison, J. 'The profits squeeze, unemployment and policy: A Marxist approach', in Maddison A. and Wilpstra, B. (eds): *Unemployment: The European perspective*, London, Croom Helm (1982).

20. Willke, G. 'The structural diagnosis and policy menu', ibid.

21. See Barker, Chapter 2, on this.

22. See Delbeke, J. 'Recent long-wave theories: A critical survey', in *Futures* 13, 4 (1981).

23. Mensch, G. *The technological stalemate*, Cambridge, Massachusetts, Harvard University Press (1979).

24. Freeman, C., Clark, J. and Soete, L. *Unemployment and technical innovation: A study of long waves and economic development*, London, Frances Pinter (1982).

25. OECD, *Economic Outlook* 33 (1983).

26. Ibid.

27. Boyer, R. and Petit, P. 'Employment and productivity in the EEC', in *Cambridge Journal of Economics* 5, pp.47–58 (1981).

28. OECD *Policies for manpower and social affairs*, Paris (1983).

29. Ibid.

30. In the United Kingdom, for example, older unemployed workers unlikely to find jobs are no longer asked to sign on at an employment exchange. Benefits do not change but this measure has the effect that 'registered' unemployment is one or two percentage points less than 'real' levels of unemployment.

31. Some thoughts on alternatives to unemployment in developing countries I have given elsewhere. See Hopkins, M. and Van Der Hoeven, R. *Basic needs in development planning*, London, Gower (1983); Hopkins, M. *Alternatives to underemployment and unemployment in developing countries: The case of Colombia*, Westview Press, Boulder, Colorado (1985).

32. See, for example, Frank, André Gunner, 'Global crisis and transformation', in *Development and Change*, 14, 3 (1983).

33. See Roe, A., Renshaw, G. and Ahmad, I. *The international aspects of*

Britain's economic recovery, Coventry, University of Warwick, Department of Economics (1982).

34. See also Galtun, J. *What economists ignore in their forecasts*, ILO (1984).

35. Keynes, J.M. *Essays in persuasion*, London, Macmillan, p.372 (1931).

36. This has been proposed by Louis Emmerij; for more detail, see Emmerij, L., 'The social economy of today's employment problem in the industrialised countries', in Malinvaud, E. and Fitoussi, J. (eds) *Unemployment in western countries*, London, Macmillan (1980).

Index